VIRTUAL PROJECT MANAGEMENT

Software Solutions for Today and the Future

PAUL E. McMAHON

S^t_L

St. Lucie Press

Boca Raton   London   New York   Washington, D.C.

Library of Congress Cataloging-in-Publication Data

McMahon, Paul E., 1949–
    Virtual project management: software solutions for today and the future / by Paul E. McMahon.
        p. cm.
    Includes bibliographical references and index.
    ISBN 1-57444-298-8 (alk. paper)
    1. Computer software—Development—Management.   I. Title.
    QA76.76.D47 M3975 2000
    005.1′068—dc21   00-059086
                                                                                  CIP

© 2001 by CRC Press LLC
St. Lucie Press is an imprint of CRC Press LLC

No claim to original U.S. Government works
International Standard Book Number 1-57444-298-8
Library of Congress Card Number 00-059086
Printed in the United States of America 1 2 3 4 5 6 7 8 9 0
Printed on acid-free paper

VIRTUAL PROJECT MANAGEMENT

Software Solutions for Today and the Future

Preface

If you work on an advanced technology software intensive project today, you probably feel as if you're being asked to do the impossible almost daily. Developing from scratch is out! Integrating existing components rapidly is in! But how do you rapidly integrate products that weren't originally developed inside your organization when the critical skills you know you need to succeed are not easily accessible? Your first thought might be to look for a subcontractor, but then you take another look at the project schedule and your heart begins to race.

Does this scenario sound familiar? If it does, consider stepping outside your box — for just a moment.

Now, imagine the possibilities. Imagine working on a project where critical skills are rapidly accessible and the personnel assigned know exactly what it is you need. Imagine not having to devote valuable schedule time to developing detailed subcontractor specifications before the "real" engineering work can get moving. Imagine your project hitting the ground running the first day after contract award with a productive, skilled team possessing just the right mix of engineering personnel in place and ready to go.

On this project there will be no lengthy integration due to task miscommunication. This time all your subcontractors operate as an extension of your own workforce, using the project's "agreed-to" tools, support infrastructure, and technical and management procedures and strategies. In fact, the project runs so smoothly that one year after contract award you can't tell your subcontractors from your own employees. By the way, some of your teammates aren't located just down the hall. Some are 3000 miles away. But on this project physical location doesn't matter because distance isn't an issue.

What's that? Do I sense just a bit of disbelief? All right, while it is true that the project described is somewhat unrealistic, advances in virtual technologies and changes in the way organizations are approaching new business opportunities are dramatically affecting how engineering work is actually getting done. These changes are being driven equally by technology advances as well as changing customer attitudes toward the use of existing solutions to solve new challenges.

Today, customers are unwilling to wait years to see the results of their investments. Increased competition is demanding rapid capability that can be changed, and then changed again quickly. This is not easily achieved. While applying existing solutions is sound in theory, few companies maintain all the necessary piece-part solutions and related expertise inside their organization to solve most of today's complex challenges.

In response, many high-technology organizations are turning to strategic collaboration employing physically distributed — but integrated — teams. While just a few short years ago this approach would have seemed inconceivable, modern technologies like e-mail, the world wide web, netmeeting, and tele- and videoconferencing are providing new possibilities for distributed teams to work more efficiently and effectively.

What This Book is About

This book isn't about virtual technologies. It's about the technical-management issues involved in moving to a revolutionary new way of building complex software-intensive systems faster and cheaper by employing the power of distributed operations. We know the potential is great. But from experiences encountered in the mid/late 1990s and early twenty-first century, we also know related implementation issues cut deep inside present day engineering organizations. This book describes and examines critical management issues commonly found on high technology software-intensive virtual collaborative projects. It also recommends practical and affordable actions to aid organizations seeking increased productivity within this rapidly changing dynamic environment.

Who This Book is For

This book was written for busy project leaders and project engineers (first and second level engineering managers, senior project engineers, and project managers) who know the fundamentals of project management, but don't yet know the underlying root causes of nor the solutions to many of the difficult issues being faced today on virtual collaborative projects. This book may also be useful to anyone interested in understanding the impacts on software-intensive projects when multiple organizations and/or sites are involved. The book assumes the reader is familiar with traditional software management issues faced on large-scale projects.

Organization of This Book

This book is organized into seven sections: introduction, overview, traditional collocated environments, tales, 8-step plan, conclusion, and appendices.

In the introduction we characterize the projects where we first began to notice the issues that are the subject of this book. We soon discovered that the lessons were applicable to a much broader range of projects. The introduction also discusses fundamental effects of virtual collaboration on productivity, why you should care about virtual projects, and specifically how this book can help you.

The insights behind the recommendations in this book are best conveyed not by telling readers what they should do, but by describing the situations that arise on virtual projects. Comprehending the nature of many of the new dilemmas faced must precede real acceptance of the need for change. This is the purpose of our tales.

At the same time, however, few busy project leaders have the time to wade through all of the details in a book of this size. With this in mind, an overview section is included. It was the last section of the book to be written, and presents in summary form the key points that are most important for virtual project leaders to know including the identification of 11 common virtual project pitfalls, and 14 recommendations.

To keep the overview as concise as possible, we don't provide all the background and rationale, but do provide references to places in the book to gain more detailed information on specific topics. The overview is based on an 8-step practical and affordable plan that can be used as a framework for setting up and executing a new virtual project, or instituting improvements to a project that has drifted off course.

Chapter 1 focuses on critical characteristics underlying how work actually gets accomplished in traditional collocated engineering environments. This chapter is based on the premise that fully comprehending the changes taking place in advanced distributed operations today first requires a deeper understanding of past collocated successes.

The next five chapters examine the changes taking place on virtual projects through a series of tales based on real project experiences. These experiences occurred for the most part between 1994 and 2000. Observations, analysis, and insights are included, along with recommended solutions to common pitfalls.

Chapter 7 synthesizes the results of the previous chapters, and provides greater depth on the 8-step plan discussed in the overview.

In Chapter 8, Conclusion, we return to productivity, reminding the reader of the goals discussed in the introduction. Key points are summarized. What the reader should do next to get a new virtual project going, or to initiate focused improvements to an ongoing one, is discussed.

A number of appendices are provided with supporting information. Thirty-four (34) specific virtual project insights and fifty (50) specific solutions are highlighted within Chapters 1 through 8 and summarized in Appendix L. We recommend that busy leaders also read the Frequently Asked Questions provided in Appendix J.

While this is not a methodology book, its recommendations are consistent with current system and software thinking. The solutions offered are supported by references to published works by recognized experts in related fields.

If you are facing a software-intensive project involving multiple organizations and/or sites — and indications are that more and more companies will be doing so in the future — then this book can help get your project moving in the right direction avoiding many of the most common pitfalls encountered by others.

The Author

Paul E. McMahon is an independent contractor providing technical and management leadership services to large and small engineering organizations. Mr. McMahon began his career in the early 1970s as a flight simulation programmer. Before initiating independent work as PEM Systems in 1997, Mr. McMahon held senior technical and management positions at Hughes and Lockheed Martin.

Today, McMahon employs his 27 years of experience in helping organizations deploy high quality software processes integrated with systems engineering and project management. He has taught Software Engineering as an adjunct at Binghamton University, published over a dozen articles, presented at industry conferences, and has been a featured speaker at NASA. Mr. McMahon can be contacted at pemcmahon@acm.org. For more information refer to www.PEMSystems.com.

Acknowledgments

T his book would not have been possible without the support of colleagues, clients, friends, and family.

I thank Bill Bail, Bill Bennett, Walter Burkhardt, Dave Clutz, Bruce Crandall, Robert Daniels, Dr. Jorge Diaz-Herrera, Bob Epps, Dr. Rodger Fritz, Lenny Genna, Ron Hendricks, Keith Hickling, Dr. Jeff Kleinwaks, Dr. Les Lander, Jan McMahon, Dennis Meehl, Paul O'Neil, Dave Pochily, Dr. Jeff Poulin, Don Procuniar, Sue Pope, Don Reifer, Art Rusch, Serg Spak, Dave Sundberg, Tony Syme, John Torres, John Troy, Dr. Frank Tsui, Kathy Walsh, Larry White, and Bob Wuestner.

Many have taken time out of their busy schedules to share their wisdom, insights, and challenging perspectives in reviewing this manuscript. Others have provided invaluable guidance, encouragement, and support over many years.

Dedication

To Jan, Lindsey and Patrick —

for helping me to see what matters

Contents

Introduction

Much has been written on the subject of productivity. We all want to produce a high quality product for our customers and do it faster and less expensively than our competitors. But what is high quality in today's world and how does it relate to productivity? Historically, inside many organizations, productivity has been viewed as a counting game.[1] That is, productivity has been associated with the number of "widgets" one can produce in an hour.

With productivity improvement in mind, recent years have found many organizations working diligently to establish stable and repeatable internal engineering processes. In many of these organizations the thinking has been that a repeatable internal process will hold a key to future productivity.[2] Despite this longheld belief, in today's world the path to real productivity requires a close reexamination; for example, what good will increasing your widget-per-hour count do when your competitor already owns the product your customer wants?

Inside today's downsized and consolidated organizations the rules of the productivity game are changing. Organizations that yesterday stood successfully and alone are now taking a closer look at the products they produce along with their relationships with external organizations. In the process, many of them are recognizing that the speed which solutions require no longer affords them the opportunity to look solely inside for all their answers.

As a result, inside today's successful organizations real productivity is no longer viewed as just a number. These organizations are finding new and creative ways to turn traditional rivals into close, working collaborative teammates.[3]

Why Do Many Collaborative Ventures Fail?

This book focuses on a new way to construct advanced technology software intensive systems that fit our rapidly changing external environment. In particular, it emphasizes the issues involving projects that are integrating existing products, along with new development through the utilization of engineering personnel with diverse skills, knowledge, and backgrounds.

Research done by Booz-Allen[4] indicates that many collaborative efforts fail because of a combination of four reasons:

■ Cultural incompatibility
■ Leadership struggles
■ Lack of trust
■ Inbred notions of competition

Based on our experience with a number of collaborative engineering ventures that took place in the 1990s and early twenty-first century, we view this list as one of symptoms. The real reason behind many collaborative failures rests in a failure to take timely and effective action to resolve the real underlying root causes of problems that are actually not as complex as imagined. Furthermore, by looking deeper into real collaborative experiences, these root causes can be identified, along with practical and affordable solutions.

Background

We first noticed the issues that became the subject of this book on a number of distributed development projects that shared a common set of characteristics. These projects occurred between 1994 and 1998. Initially we thought the material we were developing would only be relevant to projects that fit the same model. After being involved in a number of additional distributed projects (1998 to 2000) with differing characteristics, we concluded that the applicability of many of our observations was much broader than originally thought.

We do not recommend that our clients attempt to apply everything in this book to their virtual projects. This book can help if your project includes multiple sites and multiple companies with hundreds of people spread around the world. But it can also help much smaller organizations as they look for the most effective strategies to operate in the virtual world.

What Do We Mean by Virtual Collaboration?

When we began to study virtual projects in the mid 1990s we defined *Virtual Collaboration* to be

"Uniting critical skills to solve a problem without physical collocation."

Today there is a new kind of distributed development project emerging that has led us to a revised definition.

In most traditional subcontract relationships the prime contractor develops a formal specification for the subcontractor. This specification normally establishes detailed requirements of the product to be produced. Traditional subcontractors often accomplish the required work within their own facility, employing their own management personnel, support infrastructure, internal processes, and technical approach.

As long as the specification is met, the subcontractor is free to operate within his own facility as he desires using his own tools, methods, and supporting infrastructure. Using the broad definition above, this relationship between prime and subcontractor could be viewed as virtual collaboration.

The virtual projects that we emphasize in this book involve multiple organizations and multiple sites. However, the relationship between these organizations differs from traditional subcontract relationships.

In contrast to the traditional prime–sub relationship, the projects of interest to us are those utilizing virtual teams that operate more as a *single integrated* team employing some level (to be discussed) of common processes, support services, and technical strategies driven through a streamlined management chain. A key distinction of these virtual collaborative projects centers around the methodology employed.

Oftentimes insufficient time and knowledge exist at the start of a project to develop a comprehensive detailed specification before initiating engineering development activities. Furthermore, customers are looking for value added starting on day one of the project. In most new high-technology arenas few organizations have just the right set of off-the-shelf solutions to meet this need. In response to this market demand a new form of virtual collaboration is emerging which we define as:

"Uniting critical skills into a single integrated team across multiple physical locations to solve a new and complex software-intensive challenge rapidly."

Today's Virtual Collaborative Project Characteristics

We have identified seven key characteristics exhibited by many of today's virtual collaborative projects. If you are currently involved in a distributed software effort, or are working in the proposal stage of a potentially new effort, compare the characteristics below to your own project to see if the material in this book can benefit you. These characteristics include

- Multiple organizational involvement
- Software intensive
- Aggressive schedule
- Integration/reuse focus
- Advanced technology
- Physically distributed team members
- Diverse technical backgrounds of engineering personnel

Each characteristic is described below.

- Multiple Organizational Involvement. All the virtual projects involve multiple organizations. This doesn't necessarily imply different companies. Some of the projects had different sites within the same company collaborating, each with its own distinct organizational structure and culture. We consider most virtual projects to be large projects, but this is not meant to imply a specific number of engineers. Large — in the context used here — means that the project requires multiple skills and multiple departments, sites, or organizations. Some of the projects analyzed actually started out with a small team (3 to 7 people) and continued to operate in a lean manner throughout the project's lifetime. Projects that operate this way keep costs down by pulling in critical skills only as necessary. The important characteristic is the multiple organizational involvement, which brings diversity of organizational structures, cultures, and methods. On single organizational/site projects many of the issues we deal with in this book may not surface.
- Software Intensive. All the projects we examined are software intensive. This is a key characteristic because many of the issues faced involve the production of software-specific artifacts, their relationship to system engineering artifacts, and their relationship to other dependent software artifacts produced by interfacing team members. While the projects are software intensive, many of the issues involved and discussed in this book extend beyond what have traditionally been viewed as software boundaries.

- Aggressive Schedule. Aggressive schedules seem to be more the norm than the exception on most projects today. Nevertheless, it is important that this characteristic be stated explicitly. Aggressive schedules are one reason for moving away from traditional large-scale development approaches in favor of integration/reuse focused approaches. Traditional development approaches do not produce capability rapidly enough in the hands of customers to meet tomorrow's market demands. Rapid capability is another way of expressing the aggressive schedule characteristic. When customers fail to see rapid progress, projects can quickly find themselves at risk of termination or at least funding cuts before they even have a chance to get off the ground.
- Integration/Reuse Focus. This characteristic may actually be a result of the previous one — aggressive schedule. An integration/reuse focus is necessary because of the challenging demands for rapid capability. Few projects today — virtual or collocated — can afford long development cycles. Today, existing solutions must be leveraged and integrated into a single functioning system.
- Advanced Technology. Most virtual projects involving multiple organizations with multiple skills are trying to solve a new and complex challenge. This is an important characteristic of virtual projects because it raises the critical issue of creative design alternatives. This is discussed at length in Chapter 2.
- Physically Distributed Team Members. Engineering interactions are affected by physical location. New technologies (e.g., electronic-mail, teleconferencing, netmeeting, world wide web) allow for physical distribution of team members, but they also affect personnel interaction dynamics creating a new set of non-technical issues to be managed. These issues are discussed at length in Chapter 5.
- Diverse Technical Backgrounds of Engineering Personnel. When we rapidly pull together individuals from different organizations with differing backgrounds and experiences we increase our breadth of knowledge, but at the same time increase the likelihood of internal project conflict. This conflict if often compounded by physical distance, which must be carefully considered as it can influence the optimum approach to conflict resolution. This subject is discussed at length throughout the book and, in particular, in Chapters 2 and 7.

Why Should You Care about Virtual Operations?

Today, the demand for software solutions, driven by computational equipment price reductions, along with interconnectivity performance improvements, has never been greater. At the same time there exists a growing awareness among savvy customers that each new software job need not start from scratch.

Unfortunately, many of the partial solutions that exist are not found in a form readily usable by a new customer. To make the necessary changes requires specialized software skills, as well as experience and knowledge of strategic existing products. Many software organizations are finding themselves operating with a shortage of these critical skills, and therefore are unable to compete in certain markets.

Employing distributed development provides a vehicle that can dramatically increase a company's opportunities to create new business in markets normally inaccessible to them. This is because we have a broader skill and product knowledge base coupled with a deeper pool of personnel to potentially use. Company affiliation and physical location — two of the prime hindrances in the past — are removed as barriers.

It is important to understand that operating virtually with personnel from diverse backgrounds isn't something we necessarily want to do. It does complicate the management task. These issues are discussed throughout this book. Nevertheless, collocation is not always possible, or practical.

In today's rapidly changing business environment it is critical for high-technology software-intensive organizations to position themselves to take better advantage of new opportunities that might not be possible through traditional approaches. It is no longer feasible for individual organizations to maintain all the key skills potentially needed to compete in the many diverse domains where software-intensive solutions are in demand.

In theory, given the technologies available today, operating in a virtual fashion should not be all that difficult. Managers should be able to task and monitor work equally effectively whether an engineer is sitting outside his (her) office or thousands of miles away. In practice, however, this is not the case. Oftentimes, unexpected issues surface only in the midst of battle. These are the issues, along with proven solutions, that are the focus of this book.

Why Was This Book Written?

There were many occasions in the past when I wished I had at my fingertips the material in this book. It was written to move one step beyond an introduction to distributed development. While it can be used by those just looking for a glimpse into the future, my primary motivation in writing this book was to provide others with the guidance I wished I had when helping clients set up and execute a virtual collaborative project.

Others have lived through the pain of learning lessons the hard way. You don't need to follow their path. My hope is that through the insights and proposed solutions offered this book will help answer many of the questions virtual project leaders will be asking well into the twenty-first century.

Specifically, What Problems Will This Book Help Solve?

Through this book you will gain insight into how virtual collaborative projects differ from traditional collocated projects, and hopefully you will be able to relate those insights to your own experiences. You will learn about a fundamental dilemma faced by project leaders on almost all collaborative efforts. Specifically, you will learn:

- A major cause of remote tasking miscommunication and an effective and easy-to-implement technique to remedy it.
- Critical rules to avoid the most common pitfalls applying virtual communication technologies (e-mail, teleconferencing).
- Advantages and disadvantages to different approaches to work splitting.
- A technique to allow sites at different process maturity levels to operate effectively together.
- A method to reduce the cost of project-unique process tailoring for virtual collaborative efforts.
- A strategy to handle site-unique infrastructure issues.
- An 8-step plan to systematically set up and execute a virtual collaborative project while avoiding 11 common pitfalls.

A Note about The Recommendations in This Book

It is worth noting that the recommendations in this book to help your virtual project succeed are based on the assumption that your team members want the project to succeed; sometimes people often behave for selfish reasons. The recommendations provided are likely to fail if a team member is intentionally committed to sabotaging the project. Also note that throughout the book the terms *virtual* and *distributed* are synonymous.

What Does The Future Hold?

Through virtual collaboration multiple remote locations can potentially operate more productively together than traditional single location operations. Unlike traditional subcontract relationships, in which each team member adds its own layer of management and support costs and operates to a large part independently, virtual projects can potentially function more efficiently. This provides the opportunity for a dramatic improvement in real productivity.

Real productivity, as we anticipate it being measured in the future, will no longer be separated from the outside world. We are already finding that real productivity is increasingly tied to the effectiveness of our relationships with external organizations traditionally viewed as competitors. These new relationships, however, are not easily developed, nor do they fit well within traditional internal engineering processes. To understand the issues involved — both technical and non-technical — we must first look inside at our traditional internal engineering operations. This is the subject of Chapter 1.

References

1. Brynjolfsson, Erik and Hitt, Lorin M., Beyond the Productivity Paradox, Communications of the ACM, August 1998, Vol. 41, No. 8, pp. 51.
2. Paulk, Mark, Curtis, Bill, Chrissis, Mary Beth, and Weber, Charles V., Capability Maturity Model for Software, Version 1.1, p. vii.
3. Brandenburger, Adam M. and Nalebuff, Barry J., *Co-opetition*, Bantam Doubleday Dell Publ., New York, 1996.
4. Norton, Bob and Smith, Cathy, *Understanding the Virtual Organization*, 1997 Barron's Educational Series, Hauppauge, NY, pg. 68.

An Overview and Roadmap for Busy Project Leaders

This overview was written for busy leaders. It focuses on the keys leaders need to know to achieve virtual project success. An eight-step plan to set up and execute a distributed development project is provided in summary form, along with common pitfalls, key recommendations, and a roadmap to where more in-depth information can be found within this book.

While the identified steps, shown in Figure 1, may appear traditional and relevant to any project, our focus is on the specific issues related to distributed operations. The common pitfalls and recommendations provided are based on experiences derived from eight virtual-type projects that occurred between 1994 and 2000.

If you are a busy leader, it is our hope that you will find the time to read more than just this brief overview. But, if you do run short on time, we recommend giving a copy of the book to a few of your project engineers. Let them study the tales in the later chapters that most closely fit your project's situation.

Keep in mind, as you think about the common pitfalls and how they might relate to your own project, that the material provided within these pages is not intended for just new projects, nor do we expect everything discussed in this book to be applicable to every reader.

It is also worth noting that many of the issues faced on virtual projects and discussed throughout this book are complex. Don't expect each pitfall to have a simple solution. Often there exists a complex web of interconnected activities that must be understood.

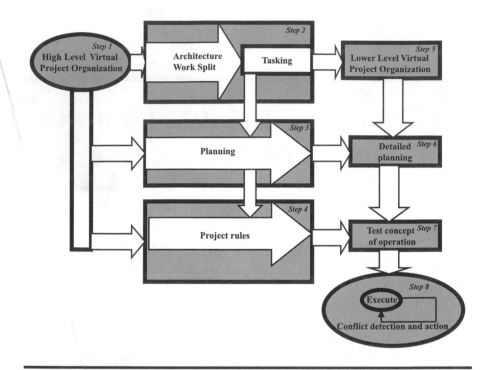

Figure 1   High Level View of Eight-Step Plan

Discuss the issues facing the project with key team members before making any changes. Then establish your own integrated plan based on the project's specific strengths and weaknesses.

Questions

- What skills are the most critical to the success of a Virtual Project Leader?
- What single issue underlies many virtual project leadership struggles?
- Why do traditional approaches to conflict resolution often fail in a virtual environment?
- What techniques have proven effective at resolving virtual project conflict?
- What is a virtual culture and why do we need one?

Step 1 — The High Level Virtual Project Organization

In Chapter 7 organizational structure, guidelines for charters, and criteria for the selection of team leaders are discussed. In this overview section we focus on the most important decision you will make toward the ultimate success of your virtual project — the selection of team leaders.

It should not be a surprise to anyone who has worked on a virtual project that among the key criteria for the selection of leaders you will find strong conflict management skills, and a willingness to consider alternative approaches. While it is true that these skills are desirable for any project leader, they are critical on most virtual projects.

About Virtual Project Leadership Struggles

It is a well-documented fact that one of the prime causes of collaborative failures is unresolved leadership struggles. We don't want to mislead you with respect to what this book can do for you. We can't guarantee that if you follow our guidance all your leadership struggles will go away. Most likely they won't. But we have found — by digging a little deeper into real situations — that underlying many leadership struggles is the issue of control. Furthermore, on many virtual projects, control issues are often rooted in divergent technical expectations. More importantly, most of these divergent technical expectations can be resolved, but often are not due to a breakdown in communication.

Conflict and Informal Activities

> *Virtual Project Pitfall 1: Failure to address the loss of traditional collocated informal activities*

Conflict is not unique to virtual projects, but it is not uncommon for traditional approaches to conflict resolution to fail in a virtual environment. To understand why we need to know more about communication in the organization.

In the early 1980s Alan Cox conducted a survey in which he found that over 66% of middle managers believed that more than half of the communication in their organizations occurred informally.[1] Our experience indicates that this is not only true, but the most important communication, when it comes to conflict resolution, occurs in this manner.

The critical role of informality to success in traditional collocated engineering operations is explored in Chapter 1. In Chapter 2 we delve deeper into the subjects of conflict, informality, and culture. We discuss how conflict is handled differently inside traditional organizations and on virtual projects. Through this investigation we uncovered three factors that often contribute to failed conflict resolution in virtual environments. These factors include distance, differing experiences, and competition.

While there does not exist a simple cure-all for this pitfall, a number of partial solutions are identified throughout the book. Two examples include the collocation of key personnel during critical project stages, and training managers in the warning signs of unhealthy virtual project conflict and associated recommended actions. Many of the partial solutions discussed are product oriented. This has led to our notion of a "Virtual Culture."

Recommendation 1: Support the Virtual Culture Concept and the associated products that fit your project's needs.

The Virtual Culture — A Practical and Affordable Approach

Understanding the root of a problem is the first step to implementing an effective solution — and the good news for virtual projects is that practical and affordable solutions do exist. In step 8, and later in the book, we discuss the concept of a product-oriented *Virtual Culture* to aid in resolving many of the identified pitfalls. You can think of the Virtual Culture as a framework that supports effective communication across the distributed sites of a virtual project.

Question

■ What techniques have proven effective at reducing miscommunication of task assignments with remote team members?

Step 2 — Architecture, Work Split, and Tasking

The placement of architecture, work split, and tasking in the same step may surprise some readers. Traditionally many think of architecture as a technical issue, and work split as a management issue. But in practice work-split decisions can fracture a sound architecture, and a sound technical architecture can provide one of the best task communication and coordination techniques. Often on virtual projects there are three common pitfalls related to work split and task management.

Virtual Project Pitfall 2: Forcing the definition of work split prior to architecture definition.

When work split decisions are forced prior to architecture definition, projects often suffer from fuzzy task responsibilities and technical leadership struggles. Without a well-defined architecture, remote groups often find themselves heading down inconsistent paths leading to project conflict and project control struggles. This common virtual project pitfall can be witnessed in many of the book's early tales.

Virtual Project Pitfall 3: Delaying the definition of work split too long.

Delaying the definition of work split too long can quickly lead to internal team mistrust. The right answer to the problem of fuzzy task responsibilities is not always simply delaying the work split definition until the architecture is defined.

When work split decisions are delayed too long, internal team mistrust quickly builds. Be aware that the consequences of defining a work split that leaves tasking gray in certain areas have proven to be poor solutions to this dilemma.

Recommendation 2: Understand the advantages and disadvantages to different approaches to work split, then define your work split in a fashion that supports clear tasking — and do it in a timely fashion.

If you are struggling with work split issues on your project we recommend first learning more about the advantages and disadvantages of different approaches to work split. There are a variety of ways to split responsibilities across sites. Some are fraught with difficulties, especially when it comes to task definition and management. Refer to Chapter 6 for more information on this subject.

While your architecture needs to be in place when you define your work split, you should also know that an architecture is an evolutionary product. Don't wait for the architecture to be 100% complete because the work split will never get defined.

Virtual Project Pitfall 4: Failure to clearly and unambiguously define remote site tasking responsibilities.

The communication of task responsibilities traditionally has relied upon both formal and informal methods. The breakdown of traditional collocated tasking models in the virtual world is the subject of Chapter 3 and our Architecture Tale. In the virtual world new task management techniques are required.

> *Recommendation 3: Utilize the Task Assignment Record (TAR) and the Component-Product Development Matrix (CPDM) to aid in the clear definition of remote tasking assignments.*

The Task Assignment Record (TAR) and the Component-Product Development Matrix (CPDM) are two important product-oriented remote tasking aids discussed in Chapter 4. You can think of the CPDM as a bridge linking the technical architecture to the task assigned to a remote engineer. By linking the task to the architecture we reduce the risk that the remotely developed product will not successfully integrate. This technique also reduces the risk of task definition ambiguity.

Question

■ What practical techniques can our virtual leaders use to reduce integration risk on a distributed project?

Step 3 — Planning

Planning and coordinating the builds across distributed sites may be the single greatest challenge faced on virtual projects. You can think of a build as a set of hardware and software that meets a subset of the functionality of the final deliverable product. Incremental build approaches are common today — especially on virtual projects — because they reduce integration risk. One of the keys to effective build coordination is found in the technical infrastructure.

Competing Virtual Project Infrastructure Visions

Often on virtual projects we see two competing infrastructure visions. They are referred to as the *Maximize Capital Equipment* vision and the *Seamless* vision.

The *Maximize Capital Equipment* vision is driven by those who demand that the project's infrastructure costs be kept to a minimum. While driving hard toward this vision does reduce the upfront project expenditures, it can also increase the project's integration risk and overall project cost.

The *Seamless* vision, on the other hand, is driven by those who believe that engineers should be able to log-on and do 100% of their engineering work using identical tools and processes from any workstation at any remote project location. While the advantages of the seamless vision are evident, the cost of common hardware, common software tools, and software licenses can quickly become prohibitive. There also exists another, less obvious, cost factor embedded within the seamless vision. This factor can best be seen through our "Let's Use the Most Mature Process" pitfall.

Virtual Project Pitfall 5: "Let's Use the Most Mature Process."

One of the most common pitfalls we have witnessed on virtual projects is the *"Let's Use the Most Mature Process"* pitfall. It usually starts with project leadership's decision to mandate that all project sites employ a common set of procedures. The common set chosen is usually supplied by the highest software-maturity-rated organization on the project.

While it is natural to look to the teammate with the highest process maturity for software guidance, this common process strategy has been proven time and again to be fraught with pitfalls. At the core of the difficulties lies the fundamental fact that procedures represent only a small part of the complete process maturity picture.

When attempts are made to drive process commonality too deeply into a virtual organization the lack of an enabling organization, supporting infrastructure, and a supporting culture at each of the remote sites is almost certain to lead this initiative to failure. More information on the difficulties faced in moving processes to remote sites is provided in Chapter 6 and in the Tale of "Down Here, and Up There."

Recommendation 4: Understand your teammate's strengths.

Instead of looking first to the organization with the most mature process, examine closely the processes employed by each teammate. These organizations were selected to be part of your team. Understand what strengths they bring and, most importantly, upon what those strengths depend. The last thing you want to do at the start-up of a new virtual project is to tell your teammates — with whom you probably don't even have strong relationships yet — how to do the job you chose them to do as part of your team.

> *Recommendation 5: Leverage your teammates' strengths.*

Once the strengths of your teammates — along with what those strengths depend upon — are known, define a common project process at the level where people and products must come together across distributed sites. You don't need to go any lower, and if you do it will probably get your project in trouble. Key to our recommendation is the definition and maintenance of a project's process freedom line.

> *Recommendation 6: Utilize global component criteria to aid in defining and deploying an effective process freedom line.*

Global Component Criteria

Global component criteria concisely define the rules that must be followed by a remote site that is developing a product for project level integration. The global component criteria answer the real questions that engineers need to know to be confident they are accomplishing the right task that will meet the expectations of their remote teammates. The notion of global component criteria supports the effective use of a local and a global process.

The term "global" in this book reflects process level information that is relevant across all remote development sites. "Local" implies a level where each site is free to take advantage of locally available supporting organizational structures, infrastructures, tools, and associated informal cultures. Refer to Figure 2.

How to Leverage Your Teammates' Strengths while Managing the Integration Risk

The concept of a process freedom line allows virtual teaming organizations to do work remotely, while being confident that their products will comply with the overall project requirements. Because the global component criteria define exactly what the requirements are to hand-over products for integration, local proven processes can be leveraged to the maximum extent. This strategy allows us to leverage our teammates' strengths, while at the same time managing associated integration risks.

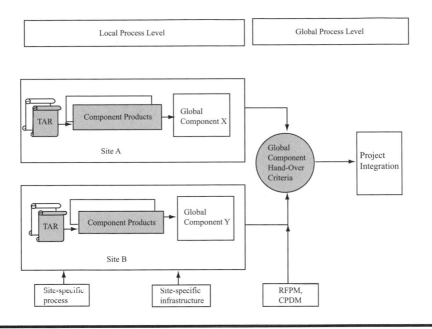

Figure 2 High Level View of Local/Global Process Strategy

The global component notion fits well with our virtual culture concept. Global component criteria are one of the products we recommend for inclusion in a given project's specific implementation of a virtual culture. For more information on global component criteria refer to Chapter 6. Sample global component criteria are also provided in Appendices D and E to this book.

Question

■ Are there specific techniques our leaders can use to guide team members in working more productively in a distributed environment?

Step 4 — Project Rules

There are plenty of good books available today on teams and it is not our intention in this book to duplicate that information. Nevertheless, for virtual teams to succeed there exist key rules that become increasingly important for the team to follow. It is also worth noting that due to the virtual environment some of these rules become more difficult to achieve.

Virtual Project Pitfall 6: Failure to define and deploy critical virtual project team rules.

In Chapter 5, through the use of a number of tales, we present and discuss a number of challenges facing virtual teams. Most of these challenges are associated with team members being physically separated. The effective use of virtual communication technologies such as e-mail, teleconferencing, and video-teleconferencing is also addressed.

Our purpose is not to describe the latest virtual communication technologies, but rather to point out fundamental methodology errors in the use of these technologies. While many of our points may seem obvious, our experience has been that associated productivity losses are real and are significant. More importantly, they are continuing in the twenty-first century.

Recommendation 7: Define and deploy critical virtual team rules and virtual communication rules.

Virtual communication is in its infancy. First-generation lessons must be understood and communicated before improvements take hold. Our objective in Chapter 5 is to accelerate this process by sharing fundamental "first-generation" virtual communication lessons along with providing a set of recommended rules that a new virtual project could use as a starting point.

When you read the tales in Chapter 5 you may conclude that the lessons are not new. But I challenge the reader to honestly assess the degree to which your virtual team is experiencing similar situations that are costing your team more than you would like to admit.

Does your project have rules for the use of e-mail and teleconferencing? More importantly, have your people been trained and are they following the guidance provided?

It has been our experience that while few disagree with the pitfalls and recommended rules provided, most virtual projects in operation today are not doing the best job of deploying effective virtual communication — and the unfortunate part is that it could be costing you plenty in human resources. Furthermore, the recommendations are simply not that expensive to deploy!

Questions

- Are there practical techniques to aid communication at the lower levels of a virtual organization?
- Do Integrated Product Teams (IPTs) work well in a virtual environment?

Step 5 — Lower Level Virtual Project Organization

In this book we employ the terms "component-product" and "global component." A component-product refers to any piece-part artifact produced by one group in the organization that another group depends upon. A global component is a logically related set of component-products meeting a specified criteria geared toward product integration across sites.

Virtual Project Pitfall 7: Failure to establish clear lines of product responsibility deep into the virtual organization.

When we find task responsibility fuzzy at the lower levels of a virtual project organization, we also tend to find an increased integration risk.

Recommendation 8: Utilize the global component criteria to aid in communicating responsibility assignments to remote sites within the virtual organization.

Besides aiding deployment of an effective process freedom line the global component also helps define clear lines of product responsibility within a distributed project environment.

Recommendation 9: Collocate personnel assigned to the same global component (to the maximum extent possible).

Studies have shown that when team members must interact frequently and for short durations (usually the case during global component development), collocation offers the best opportunity for success.[2]

If it is not possible to collocate team members permanently, at a minimum, senior leaders should be collocated during the early critical creative design stage. If the global component team cannot be totally collocated, we strongly recommend that the responsibility for each global component lie within a single site inside the virtual organization.

If your project is facing issues with respect to lower level product responsibility and personnel location, we suggest reading the section on the creative design process in Chapter 2.

Virtual Project Organizations and Integrated Product Teams (IPTs)

Virtual Project Pitfall 8: Utilizing a pure IPT organizational structure on a virtual project.

At the top end of the organization where a breadth of issues must be addressed, the IPT structure tends to function well. This is the level where heads-up activities exist. But we have also observed — and many of our clients concur — that IPTs are weak when it comes to producing executable products that include detailed design, code, and test cases.

Recommendation 10: Employ a hybrid IPT-Functional organizational structure for best results on virtual projects.

Our recommendation for the role of Integrated Product Teams (IPTs) on virtual projects may not be a popular one. It has been our observation that on distributed efforts the most effective engineering organizational structure for getting "real work" accomplished is actually a hybrid IPT-Functional organization.

Where the real engineering — or "heads-down" work — occurs, a more traditional functional structure is often more effective. An example of this can be seen in the need for an infrastructure implementation group that provides common services that multiple sub-product development teams may need across remote sites.

Too often, when virtual projects try to drive a pure IPT structure deep into the organization, responsibility for critical common services is lost.

Question

■ What underlies excessive rework on many virtual projects?

Step 6 — Detailed Planning

Detailed planning is certainly an important step on any project. But on virtual projects its critical relationship to work split is often misunderstood.

Virtual Project Pitfall 9: Failure to establish clear work split prior to detailed planning.

Often on virtual projects work-split decisions get delayed. This can occur for a multitude of reasons — most are not technical. But, all too often, great pressure continues to be brought on the engineering team to complete a detailed project plan despite the uncertainties of where work will actually get done. What is misunderstood in these situations is the extent to which detailed planning depends directly on work location.

While some project planning can be done independent of location, think about the real issues an engineering manager faces when it comes to developing a detailed plan that is actually executable. Here are just a few of the critical questions to be asked:

- Is the development hardware available?
- Have the software tools and licenses been procured and installed?
- Have we identified the engineering personnel who will do this job?
- Have the identified personnel been trained on the chosen platform, language, tools?

To develop a detailed plan that is executable, managers must make assumptions with regard to each of these issues. These are the real issues that truly impact project performance.

Now think about how the answers to these questions are affected when work is moved to a different location. Based on our experience, if you are doing detailed planning, and the work location is still fuzzy, you can start planning right now on doing your detailed plan over again!

Recommendation 11: Raise the detailed planning effort as a risk, if the work split is unclear or uncertain.

If you are driven to do detailed planning and you know there is a good chance the work will move, document the risk associated with your plan. State your assumptions clearly upfront in bold large type where it can't be missed. And be certain to include all of your assumptions with respect to infrastructure, hardware and software, personnel availability, and skills requirements.

Question

■ What practical technique can leaders use early in a virtual project to reduce miscommunication and costly rework?

Step 7 — Test the Operation Concept of the Virtual Organization

Virtual Project Pitfall 10: Failure to test the operation concept of a newly established virtual organization.

In Chapter 1 of this book we explore different ways organizations communicate task expectations in traditional collocated environments. We do so not to judge them, but rather to identify common traits among successful organizations. In particular, while significant differences in terminology and task partitioning exist, in all the successful organizations we have observed the following key common characteristic:

Individuals inside the organization understand their roles and they understand the organization's expectations of them.

In many of these same successful organizations there is a strong subculture utilized as a powerful mechanism — although unwritten — in communicating task expectations deep into the organization.

It is unreasonable to expect new virtual organizations to instantly operate as effectively as strong-cultured, time-tested collocated operations. Effective organizations — collocated or virtual — don't just happen. But techniques do exist to aid in accelerating the growth of effective virtual operations.

Recommendation 12: Employ walkthroughs of the Organization's Operation Concept to uncover potential problem areas early.

Newly established virtual project organizations should set aside the time to walk through the key organizational scenarios that are most likely to cause leadership friction. When leaders take the time to discuss openly their visions of the virtual organization, potential problem areas can often be uncovered and resolved quickly.

Often, at the start of a new project, leaders are uncertain where the most likely "hot-spots" may be. In Chapter 7 we identify, discuss, and recommend a number of likely problem areas based on the experiences of others.

In particular, if you are having trouble with task management of remote personnel or remote "sub-teams," we suggest reading Step 7 in Chapter 7 carefully. Take the time to understand the varying task direction and task management models presented. But don't limit yourself to the scenarios we discuss. Take into consideration the specific issues your project is facing. Then set aside the appropriate amount of time for your project leaders to discuss these issues openly — and be sure to do it in a face-to-face setting.

Is It Possible for Conflict and Common Vision to Coexist?

Throughout this book examples of virtual project conflict and leadership struggles are presented and discussed. The need for a common vision among team leaders has been stressed by many authors.[3] This raises an important question:

Is it possible for conflict and common vision to coexist?

We believe the answer is yes — but only if one sees the right common vision.

The Common Vision Tale

A few years ago we had an opportunity to work with a client who was convinced the lack of a common vision among his project leaders was pulling the team apart. The project leadership team included a program manager, a deputy program manager, an engineering manager, a deputy engineering manager, four product leads, and two senior staff engineers.

The leaders attempted to solve the problem by assigning one of the senior staff engineers to the task of drafting a project common vision statement. The initial attempt, which was rejected by the team, contained high level generalities and a number of potentially ambiguous statements. The second attempt, which took about a week to produce, was fifty pages in length, and packed with a number of real project solutions.

The engineering manager and one of the other senior staff members strongly disagreed with a number of the technical points in the document. One of the product team leads couldn't find enough time to read it all, and the program manager found the document too complex to comprehend. Soon after, the project's common vision initiative was abandoned.

The Right Common Vision

Getting your project leaders together to discuss openly and face-to-face the dynamic side of the organization has a number of potential benefits for your project. First, this activity can aid productivity by supporting the detection of organizational defects early. Second, early operation concept discussions provide a form of on-the-job training for the team leaders themselves.

Max DePree tells us, "We do not grow by knowing all of the answers, but rather by living with the questions."[3] This statement applies to our leaders as well.

Project leaders, like others, learn by listening to their teammates. Through this process they gain a deeper understanding of their teammates' concerns, but more importantly a solid foundation for building strong interpersonal bonds is formed. Common vision must start at the top. It must start with our leaders — and its technical content is less important than the lighted path it provides for others.

Question

■ Are there any easy-to-spot warning signs leaders should be on the look out for that are specific to virtual projects?

Step 8 — Execute

Virtual Project Pitfall 11: Failure to deploy an effective project-tailored Virtual Culture.

All of the planning and knowledge of the pitfalls experienced by others are of little use unless the plan is deployed. All too often we see well-intentioned projects — virtual and collocated — put plans in place that are never executed.

Recommendation 13: Ensure that your leaders know the warning signs of healthy and destructive virtual team conflict and are taking action at the appropriate time.

The first step to effective process deployment on a virtual project is ensuring leaders know the warning signs of both healthy and destructive team conflict. This is discussed at greater length in Chapter 7, Step 8, along with recommended courses of action to be taken for situations that commonly occur. While conflict management is particularly important on virtual projects, it represents only a part of the full virtual solution.

Why Do We Need a Virtual Culture?

A prime benefit of testing the virtual organization — as discussed in the previous step — is early resolution of potential problem areas, or "disconnects," in the organization. Disconnects tend to be more prevalent on virtual projects due to distance and the breakdown of traditionally relied-upon informal communication methods.

Recommendation 14: Deploy your tailored virtual culture — make it work for you!

What Do We Mean by a Virtual Culture?

The concept of a virtual culture is a simple, yet powerful idea that brings an information-age perspective to the notion of culture. The virtual culture — unlike traditional collocated engineering cultures — is product-oriented. There are more than 24 candidate virtual culture products identified and discussed throughout this book.

The virtual culture is not intended to replace past traditional collocated cultures. In fact, you shouldn't try to replace strong local cultures. Rather, our strategy and recommendations are based on leveraging the strengths of your teammates within their proven environments.

The virtual culture complements existing site-specific cultures by providing the critical information needed to coordinate and communicate key tasking information across distributed sites. This approach reduces the risk of rework when remotely developed partial products are integrated together.

See Figure 3 for a high level view of our Virtual Project Management Framework. We employ this framework to aid in helping both new and on-going virtual projects set up an effective virtual culture. This framework is discussed further in Chapter 8.

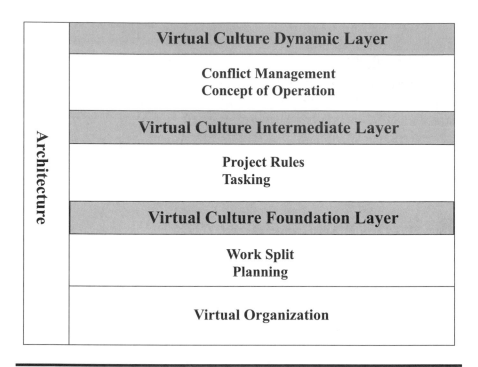

Figure 3   High Level View of Virtual Project Management Framework

It is worth noting that a key difference between a virtual culture and a traditional culture is found in its formality. Through our experience we have concluded that an effective virtual culture cannot be informal. In other words, it must be WRITTEN DOWN. We recognize that in today's world this emphasis on the written word may not be popular.

Informal Activities and the Virtual World

You will find the concept of informality discussed throughout this book. The term "informal" as used here means unplanned and undocumented. It is our opinion that in the past informal activities may not have received the attention they deserve. This occurred because in strong-cultured collocated environments the benefits of informality came to us essentially for free.

In the virtual world this is no longer the case. We cannot rely on these informal communication mechanisms to work for us at a distance in the same way they have worked for us in collocated environments. Therefore, in the virtual world, the written word takes on new and increased importance.

The Written Word in the Virtual World

Our recommendations with respect to a more formal virtual culture should not be interpreted as a step backward to the days of voluminous documentation. The virtual culture is not intended to include historical milestone type documentation, but rather it focuses on those critical pieces of information that must be coordinated and communicated across distributed sites. When you go virtual and utilize remote operations more things do need to be written down to support effective remote communication.

Think about the information that today is conveyed through unplanned meetings in hallways, at lunch, casually in cubicles, and over the tops of cubicles. If you believe that e-mail, teleconferencing, videoconferencing and netmeeting can replace what collocated teams have provided in the past, then don't put this book down until you have read at least Chapters 1 through 3.

If you're just too busy, then at least scan the rest of the book. Focus on the **highlighted "Where are we going?," "About the Tale," "Problem,"** **"Insight,"** and **"Solution"** paragraphs that let you extract key information quickly. The reader will find 34 **"Insight"** paragraphs and 50 **"Solution"** paragraphs strategically inserted throughout Chapters 1 through 8. This information takes the reader to the next level of detail beyond the 14 recommendations identified in this overview. An abbreviated form of the insights and solutions can also be found in Appendix L of this book.

After you have finished, give a copy of the book to your project engineer and ask him or her to let you know if they think the idea of a virtual culture can help your project. If they say yes, then don't just keep thinking about it. A virtual culture isn't that expensive to implement. But the potential cost of not implementing one is.

References

1. Cox, Alan, *The Cox Report on the American Corporation*, Delacorte Press, NY, 1982, pp. 112–114.
2. Gindele, Mark E. and Rumpf, Richard, "Effects of Collocating Integrated Product Teams," *Program Manager*, July–August 1998, p. 38.
3. DePree, Max, *Leadership is an Art*, Dell, NY, 1989, p. 102.

1 Traditional Collocated Engineering from the Inside

How does a manager know if a remote team member is doing the right thing? This concern has been expressed — in various forms — by many managers when surveyed about their views on virtual teams.[1] Many of us are uneasy with the thought of our teammates being apart. But how well do we really understand the driving forces behind our collocated successes? We like to look our co-workers in the eye, but do we really understand the impact on productivity when team members are separated by hundreds of miles?

In the past, the pressure to answer these questions was minimal. While there has always been high interest in productivity, its relationship to the physical location of personnel didn't seem all that important when the vast majority of the engineering effort was collocated. Today this is changing. Pressures are mounting to adopt more and more virtual-type operations. This means new decisions for managers regarding new tools, technologies, and related skills — decisions that directly affect productivity.

Too often these decisions must be made quickly without adequate time to fully analyze the cost benefit trade-offs. Also, many times these decisions are made without a firm understanding of what works and what doesn't work in traditional collocated engineering environments. It is important that we continually seek productivity improvements, but inappropriate changes place current effective engineering mechanisms in jeopardy. When decisions are made that affect the engineering process both tactical and strategic impacts must be considered.

Where are we going?

In this chapter we take a close look from the inside at traditional collocated engineering operations. We first look at what it takes for an engineer in today's collocated environments to become effective at his (her) job. Collocated engineering organizations and how the people inside them really work are discussed. We emphasize how responsibilities are communicated, and the powerful role played by subcultures down inside these organizations. Understanding — from the inside — how collocated engineering works is the first step to avoiding the pitfalls that lie before us inside the virtual world.

1.1   How Does an Engineer Become Effective at His Job?

How much of what it takes to be a successful engineer can we find in formal textbooks and documented procedures? If you pluck an engineer out of one environment where he has been successful, then insert him into another, will his formal education and acquired engineering experience be sufficient to carry him to the same level of success he has known in the past?

Problem

To be effective an engineer must first understand what he is expected to do. He must understand the expectations in his current organization.

Think about how engineers learn in your organization. Then ask yourself this question: How much of what an engineer really needs to know to do his job effectively does he learn through formal written procedures and planned training courses?

Now picture in your mind an engineer in his first week on the job. We'll call him John. Picture John's desk and the volumes of corporate procedures, policies, and plans stacked on top. Not all companies have voluminous corporate procedures, but many have found it difficult to streamline established processes that have evolved over many years. It's Wednesday — John's third day on the new job. He's looking a bit blurry-eyed as he slides one more procedure to the side, then reaches for another. But then he hesitates. Something has caught his eye. He reaches instead for the terse one page task description he received from his manager on Monday. After scanning it quickly, he turns with a puzzled look on his face to his cubicle mate.

"Hey, Jim, where do I begin?" he bluntly asks as he pushes the task description under his cubicle mate's nose. After a quick glance at the paper, Jim reaches for a manila folder in his top right-hand drawer.

"Here, John, let me show you how I do it." Jim opens the folder to a sample work product and hands it to John who then spends a few moments carefully examining it. John appears to be looking for something specific.

"Jim, I don't see anything in here about the user interface." Jim shakes his head back and forth.

"You don't need to worry about the GUIs," he replies. "Just talk to Ed down the hall. He's terrific with GUIs. Ed handles all our user interface work including the documentation." John continues scrutinizing the product.

"Jim, your diagrams look great! It must have taken you forever to create them."

"Not really," replies Jim. I just sketched them out and gave them to Mary Lou in the support group. She's a real pro with graphics. She'll correct the grammar, and format the documentation, too," says Jim swiveling back to face his monitor.

"Thanks Jim, I really appreciate it," says John.

"Happy to have been able to help," replies Jim. "And if you have more questions don't hesitate to ask."

1.2 The Role of Informal Communication

Can you sense what is happening in this exchange? While not everyone is always eager to help out, in this case in less than 10 minutes John has learned three key pieces of information.

1. Work product expectations

    First, John has learned critical information about the organization's expectations of him — information that could never be captured through formal procedures alone. John knows that Jim is a respected employee. He sees work produced by Jim. This tells John something his task description cannot convey. It conveys to him important subjective information about the content and quality expectations inside his new organization.

2. Organizational responsibilities

Second, John has gained knowledge about responsibilities within the organization. John's department is not responsible for Graphical User Interfaces (GUIs). He has also been given the name of a highly regarded contact, Ed, for user interface work. He has a clearer picture of what the organization will expect of him because he has a clearer picture of what others do in the organization.

3. Peer relationship

The simple words, "happy to have been able to help", translate into the start of an important peer relationship. John knows that Jim is going to be of great value to him during his familiarization period in the organization. He knows he can gain more critical information from Jim than he would ever be able to uncover through formal means alone.

1.3 Organizational Subcultures

Think again about how engineers learn in an organization. Part of the process includes learning how the organization works. That is, who does what and when in a formal sense. But there exists another side to each organization — a more subjective less formal side. This is where the organizational culture and its subcultures reside. The existence of industrial and organizational cultures has been well documented.[2,3] Inside each organization *subculture groups* based on common responsibilities, skills, and technologies can be found. These groups are characterized by strongly held beliefs and perceptions supported by related experiences.

The existence of subcultures and the beliefs these groups hold cannot be found on organizational charts. Subculture groups may or may not align directly with formal organizational departments. Normally the beliefs and perceptions of these groups are strongly influenced by both the direct personal experiences of members and the experiences of older personnel in the organization, who have passed down, usually by word of mouth, their own experiences and beliefs.

Insight

Strong subculture beliefs and perceptions tend to mold organizational views from the inside.

Each engineer has his/her own set of experiences, which are shared with others. Over time this sharing influences coworkers, which in turn affects the perceptions and beliefs of the group and ultimately the organization. Traditionally, this process occurs slowly — over multiple programs and years. During this time an integration of beliefs occurs along with an integration of individuals who hold them.

Those who are viewed as inside a subculture group do not always agree with 100% of the group's beliefs. But being a member of a subculture group implies a fundamental conformance with the group's core beliefs.

Acceptance of an individual into a subculture group doesn't happen overnight. New engineers must listen to stories, including those legendary experiences of former group members. As one hears more and more stories, over time, buy-in and acceptance either occur, or do not. Those who buy-in, in turn, relay the stories to others, which causes the subculture to thrive.

1.3.1 Engineering Effectiveness and Subcultures

Part of the process of an engineer becoming effective at his job requires an awareness of the subcultures within the organization. This doesn't mean a new engineer must become a member of a subculture group to gain the group's support. But we have found through our experiences with multiple organizations that acceptability of a given engineering solution is oftentimes wrapped up in the perceptions of key subculture groups within the organization. Like it or not, gaining buy-in from critical personnel in an organization plays a major role in the success of each engineer.

Successful engineers, while they don't need to agree with a given subculture group's beliefs, must demonstrate openness to the group's ideas. They must take the time to listen not only to the groups' beliefs, but also to the experiences that led to those beliefs.

Insight

The perception of key subculture groups inside an organization is often crucial to the ultimate success of individual engineers.

Clearly, new engineers in an organization have a great deal more to learn than what can be found in textbooks and formal organizational procedures.

They must also take the time to listen and honestly consider the experiences of their teammates.

In the early 1980s Alan Cox conducted an extensive survey on communication in corporate America. Over 66% of the middle managers surveyed indicated a belief that more than half of all communication in their organizations occurred informally.[4]

Insight

Our experience indicates not only that the majority of communication within organizations occurs informally, but also some of the most critical information required to succeed is transmitted through such means.

1.4 Organizational Variation

It is now time to turn our attention from the informal influences an organization places on its people to the organization itself. If a manager or senior engineer working today in a large advanced technology software-intensive organization were asked to examine the chart in Figure 1.1, he would likely shake his head up and down, reflecting familiarity with the functional organizational structure and terminology employed on the chart.

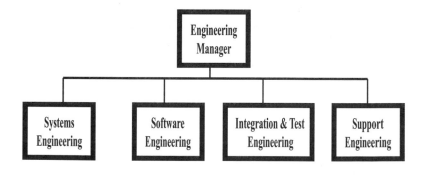

Figure 1.1 Traditional Functional Engineering Organization

Each rectangle on the referenced chart below the engineering manager is a department, each with its own manager and pool of skilled engineers.

Integration and Test in some organizations is merged with Systems Engineering, while in other organizations it is broken out with its own manager and resource pool. At this level, similarity across diverse organizations is evident. Nevertheless, when one looks a bit deeper a different picture emerges.

1.4.1 Large and Small Engineering Organizations

Consider Fred, a new hire at the multi-billion dollar ABC Corporation. Fred has never worked for a large company before. His last job was with a commercial firm with a total staff of less than 10 software engineers. His new manager, Charlie, has given Fred his first assignment and is just now introducing him to his cubicle mate Tom. Tom has worked for ABC for 3 years. Fred and Tom are both in Charlie's Database Department. The scenario goes like this:

"Good to have you on board, Fred. Have you done database work before?" asks Tom. Fred nods his head.

"On my last job I was the only engineer on the project. I worked directly with the customer, and I designed the user interface, modeled the database, and wrote all the application code."

"You did all that alone?" responds Tom incredulously.

"I had to," continues Fred, "there was no one else. I did all the documentation, too, including the graphics and final production."

"You'll find things different here at ABC," replies Tom. "Systems Engineering will handle the customer, and we have a separate group to handle all the application code. Here at ABC the Database group sticks to modeling and implementing the database."

"I like to get my hands into a lot more than that," replies Fred eagerly, but Tom cautions him.

"If you want to be successful here at ABC you need to work closely with systems engineering, and the application group." Tom notices a puzzled look on Fred's face.

"Look, Fred, it's just the way things are around here. It's the way the system works."

We've all known people who for one reason or another just seem to fit better in either a large or a small organization. Some just seem lost in the world of mega-corporations. Often, these same individuals thrive in a small start-up company environment. On the other hand, there are those who yearn for the structure large organizations provide and feel lost without it.

1.4.2 Systems and Software

While many organizations have a similar top level structure, inside these organizations implementation can vary greatly. The term *component-product* is used in this book to mean *any piece-part artifact produced by one group in the organization upon which another group depends.* Most large systems are viewed as composites of *component-products.*[2] As an example, Systems Engineering may be responsible for producing a Software Specification on which the Software Engineering department depends. In this case, the Software Specification is a component-product produced by Systems Engineering.

While the notion of component-product seems clear, when examining implementation across multiple organizations there are many subtle, but important, variations. The following is an example of three organizational variations with respect to the ways systems and software engineering interact. Our three variants are:

- Strong systems variant
- Collaborative variant
- Guidance variant

1. *Strong systems variant*

In the strong systems variant case, Systems Engineering is responsible for the complete production of the Software Specification component-product, which — when complete — is formally handed over to Software Engineering for implementation. In this model Software Engineering has no responsibility for the production of the Software Specification.

However, in one organization where we saw this model employed, the Software Engineering group oftentimes loans personnel to Systems Engineering to work on the Software Specification. After the specification is reviewed and approved, these individuals move back to the Software Engineering organization where they take responsibility for implementing the specification. This implementation, while not originally planned, evolved within the organization based on lessons learned. The process supports the separation of Systems and Software organizational responsibilities, while minimizing problems associated with the "throw-it-over-the-wall" phenomenon. It also has been found to be more responsive to staffing needs.

2. *Collaborative variant*

In the collaborative variant case, which we believe to be the most common approach, Systems and Software collaborate, with Systems being responsible for — but not actually producing — the complete specification. In one case where we saw this variant work the project produced a software specification through the use of an object-oriented analysis tool. Software personnel tasked from the Software Engineering department produced most of the Specification, while Systems personnel provided critical input data (i.e., algorithms) and maintained overall review and approval responsibility.

3. *Guidance variant*

The guidance variant case is a variation of case 2. In this situation, Systems Engineering responsibilities take the form of guidance, review and approval, with the complete specification produced by Software Engineering. This variant is used in organizations that tend to maintain a lean Systems Engineering staff. Systems Engineering maintains responsibility for the accuracy of the algorithms, and works closely with the Software team, but the algorithms are produced directly in the final specification by personnel from Software Engineering.

In all cases described Systems Engineering maintains responsibility for ensuring the accuracy and completeness of the final specification.

1.4.3 Support Functions

There are significant variations in the services provided by groups referred to as Support Engineering. In some organizations Support Engineering borders on being non-existent. This is often the case in commercial operations. At the other end of the spectrum, Support Engineering may provide technical editing, professional graphics services, document formatting, production and configuration control and management. When these services are not provided by a support engineering group, the responsibility usually falls back to the systems and software engineering groups.

1.4.4 Architecture, User Interface, and Databases

To further demonstrate organizational variation we have selected three examples to discuss briefly. These examples have not been chosen randomly, and will be discussed further in later chapters when we examine more closely virtual collaborative operations.

- Architecture
- User Interface
- Databases

Architecture

Today there is no industry-wide accepted standard definition for the term *architecture*. We have found through experience working with multiple organizations a great variety of both expectations and responsibility of architectural component-products. Some organizations assign responsibility of architecture component-products to a separate architecture group, while others distribute this responsibility in different ways across the systems and software departments. A common pitfall on virtual collaborative projects related to architecture is discussed at greater length later in this book.

User Interface

Two primary organizational variants exist with respect to user interfaces. These include

- User interface separate department
- User interface merged with application

User interface separate department

In organizations that focus on real-time and embedded applications, user interface software responsibilities are often split off and owned by a specialized User Interface department. Rationale for partitioning user interaction software includes

- Need for specialized skills
  User interface development requires unique training and skills. Productivity can be enhanced by training and supporting a core group that provides all needed user interface services.
- Style consistency
  Isolating the responsibility to a single group provides greater assurance of style consistency across all applications.
- Reuse
  Experience has shown that reuse increases when responsibilities for similar types of software are grouped together.

User interface merged with application

In applications where there is heavy user interaction responsibilities for the user interface are often merged with those of application design. Our second variant, user interface merged with application, is described in more detail as part of the database example which follows.

Databases

In organizations that specialize in database-intensive applications, the optimum placement of user interface responsibilities is frequently viewed differently for real-time and embedded applications. In the database world fourth-generation languages tend to tightly couple data to the user interface. By merging the user interface and data responsibility into the same department, a major organizational interface can be eliminated.

In organizations that develop large databases where the majority of the data accesses are through a user interface, this grouping of responsibility is predominant. It is also common in smaller organizations to find more responsibilities, such as database, user interface, and systems engineering grouped together.

In large organizations and those that build applications with complex database interfaces, systems engineering is often responsible for data definition, and a separate database department is responsible for database implementation.

In large organizations it is not uncommon to find systems engineers without database modeling skills being tasked with defining database requirements. In these cases systems engineering provides a data requirements component-product to the database group.

Insight

An engineer, if he is to be effective at his job, must understand more than how the organization is described on paper. He must understand how the organization works in practice. And he must understand the organization's expectations with respect to his specific task.

Some of the information an engineer needs to know can be learned by reading organizational descriptions and charters, but much can only be acquired through other less formal means.

1.5 Organizational Evolution

How do engineering organizations become what they are? If you've lived through the creation of an organization you're probably well aware of this painful process. During the early stages tasks often fall through wide open cracks. Organizations that survive this stage do so because task responsibilities get picked up. But this doesn't always happen as you might think.[5] In the end, two organizational views often emerge:

- The original (goal) vision for the organization
- The actual evolving operation of the organization

The original (goal) vision for the organization includes a description of each department (or integrated product team), its responsibilities, and its hierarchical relationship to other departments in the organization. Responsibilities are usually captured through written charters.

The actual operation of an organization may evolve in many ways. The following examples have been chosen to demonstrate how organizations evolve in practice.

1. Doing whatever it takes

   In young organizations we often find personnel with unlimited enthusiasm coupled with an attitude of "doing whatever it takes" to get the job done. In this environment formal organizational boundaries are rarely viewed as hard and fast. In one case a manager's career path along with his departmental responsibilities were drastically altered simply because he volunteered to get a document out the door and into the customer's hands by a specified date. At the time he volunteered, the manager had little idea what he was signing up for. He just wanted to help. Rapidly, however, the issues related to quality control, configuration management, and technical publications caught hold of him. Since no one else in the young organization owned these responsibilities, his department quickly grew to include support services for the entire organization.

2. Personnel availability

   A junior programmer discovered an intense desire to learn as much as possible about computer operating systems and real-time executive software. Unfortunately, his department wasn't responsible for this kind of work. Nevertheless, his energy and interest allowed him to complete his formal assignments, and still have time left to pursue other interests. Soon his department found its boundaries of responsibility expanding. The following scenario demonstrates how this can happen.

1.5.1

The Push-Pull Organizational Tale

The setting for this scenario is an engineering management meeting called by Jack, a manager responsible for multiple engineering departments. Fred works for Jack as the manager of the Computer Systems department.

"Fred, aren't you done with that test tool assignment yet?" asks Jack peering across the table.

"That job is falling behind schedule, Jack. I don't have anyone to work the plot feature. All my people are fully tasked through next month," replies Fred.

"That task is critical. It's got to get done this month," replies Jack as he glances around the room at his other managers. "We must have someone in this organization who can help."

"Tim could do it," responds Gary, the manager of the Avionics Department.

"Tim has been showing a lot of interest in that test tool and has already offered to help check it out when it's ready. He's also running ahead of schedule with his APU assignment," adds Gary.

Sharing human resources across department boundaries is not unusual in high technology organizations. In this case, Tim could be loaned to the Computer Systems Department. More permanent shifts in departmental responsibility can also result.

Frequently personnel, like Tim, who pursue additional work are not only energetic, but are often found to be among the most sought after engineers in the organization. Through his enthusiasm and informal peer interactions, Tim may ignite more interest and enthusiasm among his department coworkers. High energy workers often trigger greater interest inside organizational subgroups thereby fostering both individual and organizational change. Often, weaknesses or unclear responsibilities in the current organization provide the conditions that stimulate these changes.

As Gary observes this growing interest within his department he could be motivated to push the organization to increase his department's responsibility. In this case, Gary already has at least one individual with the interest and skills and Tim may have motivated other department peers. The stage is set for a win-win. The organization needs stronger test tool support and Gary would like to keep his highly skilled work force together and challenged.

When one department is overloaded with work, and another department has available and qualified personnel, shifting task responsibilities can aid the overall strength and vitality of an organization. The right mix of interest, need, and available skills often sets the stage for organizational change involving responsibility shifts. Depending on the extent of the change, these shifts can occur without formal announcement or documentation.

Insight

Organizational structures are never permanent. They continually evolve through a dynamic and healthy push-pull tension often initiated from inside the organization. It is for this reason that we claim — at any point in time — how an organization really works is best communicated by those who work within it.

These observations will become more important later when we examine more closely the effects of going virtual.

1.5.2 Common Key Characteristic of Successful Organizations

It is not our intent here to judge the merits of particular organizational approaches, but rather to acknowledge their existence and to point out a key characteristic common to all successful organizations.

Key characteristic of successful organizations

In each case, when a collocated organization functions successfully to produce an end-product, individuals within that organization understand their specific roles. That is, they understand the organization's expectations of them.

As an example, in a successful organization that employs the case 2 variant described in Section 1.4.2, both Software and Systems Engineering understand that Systems Engineering will produce the algorithms. Both groups understand their component-product interdependencies. But what would happen if Software Engineering was assuming variant 2, and System Engineering was assuming variant 3? In this case, the software team would expect a component-product from Systems, but the Systems team wouldn't be planning on producing one.

While component-products can vary substantially across different organizations, inside each successful organization the *definition of* and *responsibility for* that organization's specific component-products clearly exist. This mutual understanding of roles, responsibilities, and expectations leads to operational efficiency with minimal duplication of effort. The successful organization appears from the outside to function as a single unit. Its piece parts (component-products) may vary on the inside, but in each case they come together without major surprises into a final integrated product.

It is worth noting here that in our experience many successful organizations do not oftentimes write down or describe formally the *definition of* and *responsibility for* each component-product. Be aware that component products are not formal deliverable products, but rather represent dependencies across departments inside an organization.

In large software-intensive organizations with long histories of development and evolution this knowledge may have been written down at some point in time but due to organizational evolution its current state is most often passed on through less formal means.

1.6   Organizational Expectations

Insight

The existence of organizational expectations isn't something that can be found in formal organizational procedures, yet they are highly influential in the ultimate determining of the degree of success achieved by an engineer.

Organizational expectations are intertwined with the unwritten subcultures of an organization that have evolved over years based largely on composite team experiences. Task assignment records, on the other hand, are formal records serving a different purpose.

1.6.1 Task Assignment Records (TARs)

Much of the preceding discussion on how engineers become effective at their jobs has focused on the informal side of the organization. In many organizations task assignment definition is also communicated through formal means. Task assignment records, referred to as TARs, are employed in some organizations to define formally an engineer's task. TARs vary in format across different organizations, but their content is similar in most companies that use them. The purpose of a TAR is to communicate critical task information in a formal and crisp manner. A TAR is usually a single page (paper or electronic) containing the following information. See Table 1.1 for a sample TAR.

1. Task identifier
2. Work authorization
3. Assigned engineer
4. Manager
5. Allocated budget
6. Planned start and complete dates
7. Brief description of task

Table 1.1   Task Assignment Record (TAR)

Project Identifier
Department Identifier
Task Identifier
Task Authorization
Responsible Manager
Assigned Engineer
Budget
Planned Start Date
Planned Complete Date
Actual Complete Date
Task Description

1.6.2 Task Expectations

In organizations that are not functioning as well as they would like there is often a misconception that formal TARs capture the essence of what an engineer needs to achieve task success. In practice the informal side is at least equal in importance.

Whereas TARs focus on objective task management information, task expectations are more subjective flowing from organizational level expectations and subculture group beliefs and perceptions. Unlike organizational expectations which are general in nature, task expectations are very specific and relate directly to how a manager will actually determine the degree of success achieved by an engineer on a given task. The following scenario demonstrates how task expectations work.

"John, how is your task going?" asks Frank, the Applications group manager.

"I've been reading quite a bit, Frank. I have a good idea how I'm going to design it," responds John a recent new hire in the organization. Frank takes a long look at John, then continues.

"Have you talked to Fred." Frank is looking directly at John as he speaks. "Fred did a great job on a system that is very similar. The customer loved Fred's approach."

"I've haven't talked to Fred yet, sir. But I plan on discussing my approach with him next week." Frank nods his head. "Be sure to do that. Fred's been with us a long time. You can learn a great deal from him."

It is clear from this exchange that Fred's opinion carries a great deal of weight in Frank's eyes. Fred has proven himself. He is a recognized expert in the firm. Fred's success with a similar design is an important piece of information that John needs to be aware of in executing his task. Other organizations have their own recognized experts with their own histories of successful and less than successful experiences. These experiences all play heavily into a given organization's perceptions and expectations.

Although it is not identified formally on his TAR, John is expected to talk to Fred and consider *strongly* the approach that Fred used. This is a specific task expectation that Frank has and it will undoubtedly affect not only Frank's view, but ultimately the organization's view of the success of this task. If John chooses a different design approach, he better have done his homework, documented the reasons for his decision, and be prepared to defend his decision. It may well be an uphill battle to succeed with a design that has not been proven within the company, especially when one already exists and is believed to be the right solution for the project.

1.7 Formality and Informality

In this book the term *formal* means *planned and/or documented*; the term *informal* means *unplanned and undocumented*.

The intent is not to imply that formal corporate procedures and training material are failing to meet their objectives in guiding engineers to understand what they are expected to do. Formal training, procedures, and plans provide necessary components that help an engineer understand his responsibilities. However, experience indicates that formal processes and procedures, by themselves, are insufficient for engineering success.

Insight

In the past the importance of the process's informal side may not have received the attention it deserves due largely to the high visibility of an organization's process maturity goals and its focus on the formal side.

1.8   Process Maturity

When speaking of formal processes and procedures it is often in the context of an organization's process maturity. The Software Engineering Institute Capability Maturity Model (SEI CMM) provides assistance to organizations looking to improve the effectiveness of their software processes.[6] But just how is process maturity related to an engineer's effectiveness at executing his job?

According to the SEI CMM,[6] characteristics of a mature organization include

- Processes fit the work actually done by engineers.
- Managers have visibility into actual product development and quality.
- Engineers understand the value in following the processes.
- Support infrastructure exists.

Immature organizations, on the other hand, are defined in the CMM as organizations that exhibit the following characteristics:

- Even if software process has been specified, it is not rigorously followed, or enforced.
- Activities are reactionary — they focus on solving the immediate crisis (fire-fighting).
- Schedules and budgets are routinely exceeded.
- Product functionality and quality are often compromised.
- No objective basis for judging product quality exists.

The CMM states specifically that in organizations where disciplined processes are consistently followed the engineers "understand the value in doing so," and that in these organizations an "infrastructure exists to support the process."[6] The CMM also tells us that when mature organizations encounter times of crisis the organizational processes and practices don't break down.

But what is it that leads one organization to break down under a crisis, while another does not? Similarities exist between immature organizations and distributed engineering operations. This is discussed further in the next section.

1.8.1 Is it Easy to Physically Distribute a Mature Process?

A few years back an organization had an SEI level 3 process rating at its main location. For programmatic reasons it was decided that a significant portion of the development of a particular project had to take place hundreds of miles away from the main site. The project plan called for running the remote site development activities using the same SEI level 3 procedures and processes proven at the main site.

To implement this plan all the formal procedures, plans, and policies were physically moved to the remote site and the same formal training given to personnel at the main site was planned and provided to the personnel at the satellite location. To further aid in process deployment at the satellite organization, a few of the project personnel from the main location were temporarily transferred to the satellite location.

The original goal was to develop half the software at each location. Despite this seemingly sound approach, the project was never able to develop software at the remote site anywhere near as effectively as it did at the main site. The remote site continued to operate in a chaotic unpredictable manner for a period of time until the project was eventually shut down due largely to customer dissatisfaction.

1.8.2 What Makes a Mature Process Mature?

Martha Haywood, in her book *Managing Virtual Teams*,[1] defines Corporate Memory as "*Whatever systems your team has in place to retain the knowledge to repeatably manufacture your product.*"

Martha tells us that corporate memory includes both a formal and an informal side. The formal side includes project libraries comprised of standards, procedures, policies, designs, trade studies, and reports.

Experience says that organizations which have learned to repeatedly manufacture a product when collocated can quickly breakdown when faced with the challenges of distributed operation. There are many factors involved. The skill level of people available at remote locations is one factor. Martha says that based on her experience: *"When managers begin to manage distributed teams, they are most afraid of being unable to detect incompetent remote team members."*

But is it really incompetence that causes distributed teams to fail, or is it possible this is a perception resulting — at least partially — from poorly communicated expectations? Do remote team members fully understand the organizational expectations, and the subcultures that underlie them? Have they heard the legendary stories that led the team to their current beliefs. Have they listened to the experiences of their teammates?

In times of crisis, immature organizations revert to doing things that are inconsistent with defined processes. In times of crisis, people often react on instinct. In mature organizations, people feel they are part of the organization. They own the process because it reflects their own experiences as well as the experiences of their peers. They are part of the inner subcultures that give the organization its true identity. This does not mean that individuals in mature organizations do not express dissenting views or believe the organization works perfectly in all cases.

Insight

In times of crisis, personnel in mature organizations work through the organization — not around it — because they believe in it.

Underlying real process maturity there is always a strong set of beliefs backed by experiences that go deeper than formal processes and procedures. Often this is not found on distributed projects.

Problem

On many distributed projects, the divisive nature of competing subcultures — subcultures based on divergent experiences and beliefs — is witnessed.

The effects of inconsistent and poorly communicated task expectations are also seen. The following chapters examine these situations are examined in greater depth through a number of tales based on real project experiences.

CHAPTER 1 KEY POINTS SUMMARY
Subcultures mold organizational views
Perception of subculture groups crucial to engineer success
Majority of critical communication occurs informally
Engineer must understand how organization works in practice
Organizations evolve through dynamic push-pull tension
Organizational expectations highly influential in ultimate success of engineer
In past informal side has not received attention it deserves
In times of crisis personnel in mature organizations work through the organization

References

1. Haywood, Martha, *Managing Virtual Teams*, Artech House, Boston, 1998, pp. 10–11.
2. von Meir, Alexandra, Occupational cultures as a challenge to technological innovation, *IEEE Transactions on Engineering Management*, Vol. 46, Feb. 1999, p. 102.
3. Schultz, Majken, *On Studying Organizational Cultures*, Walter de Gruyter, Berlin, 1995.
4. Cox, Alan, *The Cox Report on the American Corporation*, Delacorte Press, NY, 1982, pp. 112–114.
5. Connor, Patrick E. and Lake, Linda E., *Managing Organizational Change*, Praeger Publishers, Westport, CT, 1994.
6. Paulk, Mark, Curtis, Bill, Chrissis, Mary Beth, and Weber, Charles V., Capability Maturity Model for Software, Version 1.1, p. vii.

2 The Tale of Two Cultures (The Schizophrenic Project)

Think back to the scenario on task expectations in Section 1.6.2 of Chapter 1. In it Frank, a manager, **strongly** encourages John to talk to a recognized expert about his design. What if our recognized expert, in this case Fred, was from a different organization? Do you think his opinion would still carry as much weight?

Where are we going?

In this chapter we take a close look at the effects on productivity of team personnel with diverse backgrounds and experiences. Rapidly assembled teams that possess a broad range of key skills and experiences can be a powerful resource. On the other hand, pulling together a team from distinct organizations with diverse experiences and few existing personal relationships can create unanticipated and often intense conflict. In certain cases, this conflict — if allowed to persist for even a short period of time — can result in irreparable team damage.

Teammates working in a single collocated organization have traditionally evolved relationships, common beliefs, and respect for one another over time and multiple projects. Virtual project teammates, on the other hand, often share few, if any, common experiences. In today's environment this conflict can intensify when teammates are employed by organizations that are also competing for new opportunities.

The intent is not to imply that conflict should always be avoided. To the contrary, the process of recognizing and working through healthy conflict fosters insight and is actually beneficial to effective team operation.

Insight

Healthy conflict, managed appropriately, invigorates a team by drawing it closer.

Problem

How is a manager to distinguish desirable conflict, which over time strengthens a team, from conflict which in time destructively turns on a team?

On virtual projects the benefit of strong interpersonal bonds that many of us have taken for granted from traditional collocated experiences often does not exist. When operating in a virtual environment, small conflicts often fester and grow to become large and more serious conflicts. This can produce an overwhelming drain on already stressed human resources. To effectively tap the potential of virtual operations, insight into underlying root causes along with timely management action and follow-up become critical.

In this chapter a tale involving two employees with divergent backgrounds is employed to aid investigation of this subject. Key to effective conflict management is early recognition, particularly of undesirable conflict warning signs. Critical warning signs along with recommended management action are identified and discussed.

About the tale

The purpose of this tale is to aid the reader in gaining insight into the value of informal activities that are often lost on virtual projects. The tale also provides greater understanding of the critical role that prior experiences play in technical decision-making and the importance of interpersonal bonds and trust among teammates. When reading the tale don't focus on what Glen or Bill believes, but rather on how their past experiences affect their communication. Note how easily competition surfaces.

The tale is long. It goes into a lengthy discussion on the backgrounds and personal situations of the characters. This may not seem important to the reader, but the impact of divergent past experiences on the effectiveness of remote team members is significant on virtual projects.

Some may also view the situation described in the tale as rare and unlikely to occur very often. For those who have known only projects where a common culture exists this view is understandable. As virtual projects become more the norm these situations will occur with greater frequency.

The setting for this tale is a major system design review involving two collaborating companies. SAAA is the prime, and ABC is a simulation sub-contractor developing software for SAAA at a remote location. Harry, a senior engineer at SAAA, is scheduled to present first. Harry has been working for Glen at SAAA for 6 months.

2.1

The Tale

"I will focus my presentation on the critical system design issues," stated Harry, as he gazed past the overhead projector out into the dimly lit conference room. Glen was seated in the front row.

"We will begin with an overview of the operational concept," continued Harry. It was a topic he and Glen had discussed for hours at a time at Glen's insistence. To Glen, there wasn't a more critical issue on the program. It was not paying attention to critical issues that had almost cost Glen his career. He rarely spoke about it now, but he never forgot that experience.

Ten years earlier on Glen's first project as a lead engineer he had allowed nearly 100,000 lines of code to be generated before the requirements were well understood. By the time they figured out what the customer really wanted most of it had to be re-designed and re-coded.

That experience deeply affected Glen who thought he was going to be fired because of it.

Early in his career Glen had spent little time trying to understand software. His expertise was on the systems side, but from that early career experience he learned two lessons that he would never let himself forget again. First, he would never again allow the software effort to get out in front of the systems work. And second, any new code for development would not be approved without clearly defined requirements.

In the far back corner of the room sat Bill, a twenty-five-year employee of ABC.

"In this area we have initiated an intensive reuse analysis of the real world software," continued Harry. As Glen nodded his approval, there wasn't a person in the room who couldn't hear Bill's squeaky chair as he pressed back in it hard against the wall. Making noise was a habit of Bill's when something irritated him and his strong opposition to Glen's reuse approach was no secret.

Harry continued, trying his best to ignore Bill. A few months earlier, Harry had found himself in the middle of an argument between Glen and Bill on the project's reuse approach. Ever since, Glen and Bill had spoken very little to each other. In Bill's words, "talking to Glen was like talking to the wall." He had told a number of his co-workers that the man just "made no sense".

To Harry, it was Bill and Glen's arguments that made no sense. Whenever Harry talked to either one alone he couldn't figure out what the disagreement was even about. They both knew the project budget was tight and reuse was a must. But for some unexplanable reason, whenever the two would get together, the discussion would go nowhere.

To Bill the subject was an important one.

Early in his life Bill found schoolwork difficult. He struggled through high school, barely making it to college. But he made it through and his first job offer was from ABC.

The pressure of learning a new job and becoming a father fueled self-doubt. Because of this stress he and his wife agreed it would be best for Bill to make a change at the end of the summer. But that summer something happened.

It was Bill's first summer at ABC, and Tom Jenkins' last. Tom was a senior engineer who was just finishing a stellar forty-year career.

That summer Tom worked more closely with Bill than he had ever worked with anyone before. During those few short months Bill learned from Tom the pitfalls of using real world software inside a simulation. Tom impressed upon Bill the importance of an early start to the critical simulation reset design. Bill learned Tom's favorite do's and don'ts and other rules that only a master like Tom could teach. That summer changed Bill's life.

Unlike Bill, Glen had no previous direct simulation experience. Most of his prior experience had been on real world systems. Based on his experience, Glen had become convinced that reusing real world software inside the simulation was critical to the success of the project.

Bill had tried to explain to Glen the pitfalls of using real world software in a simulation. But whenever he brought the subject up he would, for some unexplanable reason, get confused and his words would all get jumbled. Each time Glen said nothing. He just stared back. The arguing didn't start until much later.

Bill was thinking about it now. None of it had made a lick of sense to him until that very morning when he heard that Glen's company had purchased a software firm that just happened to be a competitor of ABC. It was now, for the first time, beginning to make sense, Bill thought to himself as he stared across the room at Glen.

Mary, a young software lead recently hired at ABC, was scheduled to present after Harry. Bill had been working closely mentoring Mary over the previous months.

"Now that we've seen the system operational concept, I will discuss the software side," stated Mary. Unfortunately Glen didn't have a chance to review Mary's presentation before the meeting. Normally he would never have allowed this happen, but the final days leading to the review had been hectic and it just fell through the crack.

"We have a very aggressive schedule," continued Mary, "and to meet it we need to accelerate our design work in a number of critical software areas." Glen's jaw was clenched tight. Mary continued. "We have already initiated work on our detailed reset design." Glen's eyes bulged from his head as he turned and stared toward the far back corner of the conference room. "Why didn't Bill talk to me about this?," he wondered to himself.

2.1.1 Observations on the Effect of Personal Experience

This tale demonstrates how two highly competent teammates with differing backgrounds and experiences can perceive vastly different critical issues on the same project. Glen has a design concept and reuse strategy in mind based on his experience. He also believes strongly that the software activities need to be controlled. He has personally experienced the loss of control on a project.

When Glen hears the words, "initiated work on our detailed reset design," alarms go off in his head. Bill and Glen have never worked together before and Glen knows the project has a tight budget. He believes strongly that the project cannot afford to design any software without clearly defined requirements.

Bill has years of experience, too, which are different from Glen's as are his beliefs and perceptions concerning the critical issues facing the project. Bill's experiences and guidance from his mentor tell him it is critical to get the reset design completed early.

Glen has trouble comprehending the significance of reset. He has no personal experience that indicates to him this area warrants special attention. To Glen, the much greater risk is losing control of the software. While each have years of valuable experience, their perceptions and beliefs are rooted in subcultures that have grown over the years inside different organizations.

2.1.2 Culture, Adversity, and Communication

Many engineers hold vivid and powerful memories of early career experiences. It is not uncommon for these early experiences to affect the beliefs engineers hold throughout their careers. This is especially true when these experiences involve adversity.

Mentors often play influential roles in the formation of a young engineer's beliefs. Much of what we learn from mentors is not found in books. This knowledge often focuses on practical and personal experiences and its impact can extend beyond the purely technical.

In our tale, Glen believes his career was almost ruined by a mistake he made early in his career. Whether or not his job was actually ever truly in jeopardy doesn't matter. For our purposes what matters is the effect this troublesome experience had on the way he views the world today, and the choices he now makes. Bill had his own difficulties early in his career. He was fortunate to find a mentor who was able to help him at a critical point in his career.

Insight

Majken Schultz in his book, *On Studying Organizational Cultures*, tells us that "organizational culture develops when members of organizations must cope with a number of more specific problems in the process of getting organizations to work." He also tells us that group identity, culture, and a sense of survival are all closely related.[1]

Bill and Glen are different people with different experiences. In our tale there are two examples where facing adversity and surviving it result in a strengthening of unique viewpoints. Strong-minded individuals like Glen and Bill work closely every day with young engineers sharing their viewpoints. In the process, unique and vibrant cultures grow stronger.

In the past this process occurred primarily inside single collocated organizations. Today, however, long-held subculture beliefs deep inside organizations are being challenged from the outside far more frequently. This is due largely to the varied experiences, beliefs, and associated cultures of teammates who have developed their skills in different organizations.

Clearly, today's work environment demands continual and open communication among teammates who must work through an increasing number of differing viewpoints.

Problem

Unfortunately, just when we see increased team communication as more critical than ever, in fact, more communication breakdowns than ever before are witnessed.

In the following section we examine more closely contributing factors to this condition.

2.1.3 Hindrances to Effective Virtual Team Communication

For the most part experience leads us to believe that engineers are essentially logical thinking people. Engineers want what they see to make sense and, when given the chance, they will actively seek out information that validates their perceptions.

In our tale Bill is troubled by Glen's views on the project's critical issues, and it is important to him to find a way to explain what he perceives. Since Bill does not have Glen's experiences to employ (recall that Glen rarely speaks about his experiences), Bill cannot use this information to help him. He has only his own experiences, based upon which he initially concludes that Glen's views simply make "no sense."

It seems obvious, observing this situation from the outside, that Bill and Glen need to talk to each other more. But in the tale instead of seeing increased communication, there is less. While part of this is due to the difficulty many people experience with confrontation, on virtual projects two additional factors hinder effective communication, especially when conflict is involved. These factors — distance and competition — are discussed below.

2.1.3.1 The Distance Factor

When dealing with conflict, physical distance can be a significant inhibitor to effective communication.

Problem

While technologies such as e-mail, and teleconferencing (communication vehicles discussed at greater length later in this book) can help, these vehicles are often inappropriate when the subject matter is of a sensitive nature, and particularly when conflict is involved.

Many discussions require face to face communication where body cues and language can be utilized. While travel is an option, it is not always appropriate, or possible, to plan ahead for just the right time to broach a sensitive subject.

Problem

On virtual projects corrective action designed to resolve sensitive issues may be delayed for long periods of time because of distance.

2.1.3.2 The Competition Factor

When two companies are teaming together on one project, and at the same time competing on another, it is not uncommon to hear the following message flow down the management chain:

"Be professional at all times, but don't volunteer more information than is asked for."

While on the surface this message may appear to be an appropriate business strategy, it is also a contributor to internal team mistrust, and miscommunication. In Chapter 1, Section 1.5, where organizational evolution is discussed, reference is made to the "doing whatever it takes" attitude. Fundamental to team success is team commitment to doing whatever it takes to achieve that success.

In a challenging virtual environment a 100% committed team attitude is vital to project success. This means team members must be prepared to reach beyond minimal levels of team participation. The message above flies directly in the face of this critical philosophy. It essentially tells the team member not to reach beyond while effectively encouraging less rather than more communication (teamwork is discussed at greater length later in this book).

2.1.3.3 Distance + Competition + Differing Experiences = Rumors + Communication Breakdown

When the factors of distance, competition, and differing experiences are put together, an environment is created in which effective communication becomes, at best, difficult. As mentioned earlier, engineers want to validate their perceptions. If a teammate's viewpoint seems illogical, team members will often seek out additional information to explain it.

In our tale when Bill heard that Glen's company was buying a software firm, he immediately jumped to the conclusion that Glen probably knew about the impending sale all along. Bill believed that this was the reason why Glen didn't seem to listen to him (he would just stare back). Soon the following rumor was running rampant at ABC:

> "SAAA doesn't want to work with us because they're out to steal our business."

Engineers want the pieces of the puzzle to fit, and there have been cases where they will even create a new piece to complete it. Unfortunately, rumors only serve to divert a team's energies and they contribute more significantly than some realize to team miscommunication and mistrust. On virtual projects, communication breakdown increases when conflict is initiated from outside of an organization. This is discussed further in the next section.

2.1.4 Why Conflict Resolution Often Fails on Virtual Projects

Challenges to an organization's beliefs are anticipated and even encouraged from inside most organizations, but challenges from the outside are often viewed differently. Most organizations have established and effective ways to deal with internal conflict. For example, many organizations train personnel in conflict resolution strategies. In most of these organizations the process starts at the peer-to-peer level working its way up the chain only when necessary. The goal is to solve conflict at the lowest level possible.

Insight

Inside collocated organizations peer pressure is often counted on as an effective vehicle to aid in rapid conflict resolution.

This process keeps many small problems small. Peer pressure is integrally tied to the organizational subculture as discussed in Chapter 1 and, in most cases, this process is effective inside of established collocated organizations.

Problem

When looking closely at conflict that crosses organizational boundaries, the same level of process effectiveness is not observed as is witnessed within single organizational environments.

While the written words found in organizational conflict resolution procedures often indicate that both internal and external forms of conflict are handled equally well, in practice this is not always so.

Insight

This is, at least partly, due to the fact that the same *informal* subculture pressures are simply not there to solve many of the "small" problems that cross organizational boundaries.

Team members who have developed bonds over long periods of time have more invested in solving problems and keeping their existing relationships intact. Traditional collocation also affords team members more opportunities to find the right time to bring up a sensitive subject.

Problem

One of the most insidious aspects of small conflicts on virtual projects is that they are allowed to fester for as long as they do.

There are four reasons why unresolved conflict remains unresolved as long as it does on virtual projects:

- Lack of clear responsibility
- Belief that small conflicts are not important
- Belief that in time these small conflicts will resolve themselves
- Peers not afforded the time together needed to work through an issue

Subcultures that exhibit strong bonds among team members tend to be organizational or site-specific. On virtual projects — particularly where multiple sites are involved and where personnel do not have strong relationships built up over time — small conflicts can fester for weeks, or even months.

On most collocated projects one would expect these types of conflicts to be resolved quickly and easily. Instead of seeing conflict resolution through effective communication at the appropriate peer-to-peer level, there are more frequent breakdowns in communication and small conflicts grow into larger and much more serious ones.

2.1.5 Back to the Tale

Getting back to the tale. After the system design review was completed, Glen prioritized a small team to work what he viewed as the critical system design issues. Because he didn't feel he could control the activities of the personnel working at ABC's remote site, the team was composed solely of personnel from the prime contractor SAAA who were physically located near Glen. In parallel, ABC continued working on what they believed to be the critical issues facing the project. The two efforts were not well coordinated, and soon the project had two separate design activities occurring at the two separate sites.

Recognizing the problem, a number of futile attempts were made to pull the activities together. Schedule pressures, however, soon mounted causing the systems engineering lead to mandate a single design approach. This action resulted in team members feeling that their ideas were not being listened to. Many personnel at the remote site concluded that the systems engineering lead didn't respect them, nor value their skills. Project morale degraded rapidly along with team effectiveness. The two organizations were never able to resolve the conflict, and eventually most of the work accomplished at the remote site was rejected and reworked at the primary location.

2.2   A Fundamental Dilemma of Virtual Collaboration

In our tale, the influence of mentors and personal experience is evident. Bill was strongly influenced by his mentor, and both Bill and Glen were greatly impacted by their personal experiences.

In her book, Martha Haywood warns us, "…*damage can be done by highly competent team members who don't feed into the team's system for corporate memory.*"[2]

Unfortunately, in the tale, and on many other virtual projects as well, there is no single sacred *corporate memory* system (recall the definition of corporate memory from Chapter 1, Section 1.8.2). This is because the experiences, beliefs, and perceptions of our team members have evolved from many directions within different organizations over long periods of time. On traditional collocated projects this dilemma usually doesn't occur because individual sites exhibit singular, or at least compatible, subcultures.

In the tale there were effectively two teams and two distinct corporate memory systems operating more like two separate projects than one single project. The two sites had no common history, culture, or set of experiences to draw them together through the project's difficult times.

2.2.1 The Schizophrenic Project Memory

Traditionally, when individuals find themselves far outside the beliefs of a local organizational subculture they either leave that organization or find a way to conform. Due largely to time constraints, on virtual projects where personnel are rapidly pulled together from varying backgrounds and subcultures, this normal filtering and blending process does not occur. As a result, multiple competing vibrant and growing subcultures exist within the same project each supported by multiple and conflicting experiences. This leads to what is referred to as a *schizophrenic project memory.*

Martha Haywood has noted a similar concern stating that the "Old Joe method doesn't work for distributed teams."[2] This statement is not an indictment of the knowledge or beliefs of mentors, but rather identifies a weakness in relying on *informal* methods when it comes to communicating clear and consistent project or task direction. When mentors and/or project leaders hold differing viewpoints, utilizing informal methods to communicate project direction can quickly lead to chaos.

2.2.2 The Integrated Project Memory

Due to the concern of "renegade" team members, Haywood suggests that in a distributed environment *"team members need to feed into a formal system for corporate memory."*[2] Making team members feed a formal system can work if you have a single corporate memory system that meets all your needs. Unfortunately, on most virtual projects this is not the case. But this does lead to a question:

> *Why not merge the best from our collaborating teammates into a single integrated project memory that meets all of the project's needs?*

After all, isn't this what virtual collaboration is all about — rapidly integrating disparate skills and knowledge from physically separate locations? While this is indeed the goal of virtual projects, experience has shown that merging, integrating, and collaborating on high technology software-intensive projects are significantly more difficult than one might think.

To help gain insight into this issue, let's take a closer look at the engineering design process. To aid in this examination, in the following section a brief tale, referred to as the Adjacent Cubicle Head Popping tale is provided.

About the tale

The purpose of this tale is to demonstrate the critical importance of collocation during the creative design process, which is discussed at greater length following the tale.

2.3

The Adjacent Cubicle Head Popping (ACHP) Tale

Suppose Jim, Gary, Elaine, and Pat have been tasked to work on a subsystem design for the recently awarded project F999. This new subsystem represents a challenge because it contains a number of requirements not previously faced by any of the team members. The project is being run in a traditional collocated fashion. The scene for this brief tale begins with each of the four teammates working quietly and alone in adjacent cubicles.

"Hold everything!" Pat looks up hearing the words float above her head.

"Did someone say something?" she queries.

"We've been looking at this all wrong!" She hears the same voice again, then stands up and peers over the top of her cubicle wall. At first she sees nothing. Then suddenly Gary's head pops up.

"I said we've been looking at this all wrong!" states Gary with his eyes wide open and bugged out. He and Pat are now facing each other over the top of their adjacent cubicle wall. "Think of it as a finite state machine!" proclaims Gary excited by his newly discovered thought. Then Jim's head pops up from inside his cubicle which is positioned on the other side of Gary.

"I was just reading some e-mail from Henry on the same subject," states Jim. "Henry wants us to eliminate the centralized controller." The fourth member of the design team, Elaine, pops her head up.

"We took a similar approach on the F249 project," responds Elaine. "But F249 ran into some tough integration problems. We'd better talk about it. I'll sketch it out on my whiteboard to help explain the issue."

We refer to this form of ad hoc brainstorming as an Adjacent Cubicle Head Popping (ACHP) meeting. ACHP meetings can be initiated at any time. In cases when these sessions start to run more than 5 or 10 minutes they usually move to a conference room to minimize co-worker disruption.

ACHP meetings are informal unplanned interchanges triggered by events that can occur at unpredictable times during the day. These meetings often provide the seeds for effective rapid integrated collaborative design, but that is not the only value to ACHP meetings — interpersonal team bonds can grow rapidly as well.

All engineering organizations do not use open cubicles, but the concept remains relevant in organizations that employ private enclosed offices. In the next section the reasons why ACHP meetings are so important are explored, especially on virtual projects where one might think the concept doesn't fit.

2.4   About the Creative Design Process

Process maturity implies, to many, structure and order. It means, at least partially, executing well-defined tasks in their proper sequence. The types of tasks normally associated with this view of process maturity relate to left brain activities. While the left brain focuses on *one-step-at-a-time* operations, it is inside the right brain where creativity occurs.

As the left brain proceeds methodically looking at each piece of the problem in sequence, the right brain sees images that cross individual task boundaries. The right brain is, in effect, a parallel processor and is heavily relied upon in the early creative stage of advanced technology projects.

2.4.1 Light Bulbs in Our Heads

Divergent thoughts are often expressed during unplanned brainstorming sessions. These thoughts may seem disconnected, but a disconnected thought in one engineer's head may connect in another's.

A study was conducted on the design process by Raymonde Guindon at Microelectronic and Computer Technology Corporation.[3] As part of this study three experienced software engineers were asked to design an elevator control system. Each was monitored closely to determine how they discovered knowledge.

First, the designers built prototypes in their minds. They produced mental simulations, or scenarios, expressing their view of how the system would work. Second, they continued to gain more knowledge by testing the consistency of their images against their own general knowledge. In so doing they began to abstract critical pieces of information. Third, they began to partition out certain functions.

The observers noticed that the design process began before the designers fully comprehended the problem. They also noted the existence of knowledge discovery. In their analysis the observers referred to "unplanned additions of new requirements." In analyzing this work Peter DeGrace and Leslie Hulet Stahl refer to these knowledge discovery points as trigger points or "light bulbs."[3] Trigger points are unplanned; we cannot predict exactly when the light bulbs will switch on. This unpredictability in how the creative process works has been corroborated by independent research.[4]

2.4.2 Relationship to Past Experience

Insight

Experienced engineers abstract by recognizing familiar features in current problems that may be similar to features in problems they have solved previously.

Smith and Dietrich call this process "associative memory."[5] We don't know exactly when these associations are going to take place because the acquisition of knowledge is not a smooth step-wise process. It is not like a waterfall, but rather it comes in "chunks."[3]

As the chunks arrive, each is reconciled with old patterns from personal experience and the light bulbs go off in our heads. As the light bulbs go off, heads pop up looking over the edge of cubicle walls for a teammate on whom to bounce new thoughts. It is not uncommon in this process for conflict to occur. This may lead to a reevaluation of an experience, which in turn may actually change an individual's belief.

2.4.3 Incubation and Assimilation

Returning to the first tale in this chapter, Glen's personal experience tells him he needs to maintain control. He also knows that the critical system design issues must be addressed early. This is why he prioritizes a small team. But why does the alarm trigger in his head when he hears what the remote team is planning to do?

DeGrace and Stahl[3] refer to four stages of the creative process: preparation, incubation, illumination, and verification. These stages do not always follow a rigid order.

Insight

Individuals need incubation time for their own ideas, but also to integrate the ideas of others.

During the incubation time engineers think about the problem and create images of possible solutions in their heads. Illumination follows. This is the point when our opportunity for rapid integration of critical knowledge is greatest. However, we cannot predict exactly when this is going to occur.

Assume the following about two engineers:

- They are physically separated.
- They do not share common experiences.
- They do not communicate on a regular basis.

If we give these two engineers identical design problems to solve, what are the chances of getting the best ideas from both in a single integrated design?

Teammates need not only incubation time, but acceptance time as well. This is particularly important on virtual projects because of the diverse backgrounds and experiences of personnel. The ability to pop your head above your cubicle wall and just start talking out loud is an extremely valuable technique that provides immediate two-way communication in support of a rapid integrated design.

This technique, however, will not eliminate conflict, which is to be expected during the creative design stage. On virtual projects its intensity can be expected to increase for reasons discussed earlier. This, in turn, increases the need for incubation and acceptance time, allowing teammates to integrate new ideas into their own thinking. In the tale this critical integration did not occur. Instead, there were effectively two teams operating disjointly, which is what triggered the alarm in Glen's head.

2.4.4 Virtual Collaboration and the Creative Process

The creative design process involves both technical and non-technical factors. Human feelings are affected when an individual perceives how others view his/her openly expressed thoughts and ideas. For those feelings to produce a positive effect, complete acceptance is not required. When an individual perceives his/her own thought triggering a teammate's thought which leads to a team decision, that individual often senses his/her own personal contribution.

Due to this need for spontaneity, the potential for achieving a rapidly integrated design is greatest when key players are collocated. While no one knows exactly when the light bulbs will pop on, studies, such as the one referenced, indicate that these trigger points are certain to occur. In this sense, they are predictable.

Insight

Studies examining the frequency of interactions between teammates[6] have concluded that when teammates must interact frequently and those interactions occur on short cycle times, collocation offers the greatest opportunity for success.

2.5 Collocation at the Right Time

On virtual projects there are new management factors to consider. While virtual collaboration provides the potential power of rapidly accessible skills, it does so at a cost of interpersonal team bonds built over time through shared experiences. On traditional collocated projects ensuring design approaches are integrated is not as large a problem because team members usually share common experiences and physical proximity.

Solution

Experience indicates that during the critical creative design stage of a virtual project a small team of senior system designers need to be collocated in support of rapid design integration.

This does not mean that full-time collocation is required for the life of the program. Cases where repeating cycles of intense collocated work followed by periods apart — incubation and assimilation — have worked well.

The dynamic aspect of the creative design process precludes this type of activity from being conducted at the next regularly scheduled team teleconference. For real rapid integration to happen, windows of opportunity must be seized at the moment they occur, or they may be lost forever.

2.6 An Implementation of a Virtual Culture

While collocation provides part of the collaborative solution, it will not solve all the issues faced on virtual projects.

Solution

To address the need for an integrated project memory (discussed earlier), the concept of a *Rapid Filtered Project Memory (RFPM)*, is introduced in this chapter. The primary purpose of an RFPM is to address the lack of a single integrated corporate memory on a virtual project.

You can think of the RFPM as one way to implement part of a virtual culture. To many engineers one of the most frustrating aspects of a virtual project is being told to go read the corporate procedures when they have a specific question about the job. Too often these procedures fall short in addressing specifically what an engineer really needs to know.

As mentioned earlier, we do not mean to imply that corporate procedures do not add value. The point here is only to reiterate that corporate procedures cannot replace what an engineer traditionally learns on-the-job through less formal means. This was discussed at length in Chapter 1.

Solution

Because virtual projects are composed of personnel with diverse backgrounds and experiences, it is critical that a single project memory be defined to aid in focusing the team in a consistent manner.

For virtual projects to succeed project memories must be established more rapidly than has been accomplished on traditional development projects.

Ed Yourdon in his book *Death March* states, "if you remember only one word from…the entire book you are now reading…it should be triage."[7] Triage means "to sort" and Ed's point relates to the simple fact that we don't have time to do everything. This is relevant to virtual projects as well. Because this is true, our objective through the RFPM is to focus on those things that experience tells us have the greatest payback for a reasonable investment.

An RFPM is usually implemented as a set of publicly accessible directories with critical project memory information that has been approved by the project leaders. An RFPM provides answers to issues where conflict most often exists. Effective RFPMs do not contain a massive amount of information, and most often are constructed incrementally as the project progresses through its developmental phases. The approval of RFPM information is key. RFPM directories must not be allowed to become too large or they can quickly lose their effectiveness. RFPMs are not intended to duplicate information available readily through other sources, such as process notes; these directories contain key information that traditionally has been passed on through informal means. An example RFPM structure is provided in Figure 2.1.

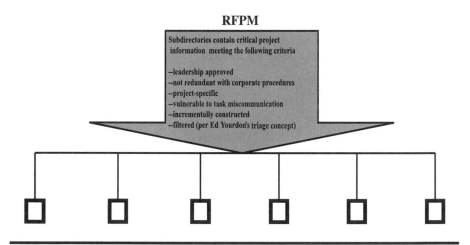

RFPM

Subdirectories contain critical project
information meeting the following criteria

--leadership approved
--not redundant with corporate procedures
--project-specific
--vulnerable to task miscommunication
--incrementally constructed
--filtered (per Ed Yourdon's triage concept)

Figure 2.1   Rapid Filtered Project Memory (RFPM) Structure

RFPMs should not be the sole responsibility of a process group. Information produced by process groups is usually general in nature, while RFPMs are project-specific. As an example, earlier in this chapter we discussed the importance of collocation during the critical creative design stage. When major design decisions have been agreed to they can be placed in the RFPM thus supporting more effective project-wide communication. The RFPM must be accessible to all sites, although we anticipate some site-specific RFPM information as well.

An RFPM cannot replace years of corporate history, nor can it create a common project culture overnight, but it can provide a critically needed focal point for addressing key issues that most frequently hinder virtual project effective team operation. More information on the type of information that we recommend placing in an RFPM and guidance in the construction and maintenance of an RFPM are provided in Chapter 4. More specific guidance on detecting unhealthy conflict and recommended actions can be found in Chapter 7, Step 8.

2.7   Conclusion

The conflict described in this chapter's initial tale is not unusual for any aggressively scheduled advanced technology project. However, on virtual projects this conflict is often intensified due to distance, lack of common engineering experiences, lack of common supporting infrastructure (discussed later in this book), and schedule pressure.

Place yourself in the shoes of either Glen or Bill and try to imagine what you might have thought if you didn't know anything about the other's background or personal experiences. The value of the interpersonal bonds created by teammates working closely and with common mentors over time should never be underestimated.

Upon first reading about Martha Haywood's "Old Joe,"[2] a picture of this legendary character instantly came to mind. He has a gray beard, age on his face, and years of corporate history inside his head. His face could be the face of any experienced engineer inside today's downsized and consolidated organizations.

On the positive side, "Old Joe" provides an important link to organizational identity. Schultz tells us that culture is deeply rooted in tradition and provides stability to an organization.[1] This may well be a crucial part of what keeps mature organizations from breaking down in times of crisis. But, on the other side, organizations with the greatest process maturity often have the greatest difficulty collaborating effectively with external organizations. This situation would not be as serious, if it were not for the critical lack of skills the software industry is facing today.

Some have expressed concern that informal activities should be discouraged because they are unplanned, undocumented, unpredictable, unrepeatable, and therefore, fuel chaos when we seek control. We do not believe informality is at odds with repeatability, nor that it is at the root of chaos. The point is not to encourage an increase in unplanned activities, but rather to recognize the criticality of key informal activities.

Insight

Key informal activities that just happen7171 when collocated require conscious management action when operating in a virtual collaborative environment.

And, as we have seen, there are certain areas on virtual projects where increased formality may be appropriate. This is discussed further in Chapter 3.

One hindrance to effective collaboration on virtual projects can be traced to the simple fact that collaboration takes time and effort. Attempts to formalize activities that can only occur spontaneously will not increase the effectiveness of virtual teams. Increased diversity of opinion should be expected on virtual projects, and this diversity can grind progress almost to a halt just when the pressures to move forward rapidly are greatest. This observation led one engineer on a virtual project to note that having multiple good ideas causes more difficulty than having just one.

In our tale there was ineffective conflict resolution. It should have occurred well before the system design review. Effective collaboration requires both listening and acceptance time. In the tale described, the root of the problem was not the activity at the remote site, but rather lack of coordination and integration with the activities at the main site. Collocating key personnel at critical times allows the creative design process to happen more effectively and more rapidly even when differences seem great.

CHAPTER 2 KEY POINTS SUMMARY
Healthy conflict invigorates a team
Organizational culture develops when coping with specific problems
Peer pressure traditionally counted on for conflict resolution
Traditional informal subculture pressures not there in a virtual environment
Engineers rely on past experience to solve new problems
Incubation time needed to integrate ideas
Need for frequent interactions drive us to collocation
Traditional collocated informal activities don't "just happen" in virtual world
Collocate key people during creative design phase
Rapid Filtered Project Memory (RFPM) = one way to implement virtual culture
Diverse backgrounds require single "project memory"

References

1. Schultz, Majken, *On Studying Organizational Cultures*, Walter de Gruyter, Berlin, 1997.
2. Haywood, Martha, *Managing Virtual Teams*, Artech House, Boston, 1998, p. 58.
3. De Grace, Peter and Hulet Stahl, Leslie, *The Olduvai Imperative*, Yourdon Press, Englewood Cliffs, NJ, 1993.
4. Blakeslee, T.R., *The Right Brain*, New York, Anchor Press/Doubleday, 1980.

5. Calvin, W.H., PH.D and G.A. Ojemann, M.D., *Inside the Brain*, Mentor Books, New York, 1980.
6. Gindele, Mark E. and Rumpf, Richard, Effects of Collocating Integrated Product Teams, *Program Manager*, July–August, 1998, p. 38.
7. Yourdon, Ed, *Death March*, 1997, Prentice-Hall PTR, Upper Saddle River, NJ, pp. 131–133.

3 Remote Task Management: Am I Doing What You Think I'm Doing?

In Chapter 1 we looked inside engineering organizations at how personnel have traditionally become effective at their jobs. In Chapter 2 we examined the powerful role played by past experience in shaping expectations.

Where are we going?

In this chapter, through the use of two tales, we take a closer look at tasking, and some of the underlying factors affecting remote tasking success.

In the first tale we examine one factor known to cause task communication breakdown on virtual projects: the "local meaning" of terms. In particular, we examine the potential impact of employing the term "architecture" or "software architecture" in a task definition when the personnel being tasked and the responsible manager have divergent software backgrounds.

Today, despite its wide usage, software architecture has no universally accepted definition. As proof, go to the Software Engineering Institute (SEI) web[1] site where pages of diverse definitions appear. While discussions on software architecture can be stimulating, what is most important here is understanding the relationship between the technical terms employed and the *real work* engineers are assigned to do.

To help in understanding the issues involved, we start with a tale. This tale has similarities to one discussed in Chapter 2, but in this chapter we dig a little deeper in search of root causes.

About the tale

The purpose of this tale is multifold. First, we see how the term "architecture" can be interpreted in two very different ways with respect to an engineer's work assignment and expected products. This provides an example of how a local meaning of a term can negatively impact remote task communication.

Second, we see how different views of architecture can affect far more than just the communication between a manager and a remote engineer. Architecture can actually affect organizational responsibilities as well. This is discussed at greater length following the tale.

Finally, it's another example of the influence of past experience; in this case, the relationship among critical issues, risk, past experience, and project control. This is discussed further following the tale.

3.1

The Architecture Tale

Usually ZBE, a large engineering firm, would have chosen one of their own employees to lead the systems engineering effort. These days the company was operating lean, and good senior systems engineers were particularly hard to free up inside the company. TTT, the small firm Laura worked for, had been brought on board specifically for their systems experience. John, a program manager at TTT, had worked at ZBE earlier in his career and had personally recommended Laura for the lead systems position on the project.

Laura was bright, energetic, calm under pressure, and not one bit hesitant to speak her mind. But today, on only her second visit to ZBE, she was finding it difficult to listen patiently as Jim struggled for over 30 minutes trying to explain the system architecture.

"This is nice, Jim, but where is the rest of the system design?" she finally blurted out. Laura had spent the previous day in a meeting with the customer who had impressed upon her the program's tight budget and their desire to run the project efficiently. They made it clear that they didn't want to micro-manage the effort.

"Just keep us informed of the critical issues, and what you're doing to manage them," the customer had told her. A puzzled look was evident on Jim's face.

"This architecture is sound," Jim replied confidently to Laura. He had 18 years of experience with ZBE where he had proven himself as one of the best senior architects in a company known for building high quality well-architected systems. He was a "big-picture" engineer and one of the best communicators at ZBE. When he spoke on the subject of architecture, it was usually with clarity, insight, and crispness. But, on this occasion, the harder he tried to explain the more difficult Laura was finding it to remain her usual calm self.

"Jim, I just don't see the system design." She was shaking her head back and forth as she said it. "Where are the products we're delivering? What about the critical algorithms?" She hesitated, then added quickly, "And I've heard nothing about performance issues." Laura had a keen mind and was quick to get right to an issue.

"Don't worry about the system design details just yet," replied Jim. "If we get the architecture right, details will fall in place." Laura stared back at Jim. The stress was evident on her face. The project was 1 week away from a major system design review with the customer and, as far as Laura could tell, the system design was missing.

That night, as Laura flew home, she couldn't stop thinking about Jim and ZBE. Something didn't add up. She knew the company had an outstanding reputation. But how could they succeed, she asked herself, when they seemed to be ignoring critical system design issues?

The next morning when she arrived at work she headed straight for John's office. She hadn't gotten half way through explaining the situation to him when he stopped her.

"They operate differently," said John, and then he began to explain how the ZBE engineering organization functioned on the inside. During the discussion Laura learned that the architecture team's responsibilities weren't exactly what she had thought.

"You should have been talking to different people," John told her, "if you wanted to get answers about algorithms and performance."

"But we're preparing for a system design review next week and the customer wants to hear about the critical issues!" replied Laura emphatically. "Why wouldn't they have brought in the right people for me to talk to?"

"The way they see it, you were talking to the right people," replied John. Then he added, "they see the critical issues differently." Laura stood up and moved toward John's door. Then she stopped and turned.

"I don't know if I can work with them." She was looking directly at John as she said it. "If I'm going to be the systems lead, I need to have more control."

3.1.1 Causes of Task Miscommunication

In this tale there exists a miscommunication of a task assignment. This is caused, at least partially, by the use of the *ambiguous architecture term*. But terminology is not the only problem in this tale. There are actually two different views of what the *critical technical issues* are and what technical information should be presented at a major upcoming review.

During the 4 weeks prior to Laura's visit, Jim and his architecture team (including two other engineers) had dedicated themselves to the architecture task which Laura had given to them. This task definition had been provided to Jim through E-mail sent by Laura. See the Task Assignment Record (TAR) that Laura provided in Table 3.1.

Table 3.1 Architecture Task Assignment Record (TAR)

Project Identifier	BAAA
Department Identifier	ZZZ
Task Identifier	TYYY
Task Authorization	Contract Charge Number
Responsible Manager	Laura
Assigned Engineer	Jim
Budget	480 hours (includes hours for supporting engineers)
Planned Start Date	August 12, 2002
Planned Complete Date	September 20, 2002
Actual Complete Date	
Task Description	Participate as a member of the architecture team developing the top-level system architecture for BAAA project

The architecture team was physically 700 miles away from Laura during this period. While it was known that this was not the ideal situation, because the architecture team had always been successful in the past, and had extensive experience, it was believed close coordination with the systems lead, Laura, would not be required. This was proven not to be the case. There was a significant disconnect between Laura's expectations of a top level system architecture as identified on the TAR, and what Jim and his team believed they were tasked to produce.

3.2 Why Architecture is Critical to Effective Remote Tasking

Communication problems are common when people from different countries who speak different languages must work together. The book *Culture Clash: Managing in a Multicultural World*,[2] is filled with stories of miscommunication due to misunderstanding or inaccurate translation of words from one language to another. Communication problems due to word misunderstanding, however, are not limited to those facing human language barriers.

While most engineers agree, in a general way, on the meaning of the term architecture, specifics about architecture and architecture-related products can vary greatly from one organization to the next.

Problem

Differing architecture views can have far-reaching effects on a virtual project's ultimate success.

The overview to this book mentioned the important relationship among architecture, work split, and remote tasking.

Insight

One's view of architecture affects not only task partitioning, task expectations, and manager-to-engineer communication, but architecture also affects organizational level responsibilities, expectations and communication.

To aid the reader in gaining a better understanding of this critical relationship, in the following pages we examine architecture in greater depth.

3.3   A View of Architecture

One popular definition of the term "software architecture" adopted by David Garlan and Dewayne Perry is as follows:

> *"...the structure of the components of a program/system, their interrelationships, and principles and guidelines governing their design and evolution over time."*[1]

A simplification of this definition views architectures as "Components, Connections, and Constraints." Note that Laura uses system design and architecture interchangeably. It is also worth noting that on many software-intensive projects today system architecture, software architecture, and simply architecture are used interchangeably. The phrase "top-level system architecture" is used on the TAR, but when Laura speaks she refers to the "system design."

3.3.1 An Organizational View of Architecture

In organizations like Jim's, architecture responsibility is often assigned to a group separate from system design. This architecture team is often given responsibility for the *common* pieces of software along with the *rules* to be employed by the users of these pieces. This team may or may not actually be responsible for defining the system components to be designed and implemented. What is important here for our purposes is that this work is actually different from the system design work that Laura is looking for.

3.3.2 A Different Organizational View of Architecture

In some organizations the distinction between architecture and system design described in the previous section is not made. In many of these organizations system design and architecture seem to be used almost interchangeably as Laura used them. In these cases, defining common architectural artifacts are simply viewed as good system design. This view is frequently found in smaller organizations that cannot afford separate architecture teams.

3.3.3 Relationship between Organizational Structure and Task Assignments

---

Insight

Task expectations are often closely coupled with specific organizational structures.

From an examination of the TAR (Table 3.1) one cannot determine which organizational view of architecture was assumed. This is not surprising. Normally, one would expect a task definition to be independent of organizational structure. As seen from the discussion on engineering organizations in Chapter 1, influential, although unwritten, task expectations frequently exist. These expectations often have their genesis in existing organizational structures that have evolved over long periods of time.

As an example, Laura's architecture task expectations are based on her past experience in a different and smaller organization than the organization Jim has operated in for 18 years. More specifically, based on her experience, Laura doesn't expect to see the system design *real work* separated from the architecture work. From Laura's view, the components, the critical algorithms, the data produced by these algorithms, and the methods used for component communication are all part of the *critical system design*. She has no historical experience from which to draw task distinctions based on an organizational structure.

Jim, on the other hand, interpreted the phrase "top-level system architecture" on the TAR based on his experience in an organization that had taught him that the "system design" would be "taken care of" (recall brief tale in Section 1.1) by a distinct department. Jim knows what it takes to be successful in his organization. He has proven himself and is simply repeating the process that has been successful for him in the past.

3.4 Evolution of "Local Meaning" of Terms and Its Relationship to Organizational Responsibilities

---

Insight

Architecture often equates to "whatever the architecture team does."

Theoretically, one would expect the definition of work products to be independent of organizational structures. Nevertheless, in practice this is not always the case.

As we saw in Chapter 1 responsibilities within organizations can evolve in various ways. In practice, the term architecture frequently equates to "whatever the architecture team does" in a particular organization. Terms well-known industry-wide tend to take on very specific local meaning inside organizations, which is often influenced by a particular organization's unique evolution.

3.5   Relationship Among Critical Issues, Risk, and Past Experience

In our tale the customer has expressed interest in being kept informed of the project's critical issues. From the dialogue at the end, it is clear the project does not have a clear view of what those critical issues are.

To clarify, Laura believes critical algorithmic work exists that should be shared with the customer at this time. In actuality, ZBE was doing some algorithm design work, but they chose not to share the status of this activity with either Laura or the customer because ZBE didn't view this work as critical. This decision was based on past experience. The company had solved similar problems before, and saw little risk in the upcoming design effort. Laura, not having shared this same past experience, took a different view on the project's critical issues.

Part of the task miscommunication in our tale is due to differing views of architecture, but this is not the only cause. There are also differing views of critical issues, which translate into differing views of project risks.

Insight
Risk, uncertainty, and critical issues depend on one's experience.

Risk is related to uncertainty, but — as we have seen — uncertainty can vary depending on one's experience. When there are differing backgrounds and experiences of project team members, we can anticipate varying levels of uncertainty in the minds of engineering personnel. Given the characteristics of most virtual projects, it should not be surprising that we have differing views on criticality of issues. What is uncertain to Laura may not be uncertain to Jim and vice versa. This factor feeds task miscommunication.

3.6 Use Architecture to Aid Task Communication

On the surface this miscommunication appears fundamental and easily correctable. Laura and the architecture team need to work more closely clarifying their use of terms and task definitions, and coordinating assumptions with respect to critical issues and related risks.

Solution

Consistently employ a well-defined and "agreed to" single architecture view when assigning lower level tasks.

3.6.1 Is Architecture the Total Solution?

While defining and deploying a clear architecture picture are certainly parts of the remote tasking solution, they do not provide the complete solution.

Given the diverse backgrounds of virtual project personnel, the types of difficulties seen in our tale should be expected in early virtual project stages. On projects that do succeed, once clear architectures are defined and deployed, team momentum often builds rapidly.

Due to increased opportunities on virtual projects for sharing of diverse knowledge, not only does project momentum rapidly build up, but personal growth accelerates. Many individuals utilize the opportunity to work with new teammates with different backgrounds to learn new skills not previously accessible. Nevertheless, a surprising number of virtual projects and personnel never reach this stage. To help understand why this is the case, let's look at another tale.

About the tale

The purpose of this tale is to provide greater insight for the reader into the role of the informal — or cultural — side of an effective organization. We provide this tale at this point so the reader understands that, while a common architecture is important, it doesn't provide the full solution for effective virtual project operations. Part of the solution is discussed later in this chapter through the use of the Task Assignment Record (TAR). This tale also provides a strong motivator for the "freedom line" recommendation discussed at greater length in Chapter 6.

3.7

The Database Process Tale

In this tale we return to our database example from Section 1.4.1 in Chapter 1. Recall that Company ABC is a multi-billion dollar conglomerate and Charlie is the manager of the Database Group. Charlie is a "people-oriented" manager. He constantly encourages his workers to keep learning and growing in their careers, and he provides a good role model for his team in this regard. Keeping up on the latest trends in database technology is one way Charlie maintains enthusiasm for his own work and his effectiveness as a manager and a mentor. His positive spirit and energetic style are infectious within the department he has led for 7 years.

In this tale ABC is teaming with another large organization, DEF, on a recently awarded new project. DEF is the prime contractor and is responsible for most of the systems engineering, while ABC is responsible for a large database implementation effort on the project. At a previous system engineering team meeting, Tim, the system engineering lead from DEF, asked Charlie for a presentation on his company's database process. Over the past few weeks people have noticed that Charlie's demeanor at work has changed. He has become unusually quiet, and his normal outgoing, upbeat attitude has been missing. His co-workers do not know what caused this change. As our tale begins, Charlie has just finished his presentation to Tim. Jack, a long time peer of Charlie's at ABC, is sitting in the back of the room.

"This was a good presentation," came Tim's muffled voice through the black box in the middle of the conference room table. "But it didn't tell me what I need to know." Instantly, Charlie's right index finger jabbed the MUTE button on the little black box.

"I haven't a clue what he really wants!" he replied. Then, abruptly, he jabbed it once more.

"I need to know how your systems people interact with your database team," added Tim. Charlie stared piercingly at the little box.

"We follow our company procedures," he replied curtly. The meeting was over. Team members, including Jack, filed out of the conference room.

As Jack approached his office, he could hear his phone ringing. Tim usually wasn't this prompt, but this time it was no surprise. Everyone knew the team wasn't working well together and Jack could hear the tension in Tim's voice as he picked up the phone.

"You guys are the experts," said Tim. "But if I'm going to be responsible I need to know how the process works." Jack wasn't surprised by Tim's reaction. The way systems engineering interacted with the database people at ABC had always been somewhat of a mystery. It wasn't that the process didn't work. It actually worked very well, but it had never been written down formally.

Less than a week later, Charlie was standing half way into the hall, half blocking the doorway to Jack's office. He was tapping his pencil on the corner of Jack's bookshelf, like he always did when he wanted to avoid a subject. Jack twisted around in his chair.

"What's up, Charlie?"

"Tim's hired a database designer." Charlie was looking at his pencil when he said it. It wasn't making any noise now. Jack slowly stood up.

"What's really going on, Charlie?" At first Charlie didn't look up.

"Charlie?" He tapped his pencil down one more time. Then he looked up directly at Jack.

"We've built complex databases before. We've done this kind of work for years." Charlie's voice began to shake.

"Charlie, do you need to sit down?" Jack asked in concerned tone. Charlie shook his head. He was looking down at the floor now. He took a deep breath.

"I'm getting too old for this," he mumbled.

"Why don't you give Tim a call and ask him how we can help him?" Charlie looked up. The usual sparkle was missing from Charlie's eyes.

"He doesn't want our help." It was all that Charlie had to say.

3.7.1 Analysis

In the above tale Charlie has been asked by Tim to explain how system engineers interact with the database group in his company. Tim is uncertain how the process works because he is unfamiliar with how Charlie's organization functions internally. This uncertainty equates to risk from Tim's perspective. This is a different form of risk than in the first tale in this chapter, but it is still a risk to Tim who is responsible for the systems engineering on the project.

In this tale Charlie has difficulty communicating with Tim. He finds it difficult to answer Tim's questions. Let's look closer at how Charlie operates on a typical day at work to uncover what might be happening.

3.7.1.1 Charlie's Typical Day

Charlie's typical day is very busy. As mentioned previously, he has led his database group for 7 years. Because his day is usually busy, Charlie tries to keep to a routine. Part of which includes devoting time to keeping current technically by reading one article each day. Keeping up on technology not only allows Charlie to continue to be an excellent role model and mentor for his people, it also invigorates him. He looks forward each day with enthusiasm to this regularly scheduled brief activity.

Charlie, like many professionals, is a structured individual who has a system. His system helps him keep his day under control. But for Charlie's day to stay under control, he must keep his system balanced. This requires him to carefully allocate and manage the amount of time he spends on each task each day. When new and unplanned activities pop up unexpectedly, it starts to throw Charlie's system out of balance.

3.7.1.2 Charlie's Reliance on the Informal Side

Part of what keeps Charlie's system in balance is his reliance on his organization. Through the years, just like other workers in the company, Charlie has learned what the organization expects of him, and what he can expect of the organization. Charlie doesn't think about this reliance much anymore, although he used to when he first came to the organization many years ago.

As an example, Charlie relies upon the organization's informal side to help train new engineers in his group. We saw an example of this reliance back in Chapter 1, Section 1.4.1 when Charlie introduced Fred, a new hire, to his new cubicle mate, Tom. Without thinking much about it, Charlie was able to walk away knowing that Fred would learn from Tom — among other things — how systems engineers and the database group interact. Charlie knows he doesn't need to take unplanned time out of his busy day to tell Fred all the things the informal system will teach him. Through the years,

Charlie has begun to take this informal support for granted, but his system continues to rely upon it as much as ever.

3.7.1.3 Relationship between Charlie's System and the Organizational System

Charlie's system is dependent upon the organizational system. For Charlie to maintain that delicate balance each day, the organizational system must continue to support him as it has in the past. Unfortunately, personnel from DEF do not tap into ABC's organizational system the same way that Charlie's own personnel do. As a result, this is causing more and more unplanned demands on Charlie's limited time.

Lately, Charlie hasn't found time to read and keep up. Charlie's balanced system has been running out of balance more and more often. His activities are not invigorating him and more and more of his days are becoming hectic and out of control.

As a result, when Tim asks Charlie certain questions alarms go off inside Charlie's head. This is not because Charlie isn't capable of answering Tim's questions, but rather because the types of questions Tim is asking don't fit Charlie's system. They are throwing his system into turmoil. Changes in Charlie's demeanor at work are a sign his system isn't working and it affects his ability perform his duties.

The book *Culture Clash: Managing in a Multicultural World*, states "each of us experiences difficulties as we attempt to function effectively in another culture."[2] Culture fatigue[2] suggests what occurs when we physically travel to another country and interact with people in a foreign culture. One needn't travel far in today's business environment to experience the symptoms of culture fatigue.

3.8   Fundamentals, Strongly Held Beliefs, and Risk

In the book, *On Studying Organizational Cultures*, Schultz tells us that culture concepts emphasize "the fundamental framework which people take for granted in their social and occupational activities."[3]

Experience on a number of virtual projects shows that it can be physically and emotionally draining when people are asked to stop and explain things they have taken for granted for long periods of time. This is especially true when schedules leave little room for such activities. Over the years Charlie has come to depend on his organization, but he has long since stopped thinking about it.

Insight

When we see things as fundamental, we treat them differently than strongly held beliefs.

There is a tendency to ignore fundamentals, treating them almost as if they didn't exist. Long held fundamentals tend to be viewed as requiring no validation, nor integration. We see them, effectively, as invariant. This type of belief can oftentimes be traced back to early influential mentors — to the "Old Joes" within our lives. Fundamentals often are set to the side, no longer thought about and believed to require no future energy. This act frees a space in our minds for other activities. Anything that invades this space can irritate us. It can become a distraction to our well-thought-out plan.

When we believe in something strongly (something not seen as fundamental), our tendency is to devote energy to it. When we know others may disagree, we prepare ourselves to defend our strongly held beliefs. In these cases, oftentimes we take the time to think about what is behind our beliefs. We consider carefully all the reasons we hold them as strongly as we do.

In this process, something else happens. By taking the time to question ourselves, we also begin to question our beliefs. Areas of uncertainty may be exposed creating opportunities to learn and grow.

Insight

By questioning our beliefs, we open ourselves to new possibilities that may be presented to us through the beliefs of others.

Sharing ideas and beliefs leads to integration and validation of our ideas with those of our teammates. An example of this process was seen in our Adjacent Cubicle Head Popping tale in Chapter 2. This is the environment in which light bulbs are most likely to pop on in our heads.

In his book, Seelye[2] tells a story about a boy named John who was blind from birth. At the age of 16 the boy was fortunate and regained his sight, but had difficulty adjusting. John found many of the objects that came within his view distracting. For example, when attempting to look at a person across the room, everything else between them would demand equal visual attention. Seelye tells us that "our culture teaches us what to see, and what to ignore."[2]

Insight

What another culture (or organization) may see as very important, or even risky, we may have been taught to ignore as inconsequential, or so fundamental as to not deserve attention.

3.9   Back to Our Tale

In our database process tale, Tim is responsible for systems engineering. This includes defining the requirements for the database that Charlie's group is responsible for implementing. In the tale Charlie became upset when he found out that Tim had hired a database engineer. In fact, Tim did hire Jeff, a database engineer, to help define the database requirements.

In the tale Tim appeared willing to use the ABC database process, but he needed to understand it. That is why he asked for the presentation. Neither Tim nor Jeff had ever worked at ABC. When Charlie heard that Tim hired Jeff he immediately jumped to the conclusion that Tim was going to use Jeff to do database work that should have been Charlie's responsibility. Let's look closer at what led Charlie to this conclusion.

Jeff has past experience from a commercial database house. He has been tasked by Tim to define the database requirements. His TAR can be seen in Table 3.2. Based on his past experience, Jeff doesn't separate requirements from design. In the commercial database organization where he previously worked, there was no need to do this. Note that the TAR provides no specific instructions on the format of the database requirements product, nor does it specify any particular tools to use. Jeff chose to use an Entity-Relationship (E-R) modeling tool to capture the database requirements because that was the way he did it in his past job.

But system engineers at ABC don't use an E-R modeling tool. At ABC, E-R modeling tools are used only by database designers. Because an E-R model was being developed by the prime contractor rumors spread at ABC indicating that the prime was taking over the database design task and wanted

Table 3.2   Systems Engineering Task Assignment Record

Project Identifier	Z234
Department Identifier	Systems Engineering
Task Identifier	TXXX
Task Authorization	Contract Charge Number
Responsible Manager	Tim
Assigned Engineer	Jeff
Budget	80 hours
Planned Start Date	June 12, 2002
Planned Complete Date	June 26, 2002
Actual Complete Date	
Task Description	Produce Data Requirements for Z234 project

ABC off the project. Note that this rumor was the result of assumptions based on the ABC organizational model, which was different than Jeff's experience at a smaller organization.

3.9.1 Use Task Assignment Records (TARs)

Solution

On virtual projects TARS, and the process required to complete the task assignment, may require more formally documented information than on collocated projects where personnel have worked together previously. This is because on these projects we cannot rely on the same informal communication mechanisms.

Miscommunication and misunderstanding occur on all projects. However, on healthy thriving projects these issues are identified, actions are taken, and resolution occurs in a timely fashion. On healthy projects these issues cause minimum impact to project momentum. On the other hand, on some technically challenging projects with tight schedules, the physical and emotional drain of culture-related clashes — if not handled in a forthright and expeditious manner — can seriously jeopardize project morale and ultimately project success.

3.10 Conclusion

In this chapter we dipped below the surface to uncover root causes of task miscommunication. Through this process we found that successful virtual collaboration requires looking to new ways to define terms and tasks more effectively across physically distributed sites.

Risk is the result of uncertainty and uncertainty can vary based on experience and background. When this simple fact is not recognized costly project tension often results. Stress can be caused when long-held fundamental views are questioned. We have also seen that what is fundamental to one, may be risky to others.

We have learned that we can no longer afford to keep our processes secret, hidden inside our collocated organizations. On virtual projects we must anticipate questions concerning long-established processes that seem fundamental to those who have been on the inside for long periods of time. When opening up our processes the price paid is the time required to answer what seem to be annoyingly fundamental questions. But this time is real and must be considered as part of the cost of doing business in a virtual collaborative environment.

With more and more projects turning to collaboration with external organizations, one need not travel abroad to witness the signs of culture fatigue. Awareness of this fact, and learning to recognize key symptoms such as those exhibited by Charlie in our database tale are an important first step. But we must not stop there. In the next chapter we look at specific approaches one can take to help tackle these new challenges in practical, affordable, and proven ways.

CHAPTER 3 KEY POINTS SUMMARY
Architecture affects task partitioning, expectations, and communication
Task expectations closely coupled with organizational structure
Architecture often equates to "whatever the architecture team does"
Risk, uncertainty, and critical issues depend on one's experience
Fundamentals treated differently than strongly held beliefs
Questioning beliefs open up new possibilities
What some see as risky, others may see as fundamental
Employ single architecture view when assigning tasks
Task assignments require increased formality on virtual projects

References

1. Software Engineering Institute Web Site, http://www.sei.cmu.edu/architecture/definitions.html.
2. Seelye, H. Ned and Seelye-James, Alan, *Culture Clash: Managing in a Multicultural World*, NTC Publishing Group, Lincolnwood, IL, 1995.
3. Schultz, Majken, *On Studying Organizational Cultures*, Walter de Gruyter, Berlin, 1995, p. 5.

4 An Implementation of a Virtual Culture: The Rapid Filtered Project Memory (RFPM)

The RFPM is one way to implement part of the **Virtual Culture** concept. As discussed in Chapter 2, it is not intended to replace project procedures, or to provide general process information. The purpose of the RFPM is to provide critical **project-specific** information that meets the following criteria:

- Information traditionally not found in corporate procedures, and
- Information necessary to effectively execute task assignments that cross organizational or site boundaries, and
- Information not readily found through other available project sources.

Often, in the past, RFPM-type information has not been formally written down (even in SEI mature organizations). Examples of such information as seen in the tales include

- Definitions of key terms as used on specific projects (e.g., architecture)
- Identification of project critical issues and agreed to related strategies (that cross site or organizations)
- Key project architecture/system design guidance
- Concise definition of key task-related information, such as

- Tools to use
- Project-specific organizational responsibility
- Product format, content

While tools may be documented in a development plan, and organizational diagrams may exist, the form in which this information is found often does not specifically give an engineer what he needs to know to successfully complete a given task assignment. An example structure of an RFPM is shown in Figure 4.1.

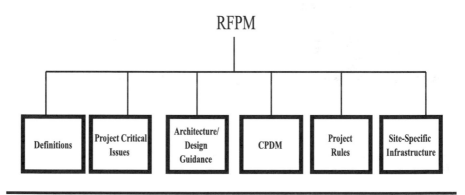

Figure 4.1   Example RFPM Directory Structure

Some of the information in this chapter and the referenced appendices may be more detailed than necessary for project leaders. It is included to ensure that the RFPM concept is well understood by those who must support and approve it.

Where are we going?

The project rules section of the RFPM is discussed in Chapter 5, and site-specific RFPM information is discussed in Chapter 6. You can also find guidance on detecting unhealthy conflict and recommended actions in Chapter 7, Step 8. In the following sections and in Appendix A we provide greater detail on how to construct and maintain an effective RFPM. Here we include greater detail about the type of information to be included in the RFPM, and the associated rationale for its inclusion. In this chapter we also define and discuss the component-product development matrix (CPDM). Lower level implementation details of primary interest to those tasked with the actual RFPM construction and maintenance have been placed in Appendix A. These details are referenced as appropriate within the text of this chapter.

Included in this chapter are also the identification of two key pitfalls (with references to our tales) and our recommendations for employing the CPDM to avoid them. Two important benefits of using a CPDM are also identified and discussed.

It is worth noting that our intention is not to imply that the mere act of including the information in the RFPM is, by itself, the solution to any of the pitfalls discussed. In many cases, it is the identified steps one must execute to attain the information that are key.

Insight

The RFPM acts as a forcing function driving us to the right solution.

By itself, the RFPM represents only a part of the solution.

4.1 RFPM Construction and Maintenance Guidance

While managers need not know the low level details of the RFPM, rules exist in its construction and maintenance which all engineering, including management, should be aware. We have identified **five key rules**:

- Maintain RFPM at a manageable size (not too large).
- Include critical project issues and agreed to strategies.
- Include architecture/system design guidance.
- Configuration manage at the increment (build) level.
- Build RFPM incrementally and through engineering team decisions (not a separate process group).

Each of these rules is discussed below.

4.1.1 Size

Our tales show the importance of key terms, project critical issues, and architecture/system design guidance. It is critical, as mentioned in Chapter 2, that the RFPM not be allowed to grow to an unmanageable size.

As an example, the definitions/terminology section should not become a general glossary of terms for the project. This is not its purpose. It must be limited to critical terms that, if not defined explicitly, are likely to cause miscommunication and conflict across physically separated project sites. Similarly, the project's critical issues section must not become a general list of issues, but rather it should be limited to critical issues where project conflict across multiple sites exists.

4.1.2 Critical Issues and Agreed To Strategies

The project's critical issues section should also provide (or reference) agreed to strategies approved by project leadership to address each identified issue. This may be accomplished through a reference to an existing project's risk abatement plan. We do not recommend duplicating in the RFPM information that already exists elsewhere within the project files. References to existing information are encouraged. What is most important are documentation of the agreement and its universal accessibility to team members regardless of their physical location.

4.1.3 Architecture/System Design Guidance

Architecture/design guidance (especially guidance that affects remote team members) should be captured or referenced from the RFPM. It, however, should be limited to those areas relevant to team members focused on completing their assigned design efforts.

Change is good, but…

With today's movement toward more evolutionary design approaches, change is not only acceptable, it is anticipated and encouraged. We discussed earlier (Chapter 2) how teams can progress rapidly when they are collocated and are able to conduct on-the-spot team brainstorming. This provides rapid turn around of validation and integration of design concepts. This form of team dynamics should always be encouraged.

However, changes — especially changes to global architectural approaches — can seriously impact ongoing designs. Nothing can be more frustrating to a designer than being told that assumptions previously agreed to are no longer valid. For this reason, baselining architectural agreements for each project increment is critical. These agreements do not need to be documented in an overly formal fashion, but they should be written down and placed in a controlled area where they are accessible to all project members.

Solution

Write down agreements that have implications across distributed sites.

Due to the demand for rapid capability and reduced cost, many projects are moving away from traditional formal documentation. In its place working engineering development folders often are being employed. While this can reduce cost, it can also complicate the communication of critical architecture/design decisions. In the absence of formal documentation, using the RFPM can help eliminate many potential communication difficulties. This is why we recommend that architecture/system design guidance be placed in the RFPM.

4.1.4 Configuration Management

Once the major architecture/design decisions have been made for a given increment (build), this does not mean the team cannot continue refining and improving the architecture. In fact, it is expected as lessons are learned from an ongoing increment that improvements are factored into subsequent increments. However, to keep the project from operating in a chaotic fashion, subsequent increment changes should be managed separately through a version control system.

Solution

Employ incremental-specific subdirectories.

Many of the topics in the RFPM will be common across all increments (i.e., key definitions); others may be increment-sensitive (i.e., design information). This can be managed by employing increment-specific subdirectories within the RFPM, as required.

4.1.5 Incrementally Built

For the RFPM to be successful it is crucial that the information included be "bought-into" by the full engineering team. In support of this objective we recommend that the RFPM be built incrementally, and represent the result of team decisions. Because of this objective we discourage the creation of a separate group to construct the RFPM. Utilizing separate groups defeats the RFPM's purpose (with the exceptions identified below) of achieving a single-team technical vision.

Each engineering team within the organization should construct and maintain the sections of the RFPM relevant to their responsibilities. A separate group may be employed to develop the CPDM, project rules, and site-specific information, but all information must be approved by the leadership team including all engineering team leaders.

In the following section task assignments are discussed at greater length. In this section we also emphasize the need for a Component-Product Development Matrix (CPDM). The CPDM is a part of the RFPM.

4.2 Why Do We Need Increased Formality on Task Assignment Definitions?

It was stated earlier that on virtual projects increased formality with respect to task assignment definition may be necessary. This is due, at least partially, to the fact that there is no single corporate culture on virtual projects on which to rely.

In Section 3.1 of the previous chapter we saw how the lack of a precise definition of a term and task products leads to serious miscommunication. In Section 3.9 we also saw a case where differing views on the use of a tool led to serious team mistrust.

These cases represent only a few of many potential miscommunication areas that exist due to the lack of precision in task definitions. Another example of potential task miscommunication can be found in Appendix A to this book where we discuss two divergent approaches and a related "hybrid" approach to specifying requirements for software-intensive systems.

These examples should make our point clear. In the following section we discuss our recommendation to meet this need for increased formality through a CPDM. On the positive side, a CPDM is not labor intensive to develop, and — more importantly — engineers don't complain about using one. In fact, engineers actually like the CPDM because it is both easy to use and crisply answers many of the questions they most often ask.

4.3   What Is A CPDM and How Can It Help?

The use of a *Component-product development matrix* (see Chapter 1 for the definition of component-product) is a powerful communication device supporting improved task assignment definition. While the technique described could be useful for many tasks the focus here is specifically on engineering tasks associated with software-intensive projects and those with dependencies that cross site, or organizational boundaries.

4.3.1 CPDM Attributes

A component-product development matrix (CPDM) is a table that lists the specific artifacts (component-products) to be developed, along with the following artifact-related attributes:

- Brief description of artifact or reference to description
- Tool(s) used to develop artifact
- What project phase artifact is developed in
- Location where artifact is maintained
- Project-specific organizational entity responsible for artifact

4.3.2 Component-Product Relationship to Task Assignments

One of the primary advantages in using CPDMs is that these tables define the piece-part products (component-products) at the same level that tasks are assigned through task assignment records (TARs). This gives the engineer the needed project-specific information that is most often found to be lacking in general corporate procedures, and is most often a source of task miscommunication.

4.3.3 Component-Products and Deliverable-Products

Component-products, as the term is used here, should not be confused with customer end-product deliverables. As stated in Chapter 1, large systems are built as composites of component-products. Many of these component-products are in actuality internal engineering products which end-users need not be aware of.

Problem

Focusing on end-products alone often leads remote team members down divergent paths.

When we focus only on end-products there are many engineering choices to be made and it becomes easy for team members who are not collocated to take divergent paths. The CPDM provides an easy-to-use method to concisely define the project's chosen directions thereby reducing the likelihood of task miscommunication. The CPDM should not be confused with project procedures.

Solution

A well-constructed CPDM can keep remote team members on a consistent path by answering many of the most common questions that arise.

4.3.4 The CPDM and Project/Corporate Procedures

Oftentimes, especially on virtual projects, there just isn't time to accomplish a complete tailoring of the corporate procedures, especially at the level needed for effective communication of all project-specific key issues that cross multiple remote sites. Furthermore when too much project-specific information is added, project procedures can become costly to maintain and difficult to use.

While we recognize the need for increased formality, we also seek to minimize unnecessary burdensome formality. We have found that using CPDMs provides the increased formality necessary, and it does so in a cost-effective and practical manner. Table 4.1 provides an example of the structure of a CPDM with two sample artifacts. For detailed examples of CPDMs, see Appendixes A and E of this book.

Table 4.1   Component-Product Development Matrix Sample Structure

Artifact	Description/ Reference	Tool/Form	Phase	Location	Responsibility
Use Cases	Ref. UML Methodology	Rational ROSE	Requirements	SEN	SE
Database Design	Ref. DB Design Proc.	E-R Modeling Tool	Detailed Design	SDF	SW

4.3.5 *The CPDM as a Bridge from Corporate Procedures to Project-Specific Information*

The CPDM is a bridge from general corporate procedures to the specific information (format, content, tool, responsibility) that engineers need to effectively complete assignments in accordance with project expectations. In particular, one of the greatest values of the CPDM has been improved definition of those tasks where dependencies exist across multiple site boundaries.

Nevertheless, it is worth noting that CPDMs can be a valuable task management aid even within non-virtual environments.

Solution

By using a CPDM the effort required to tailor general corporate procedures to the unique needs of a given project can be substantially reduced.

We view the CPDM as one piece of the RFPM.

4.4 Examples of Virtual Project Pitfall Avoidance through the Use of a CPDM

In this section we describe how a CPDM could be employed to avoid certain pitfalls observed in our tales. In the discussion that follows we reference an example CPDM (see Table A.1 in Appendix A). This example contains actual component-products.

It is important to keep in mind that this CPDM is for illustrative purposes only. This sample CPDM helps communicate our recommendations to the reader. It can also be used by readers constructing their own project-specific CPDMs. This table should not be used in its present form for the following two reasons:

- ■ It is incomplete with respect to the full needs of a given project, and
- ■ An effective CPDM must be based on project-specific information.

4.4.1 How to Avoid Pitfall One — Miscommunication Due to Ambiguous Terminology

In the architecture tale described in Section 3.1, recall that Laura expected to see critical algorithms completed as part of the architecture task. However, by referencing the task definition provided through the TAR (Table 3.1) in this tale, we see that this expectation was not clearly communicated. Laura's expectations were based on her experience, which didn't match the experience of the architecture team.

In the tale, miscommunication occurred because critical task-related information was not readily available. This information includes

- ■ Clear component-product definition
- ■ When component-product will be available
- ■ Who is responsible for each component-product

In the example CPDM provided in Appendix A-1, critical algorithms are called out as a separate component-product. Note also that availability of the critical algorithms component-product is not planned until the detailed design phase, and that it is identified as being the responsibility of the System Engineering (SE) group.

In Appendix Table A.1 one can also observe six (6) artifacts (component-products) with responsibility assigned to the architecture organizational entity (indicated through the ARCH abbreviation). These artifacts will be available in the preliminary design phase and include

- High Level Packages
- Top Level Design rationale, risks
- Process Architecture Diagram (PAD)
- Process to Class Allocation Diagram (PCAD)
- Process Interaction Diagram (PID)
- Major classes, methods, and attributes

For a description of the "High Level Packages" and "Major classes, methods and attributes" component-products, a reference to UML methodology is provided.[1] For three other component-products (PAD, PCAD and PID), a reference to the text *Use Cases Combined with Booch, OMT, UML*[2] by Putnam P. Texel and Charles B. Williams is provided.

It is not the purpose of this book to propose a specific approach to architecture, or software methodology. These references are included only as examples.

Solution

Providing well-defined component-product definitions with clear responsibility through a CPDM can substantially reduce remote task miscommunication.

By referencing a published textbook for the definitions of key component-products we further reduce the chance of miscommunication.

4.4.1.1 Use of Standards and Published Methodologies

Maximizing the use of open standards and formally published methodologies is recommended and highly encouraged. This is particularly important on virtual projects due to the issues involved in rapidly pulling together a cohesive team of engineers with divergent backgrounds.

The Unified Modeling Language (UML) is an example of a modeling language that is rapidly becoming a universally accepted object-oriented modeling standard. C++ and JAVA hold similar status at the object-oriented programming level.

By aligning our analysis and design component-products as closely as possible to UML (or a similar standard), we minimize potential task miscommunication issues especially across site boundaries.

This concept holds for methodology as well. In the sample CPDM, other software component-products are referenced (PAD, PCAD, PID) that are defined through the methodology published in the *Use Cases Combined with Booch, OMT, UML* textbook.

Endorsing any particular modeling language or methodology is not the intent in this book. Those referenced are done so merely as examples. However, we do encourage our clients to adopt published methodologies and standard modeling and programming languages on virtual projects as they simplify the communication of task assignments and reduce potentially undesirable surprises.

4.4.1.2 Using the CPDM to Aid Task Communication

Think back to the discussion in Chapter 1 about the "push-pull" organizational tale. Recall the factors that influence the evolution of responsibilities in an organization (many and varied). As seen in the architecture tale earlier in this chapter, task miscommunication was due, as least partially, to Laura's lack of knowledge of organizational responsibility at ZBE. In the CPDM example in Appendix A.1, we reference the following three organizational entities:

■ SE – Systems Engineering Team
■ SW – Software Engineering Team
■ Arch – Architecture Team

It is important for the reader to keep in mind that these are just examples. The organizational entities referenced in your CPDM must reflect the actual physical teams in your organization if your CPDM is to be effective.

If, for example, your project doesn't have an actual Architecture team that meets regularly and has defined responsibilities, then whatever team in your organization that owns the cost and schedule accountability for the identified architectural artifacts should be listed in the table. In some organizations this could be a Systems Engineering team, and in others it could be a Software Engineering team.

In our example, it can be seen that the Architecture team is responsible for the "Major Classes, Methods and Attributes" artifact in the preliminary design phase of the project. Once again, this is only an example. The responsibility for this artifact could vary on your project depending on your organization's evolution.

The main point is simply that this table needs to reflect how you are really going to execute your program. It is not an ideal table. It must reflect how you really intend to operate, and it must be kept current when changes occur.

Solution

Using a CPDM reduces the need to change standard procedures when project organizational responsibilities change.

One of the advantages of employing a CPDM is that when organizational responsibilities change, standard procedures don't need to change. This is because the hook to the project-specific organization is in the CPDM, not the procedures. In this case you just need to update your CPDM, which is much easier than updating information embedded in numerous detailed project procedures.

This is an example of how the CPDM provides the link between your corporate standard operating procedures and the way work really gets done on your project by your project organization. By using a CPDM in this fashion the type of serious miscommunication between Laura and Jim in the architecture tale (Section 3.1) can be avoided.

4.4.1.3 How the CPDM Helps Resolve Miscommunication

If early in Laura's project a CPDM had been constructed following the guidelines provided, then distinct component-products would have been developed for critical algorithms and the architecture (similar to PAD, PCAD, and PID).

Laura, as a member of the project leadership team, would have been required to buy-in to these component products and their attributes (i.e., product availability, responsibility, tools used). The TAR Laura had originally provided to Jim would have only needed the addition of the words "**in accordance with the architecture team's responsibilities for component-products found in the project CPDM.**" See Table 4.2 for an example of this modified TAR.

Table 4.2 Modified Architecture TAR with CPDM Reference

Project Identifier	BAAA
Department Identifier	ZZZ
Task Identifier	TYYY
Task Authorization	Contract Charge Number
Responsible Manager	Laura
Assigned Engineer	Jim
Budget	480 hours (includes hours for supporting engineers)
Planned Start Date	August 12, 2002
Planned Complete Date	September 20, 2002
Actual Complete Date	
Task Description	Participate as member of the architecture team developing the top level system architecture for BAAA project in accordance with the identified architecture team's responsibilities for component-products found in CPDM

Based on experience helping clients develop CPDMs, we know that by working through the CPDM approval process, Laura's concerns over the critical algorithm availability would have surfaced. Also, the more precise definition of architecture provided through an enumeration of the component-products would have forced earlier discussion of the ambiguous architecture term, thereby avoiding more costly surprises. As a result of this important team interaction, the likelihood of the produced products meeting Laura's expectations would have been greatly improved.

4.4.2 How to Avoid Pitfall Two — Miscommunication Due to Unclear Process

Recall the mistrust witnessed in the database tale (Section 3.9). It was due largely to the use of a tool (E-R design modeling tool) for a purpose that appeared inappropriate to those inside one of the participating organizations. Note that in the CPDM example in Appendix A.1, the "Database Requirements" component-product refers to a "data requirements sheet" in the tools column. A data requirements sheet is simply a form that allows communication of data requirements to the designer without using a data modeling tool. An example of a data requirements sheet can be found in Appendix Table A.2.

The use of such a form can simplify database requirements definition and communication. When data modeling tools are used in the requirements phase there is often a tendency to start the design work early, thereby constraining the design unnecessarily. This feeds project miscommunication, as seen in the tale, with regard to requirements vs. design task responsibility. Also, by using such a form the individual assigned to the requirements task need not be a proficient data modeler, or knowledgeable in using a data modeling tool.

Regardless of the actual approach chosen for requirements and design, developing a CPDM and requiring its approval force early resolution of many potential areas of task miscommunication before they can seriously impact project productivity. If a CPDM had been developed early on the project in which the database tale took place, the mistrust that ensued might have been avoided.

4.4.2.1 Enhanced Task Assignment Description

Table 4.3 provides an example of an enhanced data design task TAR. Notice in the TAR the addition of three entries:

- Component-products produced
- Dependent component-products
- Status comments

Component-products produced

By adding a direct reference in the TAR to the component-products produced and a reference to the CPDM, communication of task definition and expectations is improved. If an engineer assigned to this task at a remote location is uncertain if a particular tool is required, he/she can refer to the CPDM for this level of information.

Dependent component-products

The dependent component-product field demonstrates a method for indicating on the TAR dependencies that this task has on external tasks and products. In our sample TAR, Table 4.3, we see that the data design task start is dependent on the designer receiving the component-product, referred to as the data requirements sheet, from System Engineering (SE).

Table 4.3 Enhanced Data Design TAR

Project Identifier	Z234
Department Identifier	Database Engineering
Task Identifier	TYYY
Task Authorization	Contract Charge Number
Responsible Manager	Charlie
Assigned Engineer	Fred
Budget	160 hours
Planned Start Date	June 26, 2002
Planned Complete Date	July 31, 2002
Actual Complete Date	
Task Description	Produce Data Model for Z234 project
Component-Products Produced	E-R Data Model and DDL — refer to CPDM for details
Dependent Component-Products	Data Requirements Sheet (SE)
Status/Comments —	Week ending June 19 — Assigned engineer Anticipate two-day slip due to late delivery of dependent component-product.
Status/Comments —	Week ending June 19 — Responsible manager Slip will not inpact project critical path

Solution

Using the dependent component-products field, especially for dependencies that cross site boundaries, forces critical team communication early in areas where there is likelihood of task miscommunication.

Status/Comments

The third new entry on our enhanced TAR demonstrates a method for capturing in-process status information and feedback between a lead and assigned engineer. By using the TAR in this fashion the chances of misunderstanding are reduced, especially when the lead and assigned engineer are physically separated.

It is worth noting that when used in this fashion the TAR can be sent through e-mail back and forth between the lead and the engineer as an attached document. This added information improves our communication and increases the likelihood that the engineer will complete the task in accordance with expectations regardless of physical location.

4.5 CPDM Benefit 1 — Integration of Systems and Software

On many projects in the past, a strict separation of systems and software products existed. For example, many companies developed system engineering management plans distinct from software development plans. Inside each of these plans distinct sets of systems and software processes and products are often identified. Example systems processes and products include

■ risk management process and risk abatement plans
■ trade study process and results
■ functional analysis process and products
■ metrics process and actual metrics
■ review process and minutes of actual reviews

Examples of software processes and products include

■ requirements process and requirements database
■ design process and resultant design models
■ coding standard and resultant code
■ test approach, test cases, and test results
■ peer review process, minutes and action items from actual reviews

Strict separation of systems and software activities has, in the past, caused difficulties when related products are tightly coupled. Traditionally, in collocated development environments, these issues have been resolved through site-specific means. These solutions have often evolved through time and been highly organizational-specific.

Today we are moving toward more integrated process and product approaches. By integrating systems and software processes and products we potentially gain significant efficiencies. This potential must not be overlooked in today's highly competitive world.

This is not to say that the distinction between systems and software no longer exists. It does, and responsibilities for each must continue to be managed closely. Integrated products result from systems and software teams working closely, in one sense as a single team, but each must always maintain a keen awareness of its own distinct responsibilities.

Solution

The CPDM supports integrated development teams through communication of responsibilities across physically distributed locations.

4.6 CPDM Benefit 2 — Flexibility of End-Product Deliverables

By using the CPDM we can define and manage distinct activities leading to system or software component-products (defined through the responsibility field), while, at the same time, integration of these piece-parts remains focused on end-product deliverables.

An advantage to this approach is the flexibility provided with respect to formal end-product deliverables. As projects continue to look for ways to cut costs, the potential for reducing formal deliverable documentation continues to be appealing. A past concern in this regard has been the reliance on documentation as an engineering key activity forcing function.

Solution

Through the CPDM the forcing function moves away from costly formal documentation to the less costly management of component-products.

This provides our distributed projects with greater flexibility with respect to formal deliverables, and potentially greater cost savings without compromising sound engineering principles.

4.7 Conclusion

In this chapter we provided a number of practical, and affordable recommendations to address key pitfalls observed in the previous tales. In particular, we discussed the concepts of a Rapid Filtered Project Memory (RFPM) and a Component-Product Development Matrix (CPDM). We also discussed how these practical and affordable techniques can be applied along with enhanced TARs to address communication breakdowns witnessed on virtual projects.

To aid the reader, we provided sample component-products and related attributes (see Appendix A). What is most important isn't the component-product examples themselves, but rather the process of constructing and employing an RFPM and CPDM to help you avoid your own potential pitfalls.

Insight

The act of creating a CPDM is a major part of the solution.

This process drives us to ask the right questions, and what is key is not the answers themselves, but the forcing function that drives the project leadership to communicate early, reach agreements, and document those agreements in a concise fashion where others can rapidly access them.

Building and using a Rapid Filtered Project Memory (RFPM) and a Component-Product Development Matrix (CPDM) have been proven to be practical and affordable ways to help tackle the new challenges we face when operating in the virtual world.

CHAPTER 4 KEY POINTS SUMMARY
RFPM acts as a "forcing" function
Act of creating a CPDM is major part of solution
Write down agreements that cross distributed sites
Employ incremental-specific subdirectories
Employ a well-constructed CPDM to keep team on consistent path
Use CPDM to reduce process tailoring effort
Use component-product definitions and CPDM to reduce remote task miscommunication
Use CPDM to reduce procedure maintenance
Use dependent component-products field on TAR to reduce task miscommunication
Use CPDM to enhance distributed team communication
CPDM moves forcing function away from costly formal documentation

References

1. Quatrani, Terry, *Visual Modeling with Rational ROSE and UML*, Addison Wesley, Reading, MA, 1998.
2. Texel, Putnam P. and Williams, Charles B., *Use Cases Combined with Booch, OMT, UML*, Prentice Hall, Upper Saddle River, NJ, 1997.

5 Team Communication: The Rules of the Game Have Changed

I n Chapter 2 we discussed a number of contributing factors to virtual project conflict and communication breakdown. These factors include distance, competition, and differing experiences of personnel. Culture can also play a strong role in influencing divergent viewpoints.

Where are we going?

In this chapter we take a closer look at project conflict from another perspective — the project team.

Today there is no shortage of books available on teams, and it is not the intention in this chapter to duplicate existing published information. However, there may be no single factor more critical to virtual project success than the effective operation of the team.

In a virtual environment there are new factors involved that can rapidly lead a potentially successful team in the wrong direction. To avoid critical pitfalls there is a need for proactive management steps early in the project to establish key rules that team personnel must employ when communicating both inside and outside of the project environment. While these rules are not all that complex, they are also not well understood by many first-time virtual team members.

In this chapter we utilize three short tales to aid the investigation of key factors affecting virtual project team performance. Recommended virtual project team rules are identified at the end of this chapter. The first tale is about team loyalty. Although the scenario described could occur on any project, its likelihood of occurring increases greatly within a virtual collaborative environment.

About the tale

The purpose in telling this tale is to increase the reader's awareness of behavior that is becoming increasingly commonplace on virtual projects. If this tale sounds familiar, we ask the reader to look beyond the tale itself to its broader implications on team productivity. Note that the way this tale concludes makes the incident sound harmless. It isn't. Be sure to read Section 5.1.8.1 on Real Productivity after reading the tale.

5.1

The Team Loyalty Tale

Jim glanced up at the small clock on the wall. The last 24 hours had been crazy. The day before he had been at work all night with two of his co-workers, Sam and Ed. Jim gazed out the window, as he thought back.

It was 2 months earlier when he and Ed first decided to talk to upper management about the excessive time it was taking to prepare for the biweekly customer reviews. They were never intended to be formal, and it irked him whenever he thought about it.

It was his customer, Tim, who had agreed to eliminate those reviews, but only if another way could be found for the customer to get project insight. Jim knew it had been his idea to let the customer participate directly as a member of the design team. It seemed liked the right solution back then. He had figured that this way Tim could get his project insight, and the engineering team could focus more of their time on the "real" engineering.

For the first few weeks the plan worked. Tim attended all the design team meetings and was soon being treated by the rest of the team just like any other team member. Unfortunately, Tim was seeing more than he needed to see.

At one meeting there had been a heated exchange between Sam and Keven — two strong-minded team members with differing views on the use of a middleware product. Kevin, who was physically located at a remote site, teleconferenced into the project's team meetings. Kevin also had a reputation for being outspoken and at this meeting, in his usual unabashed style, he had made it clear that he was dead set against using a messaging middleware product that Sam had been pushing hard for the team to adopt. Kevin's views weren't a big surprise to anyone. The team had discussed the issue before and knew it was one they needed to work.

Unfortunately, before the team had a chance to solve this one, information leaked back to the customer, indicating that the "contractor had an inconsistent design approach" and that there existed serious "disconnects between team members."

Upon hearing this disconcerting status, the customer program manager immediately called the contractor program manager, Bob, who in turn called the engineering manager, Tom. After explaining the situation, Bob demanded that Tom take immediate action.

Tom responded by telling Bob that differing views were expected and encouraged among teammates and that the team should be allowed time to work it out through the "normal team process". But Bob was too upset to listen to Tom's explanation and made it clear that he didn't want another team meeting held without the issue being resolved.

It was almost three in the afternoon on Tuesday. The next architecture working group meeting was scheduled for the following day at one o'clock in the afternoon. Tom knew there wasn't time to call the full team together that afternoon because half the team was physically located at a remote site in a different time zone.

Believing he had no alternative, Tom pulled Jim, Sam, and Ed — his three best engineers who physically resided at the same location as he did — into a private meeting and explained the situation. He said he wanted them "to do whatever it takes" to get to a "single consistent design approach." And he also said that he wanted the approach completed before they went home that night.

Sam immediately objected. He told Tom that the team needed more time. He said that Kevin needed to be a part of any decision the team made because Kevin had the most experience of anyone on the team with the middleware product. But Tom wouldn't budge with his direction. He told Sam that the "issue was just too hot" to let it go unresolved any longer.

That evening Jim, Sam, and Ed worked through second and third shift doing their best to reach a consistent design approach with the information available. Sam made a number of unsuccessful attempts to contact Kevin by phone. By six in the morning the team had done what they could in the time available. Completely exhausted, the three team members went home to get some badly needed rest.

At the one o'clock architecture meeting Jim presented the approach reached by the three team members who had worked through the night. All team members heard the presentation including those teleconferenced in from remote locations.

Sam had wanted to talk to Kevin before the meeting, but was unable to contact him. During Jim's presentation remote team members listened politely, but no comments or questions were posed. Jim described the design approach as a "team" decision. He stated that alternatives had been considered, but due to time constraints an approach had to be chosen rapidly.

The following day the program manager, Bob, received positive feedback from the customer indicating that the team "disconnects" and "inconsistent design" had been resolved. The contractor management team was praised by the customer for taking timely action to resolve the issue. Bob passed the positive feedback on to the engineering manager, Tom, who in turn let the team know that their hard work had been recognized by the customer.

5.1.1   Tale Observations

This tale may sound familiar even if you've never worked on a virtual project. Nevertheless, on virtual projects there exists an increased likelihood of this type of scenario occurring because of the demand to accomplish more in less time coupled with the factors of distance, competition, and divergent personnel experiences. Regardless of the type of project, what we have heard so far about this tale gives little indication of its full impact. Let's take a closer look.

5.1.2   Categorizing Team Information

The information flowing from team activities falls into two broad categories. The first category is team results information. The second category is team in-process information.

The first category includes information that the team has agreed to make available to those outside the team. It is information that has already been through a team review and represents some level of team consensus. The second category is internal team privileged information. It is information that is not yet ready for public scrutiny because it contains in-process information. This means that the team has not yet reached a team consensus position.

Awareness of the distinction between these two categories of information by team members is critical to the effective operation of any team. Teams that function well as teams do not always agree. Part of the process of effective team operation includes taking the time to work through differences.

For teams to work through differences effectively, open lines of communication, where divergent positions can be expressed, are required. The need for this open and informal atmosphere within the team was also discussed in Chapter 2, Section 2.4.3 on incubation and assimilation time.

5.1.3   Team Rule 1 — Be True to Your Team

Solution

Keep in-process information inside the team.

It is crucial to the effective operation of any team — and, in particular, virtual teams — that during the incubation and assimilation time in-process information remains inside the team. This is what is meant by "be true to your team." While it may sound obvious — even trite — it is especially critical on virtual projects that team members abide by this rule.

Unlike traditional collocated engineering efforts, most virtual teams do not start out with strong interpersonal bonds. As a result, especially in the early project stages, when team members choose to share category two team information inappropriately with outside sources it can rapidly fuel team mistrust.

Early in the tale the architecture team functioned effectively with the customer, Tim, participating. But at some point in time Tim either forgot — or never knew — the number one team rule.

In this tale Tim betrayed a critical team trust by reporting what should have been internal working group information to an outside source, the customer program office. It also may have been that Tim just didn't understand that he had been asked to participate as a member of two distinct teams. Participating as a member of multiple teams is discussed further in the next section.

5.1.4   *Virtual Projects and Multiple Team Allegiances*

While the tale demonstrates what can happen when a customer doesn't abide by a critical team rule, there is a broader lesson applicable to all team members. On virtual projects, unlike many collocated single-organization projects, team members often have more than one team allegiance.

For example, a subcontractor on a virtual project has an allegiance to his home department in his home organization, as well as to his assigned project team. It is also worth noting that it is quite possible the objectives of these two team affiliations could conflict. This could place a team member in a difficult position. On traditional collocated projects, where most if not all team members are from a common organization, conflicting team objectives are less likely to fuel the type of serious mistrust found on virtual projects.

5.1.4.1 *Wearing Multiple Team Hats and Setting The Right Priorities*

On virtual projects there is greater pressure than on traditional programs for team members to report internal project team information at inappropriate times to outside organizational entities. On these projects it is critical that team members be aware at all times which team hat they are currently wearing and what information is sharable with outside groups.

In our experience, the trust of a project team must never be jeopardized by inappropriate leakage of information to outside sources. Home organizational managers, as well as co-workers, must be particularly sensitive on virtual projects to team loyalty issues when communicating team status through external organizational chains. On multiple occasions irreparable team damage has been done when this critical team rule was not well understood.

In the tale above, Tim should have been more sensitive to his responsibilities as a member of the design team. If, within a reasonable time period, the internal design team conflict was not solved, then the team leader should have raised the issue to an appropriate outside source for resolution. This process not only holds for customers who also wear working team hats, but is also critical for subcontractor team members who may find themselves participating on more than one team at the same time.

5.1.4.2 Are We Motivating Our Remote Team Members to be Real Team Players?

The issue of multiple team allegiances is an important one on virtual projects not only from the team trust perspective, but also from the team motivation perspective. I recently talked to an engineer from an organization that had a small role on a project. The organization the engineer worked for brought a critical expertise to the project, but due to a tight budget its involvement in the project had been severely limited.

The engineer I spoke with indicated that he originally hadn't wanted to work on the project because he didn't believe his company had a large enough role. He believed that his company would be giving away too much expertise for too little business.

Nevertheless, a manager had apparently convinced the engineer that the project held strategic importance to the organization. The manager told the engineer that through his participation on the project his organization would be kept in-the-know with regard to future related business opportunities. The manager also told the engineer to be "90% ears in the team meetings," and "to be careful what information he volunteered."

We have heard similar messages from other organizations participating as members of a virtual project (refer to Chapter 2, Section 2.1.3). We also believe **strongly** that such messages are inappropriate and serve to undermine the critical and fundamental objectives of a virtual project.

Place yourself in the shoes of the prime contractor who is trying to put together the best team possible to execute this program. Is this the kind of motivation you would want your teammates to bring to your project if you were the prime?

5.1.5 Are We Asking Too Much of Our Remote Teammates?

Inappropriate sharing of information with outside organizations impacts the effective operation of our virtual teams. In our tale we recognize that Tim may have been placed in a difficult position by being asked to wear two hats requiring him to view the project from two different perspectives.

This raises a question: Is it unfair to ask our personnel to wear multiple team hats and keep aware of what information they should and shouldn't share with others at any given point in time?

The answer to this question is no, and, in fact, many engineers have been doing this successfully in slightly different contexts for many years. Two examples that come to mind are classified programs and consultants.

Consultants have always had to deal with wearing multiple hats and maintaining a sensitivity to knowledge sharing across clients. It is critical to their businesses that they learn to be loyal to each of their customers by not using information inappropriately with one customer that may be sensitive to another. Similarly, engineers who have worked on classified projects must maintain vigilant awareness of classified information that should never be shared with those outside the project environment.

We have known many engineers who have worked on classified projects while, at the same time, working on unclassified projects. These people have been able to work effectively in both environments simultaneously, maintaining appropriate awareness of what information to share and what not to share.

5.1.5.1 Sensitivity to Information Sharing and Team Loyalty

The same information sharing mentality that has been successfully implemented on classified programs can be implemented on virtual programs. It is important to understand that we are not recommending formal and costly methods to manage information on virtual projects, but rather the adoption of a personal awareness and integrity policy.

As an example, when project team members attend home organizational meetings, just as they would not share company sensitive or classified information with others, neither should they share virtual team in-process information with non-team members. We each need to accept responsibility for guarding internal team in-process information that belongs nowhere else but inside the team.

For virtual projects to succeed, team members must understand the critical importance of team loyalty. Unfortunately, today, team loyalty is being viewed by too many as something others should hold toward them. Too often we fail to see in ourselves the inappropriateness of our behavior as we run to our home organization with the "hottest" internal project team information.

5.1.6 Back to Our Tale — The Predicament

In our tale, once the information got into the hands of the customer, the program manager felt he had to take correction action. But was the action taken the most effective way of handling the situation? Let's take a closer look.

Because the customer viewed the problem as serious, the program manager felt he could not allow the perceived design inconsistency to continue any longer than necessary. He wanted the issue to be resolved prior to the next team meeting. Since that meeting was scheduled for the following day at one o'clock in the afternoon, action had to be taken immediately. Since the complete team was not collocated, and due to the time zone difference, the engineering manager, Tom, felt he couldn't rely on the full team to resolve the issue as fast as he wanted it done. As a result, he turned away from his project-defined collaborative and self-directed design team in favor of a smaller collocated tiger team.

5.1.7 Self-Directed Teams, Tiger Teams, and Control-Oriented Managers

Over the past few years the movement to self-directed teams has received plenty of attention. Self-directed teams are the result of an integrated product team approach to solving problems coupled with a reduction of external management intervention.[1] With self-directed teams the big change is one of traditional management moving away from a controlling role into more of a supporting and coaching role.[1]

Insight

On virtual projects supporting self-directed teams is difficult for managers who have historically exerted strong control to get results.

Self-directed teams are difficult for control-oriented managers even in a collocated environment, but they become increasingly difficult when the team members are physically distributed. As a result, we often see control-oriented managers reverting — especially in times of difficulty — to the tiger team approach which allows them to exert greater influence over team direction when rapid solutions are needed.

5.1.8 The Tiger Team

A tiger team is a temporary working group formed with a specific objective and a stringent schedule. We have identified five characteristics common to most tiger teams observed in operation:

- Small
- Temporary
- Collocated
- Tight schedule
- Clear and limited objectives

On the positive side, small collocated teams with clearly defined objectives and tight schedules can often solve specific problems more rapidly than utilizing a larger team where conflicting potential solutions are more likely to be voiced. However, there exists another side to tiger teams.

5.1.8.1 Real Productivity

In the introduction the question of real productivity was raised. We questioned the traditional view of productivity as a widget per hour count. In this chapter our **definition of productivity** is given:

> *"The effectiveness with which resources are utilized."*

In this definition resources can be people or equipment. We believe this definition of productivity is more appropriate than the widget per hour definition, particularly to the types of issues we are seeing today on virtual projects. Now let's look at our tale again, only this time from the productivity perspective.

In the tale, a small percentage of the team (the tiger team of three — Jim, Sam, and Ed) ended up working close to 80 hours in one week, while the rest of the team worked roughly half as many hours. The tiger team lead, Sam, ended up getting sick from working too much and was out of work the following week.

This caused great confusion for the rest of the team. Before he got sick Sam had not told anyone else on the team how the new consistent design approach affected the rest of the team's ongoing task assignments. During that following week the productivity of many team members was impacted. Some continued working on their current task assignments although they knew rework would be required based on the new design approach. Others just stopped work, waiting for new direction. In both cases, productivity was negatively impacted.

It is also arguable whether the best technical decision was actually made. Kevin had the greatest experience with the middleware product and his experience was not effectively factored into the new approach. Small teams can make fast decisions, but fast decisions are not always the most cost-effective decisions.

5.1.8.2 The Quiet Sign — A Warning Sign

If your team is usually energetic, be on the look out for one easy-to-spot warning sign that the team may not be working well together. In some cases, when a team gets quiet it may be a sign of agreement, but in our tale the **quiet sign** is a warning sign.

Solution

The "quiet sign" is often a warning sign — be prepared to take action.

When the full team heard the presentation on Wednesday afternoon the quiet response signified feelings of being blind-sided. Also be on the look out for invalid arguments often employed to justify the use of a tiger team at inappropriate times. Those arguments include

- There just wasn't time to do anything else.
- We can't afford to design by committee.

Think about how this scenario could have been handled differently and still met the constraints of the project.

5.1.9 An Alternate Approach

What would have happened if the Wednesday one o'clock meeting had been postponed just one or two days? Just how critical is two days on any project? In that period of time the complete design team could have met with the remote team members teleconferenced in. It could have been stated at this meeting that a decision had to be made within the next 24 hours.

The tiger team could still have been utilized, but under the cognizance of the full collaborative self-directed team. This tiger team could have been directed to bring its proposed solution back to the full team within 24 hours. Then the full collaborative team could have reviewed and approved the approach recommended by the tiger team. This cross-check by the full team could have served multiple purposes.

First, it would have given Kevin an opportunity to voice his opposition if he saw a glaring problem with the new approach. Second, in parallel with the tiger team activities, another small team could have been formed to consider potential impacts to ongoing task assignments. This effort could have minimized the transition impact to ongoing tasks caused by the new design — or it may have resulted in certain changes to the approach to minimize impacts. It is doubtful that one or two days would have made much difference to the customer, but it could have made a huge difference to the trust of the project team and to overall team productivity.

5.1.10 "Having a Say Differs from Having a Vote"

Max DePree tells us in *Leadership is an Art*, that "having a say differs from having a vote."[2] The extra day or two that was recommended as an alternate approach recognizes the value of assimilation and incubation time discussed earlier. More importantly it demonstrates respect for the team.

Give your teammates the respect they deserve by listening to their ideas. This is a crucial step to building the key interpersonal bonds and team loyalty that are often missing early on virtual projects. This recommendation is not high in investment cost, but it can provide immense payback in overall team productivity.

5.1.11 More on Team Loyalty

Our experience indicates that for virtual teams to succeed it is crucial that those teams be given authority to make their own decisions and be given the responsibility to include the full team in all their decisions, regardless of where team members are physically located.

Steve Covey in *The Seven Habits of Highly Effective People* tells us that "one of the most important ways to manifest integrity is to be loyal to those who are not present."[3] On virtual projects, because of the distance factor, there are often opportunities to demonstrate loyalty to those not present, but also more opportunities to fail to demonstrate it. Our recommendation is not overly burdensome from a schedule point of view, but it does require vigilance in changing traditional collocation habits.

Experience has shown that it is easy to call a quick meeting and just forget to teleconference-in a remote team member. We do not mean to imply that small focused tiger teams have no place in a virtual environment. There are many cases where a small focused group should meet alone to work through tough issues. But there are appropriate ways to accomplish this within the full team context. Open, honest, and continual communication is critical to virtual project team success.

5.2 How to Effectively Use Virtual Communication Technologies

About the virtual communication tales

Our purpose, as stated in the overview to this book, is not to describe the latest virtual communication technologies, but to identify fundamental methodology errors in the use of these technologies. In the following tales you will hear about first-generation virtual communication lessons. Part of the solution is the deployment of rules that may seem obvious, but they can save your project plenty in human resources.

Our second and third tales in this chapter address common pitfalls in the use of virtual communication technologies (e-mail, teleconferencing). An increased likelihood exists of applying these tools inappropriately because they are relatively new and we do not yet have past proven patterns of success in their effective use.

Virtual communication technologies differ from traditional communication methods in a number of fundamental ways. On the positive side, an understanding of these fundamental differences along with the implementation of a small set of key rules can significantly improve the effectiveness in applying these technologies. In this section these fundamental differences and the issues involved are examined. Recommended rules are provided and discussed at the end of this chapter.

5.2.1 Electronic Mail

The first tale on electronic mail may seem a bit unusual, but don't be too quick to dismiss it. This tale demonstrates one of the fundamental differences between e-mail and direct personal interaction. It also shows how easily we can get into trouble if we don't understanding this critical difference.

The tale involves an engineering manager, Jen, who is responsible for leading a distributed team in the development of a large complex subsystem for project F876. Anyone who has had the opportunity to work with Jen knows that she is not only conscientious and disciplined in her own work habits, but also cares deeply about the people with whom she works. In meetings she consistently listens to others first, documents agreements, and then follows up on every point requiring action. She is the consummate professional and a true people-oriented manager, which is partly what makes this tale so difficult to comprehend.

5.2.1.1

The Tale of the Missing Teammate

"What is it, Jen?" asked Lynn as she stood in the office doorway.

"He simply refuses to work with us!" Jen replied sharply. "No matter what I do he won't return my e-mail!"

"Maybe he's on vacation," quipped Lynn. Jen just stared back.

"He's not on vacation and I know it. I called Sara and she told me he's been in the office every day this week."

Sara was the secretary at the remote Calverton site where Tim worked. And everyday, or so it seemed, there would be another incident on project F876 with someone trying to communicate with the Calverton group. This time, Sid, Jen's manager, was determined to get to the bottom of it.

Sid was a slow-moving even-tempered manager who could usually find a solution to a problem once he understood it. So far, this one just didn't make sense. Sid didn't know Tim very well, but he had talked to him enough on the phone to have formed an impression. While Sid knew that Tim's work habits weren't the best, he appeared to be a responsible engineer. So Sid started digging in.

First he called Tim, but there was no answer. He left voice mail asking Tim to call him back as soon as he could. Sid also sent Tim a quick e-mail note. After a day went by with no response, Sid decided to make a few more calls. That afternoon he got Jack Hargrove on the line.

Jack was one of the software leads along with Tim at the Calverton site. On his last trip to Calverton Sid had gotten to know Jack fairly well. Jack had recently taken up running and at lunch one afternoon the subject of running came up. That was when Jack found out that Sid was a serious marathon runner. That evening Jack and Sid ended up going for a run together. Ever since that day Jack and Sid had found it easy to talk to each other, even on sensitive subjects. So when

Sid brought up the question of Tim, he was surprised by Jack's response. He suddenly turned unusually quiet.

Sid explained why he was inquiring. He told him about Jen's difficulties contacting Tim through e-mail. Then he asked Jack if he had any idea why Tim might be angry with Jen. After some hesitation Jack finally opened up. But he asked Sid to keep what he was going to tell him in strict confidence.

Jack went on to explain that Tim and his wife had been having marital problems for some time. "About a month ago," said Jack, "Tim and his wife had made the decision to get a divorce." Jack went on to say that it was just the previous weekend when Tim and his wife finally sat the kids down to try to explain it.

Sid listened, somewhat surprised, but still didn't understand what any of this had to do with Jen. Finally he asked.

"Well," replied Jack, "for the last two weeks Tim's been coming into work and sitting at his desk, but I don't think he's logged on once or even picked up his phone to listen to his voice mail. I doubt he even knows that Jen has been trying to contact him."

5.2.1.2 A Fundamental Difference Between E-Mail and Direct Personal Contact

Inside traditional collocated engineering organizations diverse ideas are continually being shared, evaluated, discussed, and assimilated often through multiple ongoing projects and often through informal means. Interpersonal bonds and trust build among teammates as a byproduct of these activities. On virtual projects, however, these critical interactions often do not happen the same way.

The situation described in our tale may be unusual and not likely to occur often, but we chose to relay it for one reason. It demonstrates a fundamental difference between e-mail and direct personal contact.

Insight

E-mail is not a synchronous form of communication.[4]

In this tale Jen believes she is having a bad experience communicating with Tim. In the process, her mistrust of Tim grows. However, this mistrust is not the result of anything Tim believes or any ideas he has shared with Jen. There has been no assimilation of divergent viewpoints. Martha Haywood reminds us, "in our culture, it is interesting how many people think that communication is something that you do to someone as opposed to with someone."[4]

In virtual environments the root of team problems can be something that didn't occur as opposed to something that did. It takes two people for communication to take place. In reality, in our tale, Jen wasn't communicating with Tim at all.

5.2.1.3 E-Mail Flooding

The situation described in our previous tale is only one of a number of ways that e-mail can be misused. Another example is e-mail flooding, which occurs most often in the early stages of a new virtual project. To understand this condition it is first helpful to recall the following conditions which usually exist on a virtual project:

- Multiple contractor involvement
- Desire to do things rapidly
- Multiple technical challenges

These conditions create an environment conducive to blasting out large amounts of e-mail correspondence to long lists of project personnel. Below are the reasons for and ramifications of e-mail flooding.

5.2.1.4 Why So Much E-Mail?

It may sound hard to believe, but it is not all that unusual during the early stages of a virtual project for engineering personnel to receive 50 to 60 e-mails per day! Think about it. If you take just 4 minutes to process each e-mail, at this rate you could spend half your day just handling e-mail correspondence. Why so much e-mail? Four reasons for e-mail flooding are identified:

- Desire for others to know you are doing your job
- Belief that what is of interest to you is of interest to others

- It's easy to do
- New tool with lack of training

First, it is understandable that engineers want co-workers and managers to know they are doing their jobs. Second, there is a tendency to believe what is interesting and important to them will also be of interest and importance to others. Nevertheless, what often occurs is that pages and pages of technical details get electronically transmitted to people who neither need it, nor have the time to process it.

One of the reasons this happens is simply because it's easy to do. Once you have created a piece of electronic mail it is easy to just add another person to the distribution list and let the tool make another copy and send it out. It's easy for the e-mail provider, but not necessarily for the e-mail consumer.

Insight

E-mail flooding is the result of personnel being given a new tool and insufficient training in its use.

E-mail, as well as teleconferencing and voice mail are new tools for engineering use, and they require training in more than just the mechanics of their use. Recommended rules for the use of these new virtual communication technologies are identified and discussed later in this chapter.

5.2.1.5 Ramifications of E-Mail Flooding

Often in the early stages of a virtual project people become so overwhelmed with e-mail that they stop using it altogether for a period of time. If this happens at the wrong time, it can have serious consequences for your project. As in our tale above, when a teammate fails to respond to an e-mail, especially when that teammate is remotely located and a strong working relationship does not exist yet, feelings of mistrust often develop.

In reality, the cause of no e-mail response could be one of many. Below are listed just a few of the reasons witnessed on real projects:

- Overwhelmed with e-mail flooding
- Just too busy
- Not yet in the habit of logging on and reading e-mail regularly

- Out sick
- On vacation
- Only read part of message and missed the fact that a response was requested
- Local e-mail server down for system maintenance
- Local e-mail server failure
- Error in e-mail address

What is important to recognize from this list is that if we are going to rely on e-mail, then we need more specific rules on how to use this communication technology within a given project. Recommended rules for the use of e-mail on virtual projects are discussed in the following section.

5.2.1.6 Recommended E-Mail Rules

Managers need to be kept aware of engineering activities, but they don't need the same level of detail as the engineers who report to them.

Solution

Use predefined e-mail distribution lists.

To aid in managing e-mail flooding clear and simple guidance should be provided to the engineering team to help them quickly determine who on the project needs technical information. Predefined distribution lists can help in this regard.

Solution

Use e-mail templates and response rules.

Another common error with e-mail is unclear response requirements. To address this issue, each virtual project should set up its own e-mail template and response rules. We recommend a simple format that includes a response code. See Figure 5.1 for an example of an e-mail format which, if followed, makes it very easy for the reader to know instantly if there is an action required and if so, how urgently the response is needed. The code in the right-hand corner of the e-mail template in the figure indicates the response need. In our sample there are four possible codes:

Date: **99-06-21 12:25:22 EDT** **Email Code: RW**
From: **JMDoe@aol.com**
To: **JCSmith@ccc.com**
CC: **SMBrown@ccc.com**
Subject: Design Review

Joe,
Please review the attached documents in preparation
for the upcoming July design review.

Thanks, Jim

Attachments: XYZ.doc TUV.doc

Figure 5.1   Sample Formatted E-Mail

- IO = Information Only, no response required
- RY = Reply at reader's convenience
- RW = Reply requested within 1 week
- UR = Urgent reply requested within 24 hours

The code is relevant to all those to whom the e-mail is addressed. All those on Carbon Copy (CC) are assumed to be for information only.

By using a priority coding scheme similar to the one described, personnel can browse their e-mail quickly in the morning, filtering messages to be handled that day. This allows personnel to more efficiently and predictably plan and execute their daily activities.

5.2.1.7 Recommendation — Treat Lack of Trust as a Virtual Project Risk

In the introduction four reasons were identified by Booz-Allen for collaborative failures. One of those reasons was lack of trust. We believe that lack of trust frequently holds a key to many virtual collaborative failures. But, as stated in the introduction, this lack of trust is a symptom of failing to take the necessary actions to build trust where it is missing.

Insight

On virtual projects we often don't start out with either trust or mistrust.

It is important to understand that on virtual projects, unlike many traditional collocated projects, we usually do not start with either trust or mistrust. This is why we recommend that the lack of team trust be treated as a risk at project startup, and managed proactively to ensure it is replaced with trust, rather than mistrust.

Solution

Treat lack of trust as a virtual project risk.

What would you expect most project managers to do when faced with a high risk? Our experience indicates that most high risks are handled through aggressive risk abatement plans with clearly defined and closely managed actions. Nevertheless, while it has also been our experience that many managers recognize the seriousness of the trust issue, actions to build trust are not often aggressively pursued.

This is, at least partially, because trust is seen as something too intangible — or too "touchy-feely" — to attack from a project management perspective. A few years back we participated in a team-building workshop to kickoff a new project with one of our clients. The workshop facilitator stated in the morning of the first day that the team should set its own rules for conducting the workshop. The workshop participants then brainstormed a list of rules. During this process one participant suggested the rule, "No touchy-feely stuff." Everyone laughed, but the rule was accepted.

Later in the day a customer representative who was participating in the workshop voiced an objection to this rule declaring it to be unfair since individuals use different methods to communicate. My thought at the time was how difficult the virtual world must be for people who need personal contact to communicate most effectively.

Now — putting this story to the side — when treating trust as a project risk, we are not suggesting everyone stand in a circle and hold hands. Rather, we are simply recommending that practical and proven actions be taken to aid in creating an environment conducive to effective team interaction.

An example of such an action is the establishment of rules for the proper use of virtual communication equipment (i.e., e-mail, teleconferencing). This is what is meant by proactive management. While it may seem like a small thing, on virtual projects it is often small things that lead to big things.

What is critical to understand is the simple fact that on virtual projects trust doesn't just happen. In many ways we have been spoiled by traditional collocated engineering where the existence of trust has been taken for granted.

Insight

Many collaborative ventures fail because the process by which trust is achieved is not well understood, or well implemented.

Team trust is a byproduct of strong interpersonal relationships built gradually over time. Inside strongly cultured, time-tested collocated engineering organizations this benefit is available at project startup without having to work for it. On virtual projects, unfortunately, this benefit no longer comes for free.

5.2.2   Teleconferencing

Many presenters have developed unique styles. They've learned through their own experiences what works best for them to get their message across. Some raise their voices to accentuate key points, while others slow down making eye contact with their audience. Whatever techniques are used, it is likely that some changes will be necessary when teleconferencing is employed.

Experience indicates that when certain basic rules of teleconferencing etiquette are not followed, the value of this medium can rapidly degrade. Most of the rules are simple — almost too obvious to mention. However, without frequent reminders, it is easy to fall back into old collocation habits that do not fit well with this communication medium, as the following tale demonstrates.

5.2.2.1

The "Old Habits Die Hard" Tale

Don Martin had 22 years of experience in Configuration Management (CM). He understood from both a theoretical and a practical side the issues related to configuration identification, control, change management, and status reporting. But what stood out among those who knew Don best wasn't his knowledge of CM, but rather his unmatched ability to communicate, especially with new engineers.

Fred had worked with Don on a number of projects in the past, and knew he didn't need to be listening to the fundamentals of configuration management again. But Fred also knew that Don was one of the best at getting right to the most important issues and so he didn't want to miss this presentation of Don's.

The purpose of Don's presentation today was to describe the CM process to be followed on the Q879 project. Q879 was a software-intensive project involving two development sites. The project was just getting underway.

Most of the personnel assigned to the project from the main site were already familiar with the company's CM process from previous projects, but Q879 had chosen a new commercially available CM tool that hadn't previously been used at the company. Don knew from past experience that whenever a new CM tool was chosen he could expect most of the engineers' questions would be about the tool.

Anticipating mostly tool-related questions, Don developed his 2-hour presentation using actual graphical user interface screens from the new tool to describe both the sequence of CM operations, and when in the development cycle each of the operations would be required.

At the conclusion of the meeting, as he did at most of his presentations, Don asked those present for feedback on how they thought the meeting went. Don had learned early in his career the importance of feedback, and he wanted to make sure he was addressing the right issues and concerns of those present. All of those who responded indicated that the meeting went well. As usual, Don had apparently done an excellent job of communicating the CM information.

The next day Fred was talking to Bill Higgins, who just happened to have been teleconferenced in to the configuration management meeting the previous day from the remote development site. During the conversation Fred asked Bill how he thought the CM meeting had gone. At first Bill didn't respond. Then, slowly he said,

"I'm not sure." This response puzzled Fred.

"Do you have more questions?" he asked. Fred had actually been surprised that there hadn't been more questions and follow-up discussions.

"Well," said Bill, "it may have gone OK. I just don't know because we couldn't hear a thing. I don't know whether the teleconference set-up wasn't working, or if Don was just standing too far away from the receiver. In any case, a lot of people got up and left before the meeting was half done."

5.2.2.2 Keeping Aware of the Needs of Your Full Team

Don Martin was well respected at the main site. His colleagues also knew he spoke with a soft voice. They knew that to hear Don it was best to sit up front, which is what most of them did. But no one who was on the team from the remote site had ever worked with Don Martin before.

This tale demonstrates a number of points. First, when we are communicating through teleconference we miss important communication cues. If those from the remote site had been sitting in the back of the room, there probably would have been body language and/or facial expressions that would have given Don a sign that he wasn't effectively reaching his audience.

Many of us are unaware how often we modify our tone, or pace, or question our audience based on non-verbal feedback cues. When we communicate through teleconferencing, much of this important feedback is missed.

Second, there is another equally important lesson in this tale. Most of the engineers at the remote site not only didn't know Don, they were also unfamiliar with the fundamentals of configuration management. Many of the engineers at the remote site had been hired specifically for the Q879 project. The prior experiences of many of these new software engineers had been in a commercial organization where they were expected to code fast, but weren't required to follow strict configuration control and management processes. This situation is not unusual.

As a result, disciplined software processes were foreign to many of the remote team members. Because they didn't have training in the CM fundamentals — which Don jumped over thinking everyone already knew — the remote site team members viewed the CM activities as nothing more than a burden that did not contribute value to the functionality of the end-product.

Unfortunately, Don had no idea of the backgrounds of the new personnel hired at the remote site. He had been asked just to give his usual CM presentation to the Q879 team.

In hindsight, Don should have been more attentive to the needs of his audience even before his presentation started. He should have done more homework on the backgrounds of the personnel to whom he was presenting. He also should have been thinking about the specific issues that the remote site personnel would face. If he had done this, he probably would have realized that he needed a tailored presentation addressing the specific needs of the remote site personnel. Furthermore, in putting this presentation together, he probably would have realized it would have been best if he traveled to the remote site to give this presentation in person.

As the project proceeded the configuration management process and tool were never fully accepted by the remote site personnel. It might not have been accepted anyway, but it does make us wonder what might have happened if early in the project a little more attention had been paid to the specific needs of the remote site personnel.

5.2.3   Small Things and Big Things

Often on virtual projects individuals at remote locations begin to act like their own separate and distinct team. To a certain extent this is to be expected. Those who are physically close together tend to build team bonds more rapidly. However, while this may seem like a small thing, certain site-specific actions when allowed to persist can quickly become destructive to the overall effectiveness of the project team. Examples include

- Inappropriate use of the mute button to make a curt remark during a teleconference; (see Chapter 3, Section 3.7, the database process tale).
- A team teleconference that fails to consider a remotes site's perspective (see tale above).
- Failure to consider a site's specific infrastructure constraints (discussed in Chapter 6).

Many situations we have witnessed are neither time consuming nor costly to resolve. Steven Covey tells us, "the little kindnesses and courtesies are so important. Small discourtesies, little unkindnesses, little forms of disrespect make large withdrawals. In relationships, the little things are the big things."[3]

5.3 Rules for Effective Virtual Operations

We have previously discussed the need for a RFPM and have discussed in Chapters 2 and 4 some of the recommended artifacts to be maintained in this set of directories.

Solution

Set up a rules subdirectory within the RFPM that could be partitioned as follows:

- Team rules
- E-mail rules
- Teleconferencing rules
- Leadership/Manager rules

Once again, as a reminder, all information that goes into an RFPM must first be approved by the project leadership (discussed in Chapter 2). It is critical that the RFPM represents a **single agreed to** vision for the project. It is also important to understand that the RFPM is not intended to replace existing process-related procedures, or process training.

The RFPM provides supplemental project information that addresses specific problematic areas that tend to arise when operating in a distributed fashion. In particular, the RFPM provides a consistent set of project definitions, critical strategies, high-level design guidance, component-product development matrices (CPDMs), project rules, and site-specific information. The site-specific information is discussed at greater length in Chapter 6.

The RFPM can be thought of as a virtual project's answer to Ed Yourdon's triage recommendation.[5] In the following sections key rules to include in a RFPM are recommended. See Figure 5.2 for a sample RFPM structure.

5.3.1 Recommended Rules and Maintenance of an RFPM

Each project is encouraged to add its own rules based on its own experiences. However, we have one warning — do not allow the RFPM to become inordinately large, or it will not be used. We recommend the following guidelines be employed in maintaining an RFPM (also discussed in Chapter 4):

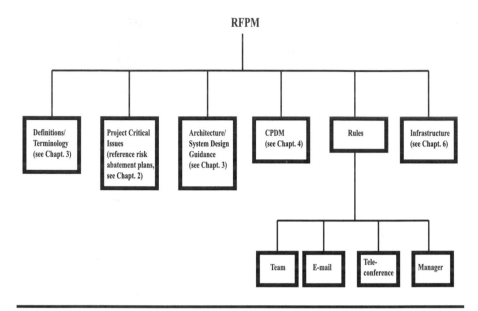

Figure 5.2   Sample RFPM Structure

- Keep it reasonably small. If it becomes too large it won't be used or maintained.
- Strictly ensure all information in the RFPM is approved by project leadership.
- Keep the information at the project-specific and task level. Do not duplicate general process guidance.
- Keep the RFPM up to date at all times.

Solution

Use the following summary of recommended rules that are based on past virtual project experiences.

5.3.1.1 Team Rules

Team rules added to the RFPM should not be general team rules. The objective of the RFPM is to address those virtual project-specific issues that hinder productivity specifically related to communication across multiple sites.

- Abide by team information-sharing policy (see Section 5.1.2).
- Use collocation for critical front-end design activities (see Section 2.5).
- Minimize the use of tiger teams (see Section 5.1.8).
- When tiger teams are employed, use full team as a check-point.
- Respect team members at all times.
- Listen to team members first.
- Recognize that "having a say is different from having a vote" (see Section 5.1.10).

5.3.1.2 E-Mail Rules

- Establish project distribution lists.
- Establish format and response rules.
- Try not to use e-mail for task assignments, but when necessary follow-up with phone call.

5.3.1.3 Teleconferencing Rules

- Ensure speaker is near receiver and all participants can hear.
- Minimize use of mute button.
- Provide hand-outs and presentation material early.
- Be aware of presentation style issues that are not conducive to tele-conferencing (i.e., pointing to slide).

5.3.1.4 Leadership/Manager Rules

- Be aware of messages to personnel that limit dedication to task or give double message.
- Give team authority as well as responsibility for team decisions.
- Use tiger teams with caution, always involving full-team participation in at least a review role.

5.4 Summary and Conclusion

Two categories of information flow from team activities. These categories include team results and team in-process information. It is critical that team in-process information be kept inside the team, especially in the early project stages when team trust has not yet been established.

Oftentimes on virtual projects secondary organizational objectives or hidden objectives of control-oriented personnel can become a distraction to effective team operation. As an example, there are cases where control-oriented managers revert more often in a virtual environment to tiger team approaches in an effort to exert inappropriate influence over team decisions.

It is important to understand that small focus groups (tiger teams) are not always inappropriate within virtual environments. Tiger teams can aid virtual projects by speeding up the decision process, but fast decisions are not always the best decisions.

When used inappropriately tiger teams can actually hinder, rather than accelerate team productivity. This is why it is crucial on these projects to continually maintain a full-team perspective. One of the most practical and affordable ways to accomplish this is to define and follow a small set of key rules to aid in effectively utilizing virtual communication technologies (e.g., e-mail, teleconferencing).

For teleconferencing the rules may seem simple and obvious, but without frequent reminders personnel often fall into old collocation habits. It is also critical to understand the fundamental difference between e-mail and direct personal contact. E-mail is not a synchronous form of communication.

Within traditional collocated engineering environments, common cultures, common site infrastructures, and common experiences are all important ingredients supporting a solid foundation of team trust. Unfortunately, this same trust doesn't just happen in a virtual environment. The process that produces trust in collocated engineering environments has in the past been taken for granted, but it is not well understood.

In traditional collocated environments trust appears to "just happen" through little more than the passage of time. In reality, there are numerous *informal* factors hard at work building trust on a daily basis within this environment. Unfortunately, what we have witnessed on many virtual projects is an environment that appears more conducive to building mistrust.

Trust will not just happen on virtual projects without proactive intervention. It is a byproduct of strong interpersonal relationships. Relationships that exist today within collocated environments will require additional effort inside the virtual world. This added effort must start with the project leaders.

On virtual projects one of the best ways to build trust is through the demonstration of respect for all teammates. This respect starts by leaders listening to alternate ideas put forth by team members who may have very different experiences from their own.

This type of leadership requires changes from old collocated habits, but they don't need to be costly. For example, just remembering to include remote team members each time a meeting is called, and keeping in mind key rules such as responding to a teammates' e-mail request in a timely fashion, and not reaching for the mute button each time the urge strikes. These are little things — inexpensive things. However, on virtual projects it is frequently the little things that build the needed trust to solve the much bigger issues.

CHAPTER 5 KEY POINTS SUMMARY
Self-directed teams difficult for control-oriented managers
E-mail not synchronous form of communication
E-mail flooding is the result of a new tool and insufficient training
Virtual projects don't start out with trust or mistrust
Process by which trust achieved not well understood
Keep "in-process" information inside the team
The "quiet sign" is often a warning sign—be prepared to take action
Use e-mail predefined distribution lists
Use e-mail templates and response rules
Treat lack of trust as a virtual project risk
Set up a "rules" subdirectory within the RFPM
Use recommended rules based on past virtual project experiences

References

1. Deeprose, Donna, *The Team Coach*, American Management Assoc., NY, 1995.
2. DePree, Max, *Leadership is an Art*, Dell, NY, 1989, p. 25.
3. Covey, Stephen R., *The Seven Habits of Highly Effective People*, Simon and Schuster, NY, 1989, p. 196.
4. Haywood, Martha, *Managing Virtual Teams*, Artech House, Boston, 1998, p. 17.
5. Yourdon, Ed, *Death March*, Prentice-Hall PTR, Upper Saddle River, NJ, 1997, p. 132.

6 The Integration Side: It Isn't a Seamless World Just Yet

Think back to our scenario in Section 1.1 of Chapter 1. What if Jim and John worked on a virtual project? Could Ed still be relied upon to do the GUIs? And what about Mary Lou? Can she still be counted on to fix the grammar, format the document, and handle all the graphics?

As organizations streamline to remain competitive and turn to virtual teaming, the role of once heavily relied upon support groups inside traditional organizations is changing. Complicating this picture, today incremental development approaches are causing us to rethink some of our basic notions of a quality product itself. In many traditional organizations support groups have provided not only a functional role, but a quality checkpoint as well. This raises a question:

Who is responsible for defining the quality standard on a virtual project?

In particular, who decides if Jim's sample work product from our tale in Chapter 1 is still acceptable in this new virtual environment? Today, many share a common vision of a seamless virtual world where it simply doesn't matter where an engineer is physically located.

This vision implies that the operations an engineer performs are independent of location. That is, our tools, support functions, infrastructure, and views on quality must be common across all project sites.

Problem

Is the seamless vision the right vision?

But is this vision the right vision? Is this approach the optimum road to improved productivity on virtual projects? Before addressing this question let's look at a tale that demonstrates a few of the related issues companies are struggling with today.

About the tale

The purpose of this tale is to describe what commonly happens in a new virtual organization. In this tale individuals do not understand the organization's expectations of them. There is no common culture to act as forcing function to ensure responsibilities are owned. This tale emphasizes the need for a walkthrough of the concept of operation of the virtual organization, and the freedom line idea.

6.1

The Document Production Disaster Tale

It was always cold in the old corner conference room, but it seemed even colder than usual to Jim as he glanced up at the oversized square clock just behind the door. On the far side of the room across the table from Jim, Frank sat staring down at page after page of the System Design Document. Every margin was filled with bright red customer comments. He had read each at least twice. Jim turned his head away as he thought back.

It had been just 3 weeks earlier when he, Frank, and Mary, along with Tom, the system engineering department manager, sat in that same room reviewing the document. It was due to be shipped to the customer that afternoon. Mary had been asked to attend the review by her manager. She was one of those engineers who always thoroughly scrutinize anything she was asked to look at — and her comments were usually on the mark. Frank and Jim worked for Tom, but they had never worked with Mary. They listened closely as she explained in detail what she had found.

"First of all," she began, " the System Overview is completely missing."

"That was Patrick Murphy's responsibility," responded Frank quickly. Jim looked up.

"I sent him an e-mail over a month ago identifying exactly what he was responsible for providing. And I sent him a follow-up three days ago pleading with him to get his assignment done on time," Frank added. Patrick Murphy worked in the architecture group.

"Second, the System-Wide Decisions section is incomplete," continued Mary. "This section has good information, but our latest critical design decisions are missing. Third, the Concept of Operation is inconsistent with what Jeff presented to the customer last week."

"Has Jeff reviewed this document?" asked Jim.

"We tried to get him on the review team, but he had higher priority commitments," replied Frank.

"Fourth, the quality of the document is inconsistent throughout. Some sections read well, but others read like a rough draft."

"That's because we told the engineers not to spend a lot of time wordsmithing. We wanted them to concentrate on getting the technical information on paper because time was short," replied Frank.

"Did the customer agree with that approach?" asked Tom.

"Yes, they did," replied Frank. "I was in the meeting when we told Will Brown what we were doing, and he agreed that the document didn't have to be pretty. And besides, technical publications will clean up the grammar." Jim shook his head.

"There is no budget for technical publications support on this project. And there isn't time for them anyway. The only way we can get this document out on time is to ship it just like it is."

"But you can't send a document like this one to a customer!" stated Mary emphatically as she pointed to the document resting on the table.

"Are we sure that the customer understands what we're doing?" asked Tom again. He glanced around the room at each of those present as he said it.

"We told them it's work in progress — just a draft. And remember, they told us they don't need formality," stated Jim.

"But you can't send a document out like this!" exclaimed Mary again. For a moment the room fell silent. Then Tom stood up.

"Here's what we're going to do," he stated confidently. "The customer wants us to meet our commitments. And it's very important for us to show them we can get our products out when we say we will. They're also looking for us to show them we can be flexible in the way we do business. Jim, I want you to write a cover letter and place it on the front of the document where they can't miss it. The cover letter needs to state clearly that this is a **DRAFT**. Make it clear that this is **WORK IN PROGRESS** and needs to be treated that way. Our customer wants to do business a new way. We're going to show them we can."

Tom's words were still fresh in Jim's memory as he gazed back down at the pages of red customer comments spread across the table. Slowly he raised his head up staring across the table at Frank.

"Do you think the customer read the cover letter?" he asked. Frank didn't reply.

6.1.1 Stepping Back — The Good News

We don't tell this tale to describe how undisciplined companies operate. In actuality, the company where this tale occurred has a proven track record for excellence and the use of mature processes. So what went wrong this time? First, if we step back, we can observe that many good decisions were actually made. The good decisions include

1. Assignment of best possible personnel to the tasks
   The best qualified personnel on the project were actually assigned to write each section of the system design document, regardless of physical location.
2. Notification of assignment by e-mail
   See Figure 6.1 for a sample of the e-mail notification that was sent to assigned personnel.
3. Single point of control designated for document production
   A focal point to coordinate document final production was assigned.
4. Review and approval
   The document was reviewed according to corporate policy, comments were written up, and a meeting was held to determine the readiness of the product prior to customer shipment.

Date: 99-06-21 12:25:22 EDT
From: FMDoe@aol.com
To: JCSmith@ccc.com

Subject: System Design Document Task
Assignment

Joe,
You have been assigned to write section 2.4 of
the System Design Document.
Please send your inputs to Fred Hammer by July
28th.
The schedule is short. What is most important is
that we get the right technical information into
the document. Do not worry about format or
grammar.

Thanks, Frank

Figure 6.1   Sample E-Mail Task Assignment Notification

6.1.2 The Not-So-Good News

While many good decisions were made, something still went wrong in getting a "quality" document produced for the customer. Let's look closer at three areas that may provide insight:

- Quality expectations
- Task communication and acceptance
- Product integration

6.1.2.1 Quality Expectations

Most mature organizations have a well-understood and expected level of quality. But what happens when personnel are rapidly pulled together from diverse organizations with varying quality experiences? To complicate the situation further, what happens when just the right combination of key skills for a new opportunity involves three different organizations at three different process maturity levels?

Insight

In mature organizations long-established cultures often provide a "frame of reference" for product quality.

Typically, in mature software-intensive organizations (as discussed in Chapter 1), engineers learn what is acceptable and what is unacceptable product quality through interactions with co-workers. In this environment the established organizational culture provides an important frame of reference for product quality. By talking to peers and by reviewing existing products, engineers learn about product acceptability within their organizations.

Problem

In a distributed environment a culture-based quality frame-of-reference method rapidly breaks down.

However, when we introduce multiple organizations, each with its own quality experiences, the individual organizational frame-of-reference method rapidly breaks down. To add to this quality dilemma, today we find ourselves moving to an incremental or evolutionary approach to building software products. This leads us to the new notion of evolutionary quality[1] as well. This makes the already difficult to manage quality issue more difficult. Martha Haywood refers to how wildly differing quality standards can affect a team from yet another aspect. She states,

> *"One of the fundamental problems we found was that the executives and the developers had very different visions of what was an acceptable level of product quality. The lead developer had extremely high standards and made it clear they would not cooperate or put their name on any product shipment that had a known defect. The executive understood, but did not communicate that they were in an industry where their products were really only useful shortly after a new technology became widely available."[2]*

Martha goes on to make the point that in today's world the quality standard is set by the customer; it is no longer an absolute, especially in a design-to-cost environment. But this thought leads us to a question:

Is the customer really setting a new quality standard?

In the tale above our engineering team clearly thought there was a new quality standard being set, but when they received their System Design Document back with all the bright red comments in the margins, they received an unexpected surprise.

In the virtual world the quality issue becomes more complex. As a result, there is another equally important question to ask:

If there is a new quality standard being set, then how do we communicate it consistently to our full team, regardless of their physical location?

Recommendations addressing these questions are provided later in this chapter.

6.1.2.2 *Task Communication and Acceptance*

Because virtual projects do not physically collocate personnel, new mechanisms of task communication and acceptance must be employed. In the tale above, where e-mail was used as a tasking mechanism, there is a breakdown in communication.

As discussed in Chapter 5, e-mail is not a synchronous communication mechanism; that is, there is no immediate feedback to the e-mail sender that the e-mail recipient received, read, understood, and accepted the assigned task. For all we know Patrick Murphy might have been out sick, or too busy to read his e-mail, or working on a higher priority task. Maybe he actually read the e-mail, but didn't read it closely enough to recognize that he was being tasked. Even if he did receive it, and understood it, how do we know he accepted the task? Maybe he simply couldn't complete it in the timeframe requested.

In any case, the point is a simple one. As discussed in Chapter 5, there are too many potential possibilities to trust task assignments to a non-synchronous form of communication. This is not to say that e-mail can never be used when tasking is involved. When there is no good alternative, e-mail can be employed, but in these cases following up the e-mail task assignment with a phone call to ensure both parties understand the task, and all its related constraints is advisable.

Back to our tale

In actuality, Patrick Murphy wasn't out sick. He had read the e-mail, but didn't respond for a different reason. Recall that Patrick Murphy worked in the architecture group. Frank, who had sent him the task via e-mail, was a senior engineer in the systems engineering group.

In our tale, Frank, who was being held accountable for coordinating the production of the System Design Document, was attempting through e-mail to task Patrick. But Patrick didn't officially report to Frank. Patrick's formal manager had been given the responsibility for supporting the System Design Document, but he was not being held accountable for the quality of the end product.

On the other hand, Patrick's manager had other tasks for which he was being held accountable — and these tasks were constantly on his mind. As a result, Patrick now had two tasks he was attempting to juggle. But every day Patrick's manager took the time to let Patrick know exactly where he felt Patrick's priorities should lie.

Problem

"Double-tasking" tends to occur more frequently on virtual projects.

This situation, referred to as "double-tasking," could happen on any project, but is more prevalent on virtual projects. This is partly due to the added conflict with regard to task priorities on virtual projects.

The fact is that managers at different sites and particularly from different organizations are often going to see the priority of issues differently, and site-specific priorities often play an influential role in the responsiveness of an engineer to an assigned task. Obviously, influenced heavily by his manager, Patrick put his System Overview task on the back-burner — and on virtual projects back-burner tasks rarely make it to the front-burner on time.

6.1.2.3 Product Integration

So far in this book the focusing has been on individual task assignments. However, virtual projects are often complex projects where multiple piece-part150150 products must be integrated together into a final deliverable product. Success in achieving individual task expectations is no assurance that the piece-parts will integrate into an acceptable deliverable end-product.

In our tale we observed both a failure of individual tasking, and a breakdown in piece-part integration. Even when individual piece-parts slip through with quality problems, deliverable products containing unacceptable defects should never be approved for a customer delivery.

In many cases there are more severe quality issues on virtual collaborative projects than seen in the past even on comparable collocated projects. To understand the root cause of this issue we first look at another brief tale.

About the tale

The purpose of this tale is to demonstrate what often happens when attempts are made to force process commonality at too low a level in a virtual organization.

6.2 The Tale of "Down Here, and Up There"

ACE is a multi-billion dollar Nebraska-based firm that has undergone a number of mergers and acquisitions over the past few years. The GRUV project is a strategically important project to the ACE company. Most of the software on the project is planned to be done at the main site in Nebraska. However, because the GRUV customer is located in Oklahoma, a small team of software development personnel has been strategically located in the Oklahoma area.

Jim was hired just three months ago by ACE at the remote Oklahoma site. Very little software development has been done at this site in the past. As our tale begins Jim is just completing his first coding assignment on the project. His cubicle mate, Tom, has been working on the GRUV project at the remote site for over a year.

6.2.1

The Tale

"I was reading in the project review procedure that I need to place my code review package in the RevRdy directory," said Jim glancing over his shoulder. Tom pushed back in his chair.

"And it also says in here that I can't hold a review without a representative from the Systems Support department." Jim was pointing at his screen as he spoke. "I can't find the RevRdy directory, and I never heard of that department. What gives?"

"I can explain it, replied Tom. "Down here in Oklahoma we're following the same procedures as the guys up at the main site in Nebraska. But the guys who wrote those procedures weren't thinking about us when they wrote them. Down here we can't get to the RevRdy directory, so we use the Rready directory. And don't worry about the Systems Support department either. We don't have one down here."

"I think I understand," replied Jim. "Thanks for the information. But now I have another question. It also says I need to include my documentation in my review package, but it doesn't tell me what documentation is required." Tom reached into the right drawer of his desk and pulled out a thin document with a blue cover.

"Here's an example of a document from up at the main site. Until I received it I always ended up reworking my documentation to get it accepted." Jim glanced through the document.

"This is pretty fancy. How much help do we get from tech pubs?" asked Jim.

"They get plenty of help up at the main site, but I've found its easier to just do it all myself than trying to work with the Nebraska tech pubs group from down here," replied Tom, as he started to turn back toward his workstation. But then he hesitated. "One more thing," he looked back over his shoulder at Jim. "When you get to the test phase, be sure and talk to me. I've had nothing but trouble getting the test tool to work. Its got bugs and no one up at the main site has been able to help because they're not using the same version of the tool. We're suppose to be using the same version, but we've got hardware configuration compatibility problems down here."

6.2.2 The "Let's Use the Most Mature Process Available" Pitfall

One approach attempted on a number of virtual projects is to transport mature processes and procedures from one project site with a high process maturity rating to another project site with a lower rating.

When thinking in terms of a "best of the best" strategy, this approach may seem logical. Unfortunately, although this strategy can have merit in certain circumstances, in most cases it is fraught with pitfalls.

Insight

Procedures are only a small part of effective process deployment.

Making existing procedures from one site accessible for use at another site is not difficult. For example, today it can easily be achieved through a common web site. However, making procedures accessible is only a small part of the issues involved with process deployment.

Often, as organizations become increasingly mature, their processes become increasingly site-specific. In other words, efficiency refinements are sometimes tightly coupled with site-specific issues (tools, infrastructure). In this environment what is called "process improvement" at one site often won't even work at another site. This can be caused by many issues including differences in hardware configuration or tool revision levels.

6.2.2.1 Examples of Difficulties Transporting Mature Processes

Examples of site specific process improvements include the embedding of specific organizational department names, or specific mass storage directory names inside of procedures. In one case we even found a reference to a specific individual and a phone number to call in case of problems executing specified configuration management functions.

Clearly, while such information may improve a given site's efficiency, it also makes the procedure less usable at a different site without costly changes. This results in frustration and reluctance to employ procedures developed elsewhere.

In the final analysis, from the process maturity perspective, rather than taking a step forward, the best of the best approach often results in a step back.

6.2.2.2 The Multiple Site Process Dilemma

Given the observations above on transporting mature processes, how are we to approach the process side of a virtual project? While one may be tempted to water down the site-specific information, this is not the best answer. Site-specific issues will continue to hold importance on virtual projects for a number of reasons. Just a few of those include

- The need to leverage existing site capital investments (i.e., workstations, tools)
- Performance issues across wide area networks
- Security issues

Oftentimes at a new project's start up the magnitude of site-specific issues is not well understood, especially when distributed development is new to the organization. Even without the site-specific issues already identified, one can anticipate resistance to the use of procedures developed elsewhere because of the lack of a strong supporting subculture and personnel with experience using these procedures.

6.2.3 Observations on Process

Today, significantly more information can be shared across multiple sites than was possible just a short time ago, and many tools can now be purchased supporting multiple site capabilities (i.e., configuration management tools). Nevertheless, experience indicates that we shouldn't be too quick to abandon many site-specific proven processes that may have taken years to mature.

Tight project budgets and continued pressure to leverage existing assets will continue to force future virtual projects to find creative ways to operate effectively with existing and varying site infrastructures, support services, and tool-sets.

At the same time, experience indicates that we cannot allow each remote site to operate in a completely independent fashion. This is a particular concern with regard to final customer-deliverable product integration. This leads to another question:

> *How do we determine which processes can vary, and which processes must be constrained at each site?*

The answer to this question is dependent upon the subject of the next section — work split.

6.3 How to Make Effective Work Split Decisions

In the book *Global Software Development*,[3] Dale Walter Karolak identifies seven different ways to divide an engineering effort. These include

- Business relations (percentage of effort/budget)
- Development phases
- Architectural considerations
- Knowledge and experience
- Leadership
- Staffing
- Tools and capital resources

In this section we discuss advantages, disadvantages, and recommendations for using two of the more common methods. These methods are

- Development phases
- Architectural considerations (subsystems)

6.3.1 Development Phases

Insight

Mature organizations often find it difficult to work effectively with phase-based work splits.

Partitioning work based on development phase is often employed when participating companies possess a life-cycle phase specialty such as systems engineering, software engineering, or integration and test. However, companies that possess higher process maturity ratings — particularly those that have in the past developed complete solutions — may actually find it more difficult to develop a product limited to a specified subset of life-cycle phases.

This is because established site processes do not always align well with traditional life-cycle phase boundaries; for example, one might think that a good split would be at the systems and software boundary. However, as we saw in our tale in Chapter 3, architecture could fall on either side of this boundary depending upon an organization's evolution.

Phase-based work splits cause particular difficulty on new software-intensive projects because of the tendency to iterate through each phase. Iteration results in phase overlap, which in turn makes the management of phase-dependent artifact hand-over significantly more difficult.

If you choose to partition work along development phases, the use of a Component Product Development Matrix (CPDM, see Chapter 4) becomes critical. We recommend, in this case, that you use a CPDM to define precisely the component-products and their phase-based responsibilities. Phase-based work splits can succeed, but they do require more formal definitions of component-products and their responsibilities.

6.3.2 Architecture Considerations (Subsystems)

Partitioning work based on architecture considerations (subsystems) is probably the most common method[3] and the one we recommend, particularly for mature organizations with a history of developing complete solutions inside collocated operations. A strong motivator to split work at the subsystem level is the opportunity to leverage proven mature processes. Subsystem work splits, however, introduce a new integration dilemma.

6.4   The Integration Dilemma

While the subsystem partitioning approach has advantages, it creates an integration dilemma.

Dilemma

If we allow site-specific institutionalized processes to be used to develop each subsystem, then how do we ensure these subsystems will integrate successfully?

6.5   Global Component Recommendations

In this section the recommendation to address the integration dilemma on virtual projects through global components is defined and discussed.

6.5.1 *What is a Global Component?*

A global component is defined as a logically related set of component-products (defined in Chapter 1, discussed in Chapter 3) that meet the following criteria:

- Contains a well-defined set of requirements.
- Includes design component-product artifacts.
- Includes source code component-product artifacts.
- Includes stand-alone test component-product artifacts (test cases, and results).
- Is executable and testable.
- Meets a set of specified architecture constraints.

6.5.1.1 *Component-Products vs. Global Components*

As a point of clarification, recall that a component-product is defined to be "any piece-part artifact produced by one group in the organization that another group depends upon." A component-product could be as simple as a block of text providing an overview description of a system. A global component, on the other hand, could never be this simple. You can think of a global component as a chunk of software that can be executed and tested, along with its related documentation.

Insight

Think of component-products as the piece-part products of individual tasks, while the global components are the products of individual sites within a project.

6.5.2 *Advantages of Using Global Components*

Global components provide two primary advantages.

Solution

The use of global components reduces system integration risk.

First, they provide system integration management support. Because global components are executable and testable, formal global component hand-over criteria (to an integration team) can be effectively achieved. Having specified architecture constraints as a part of the hand-over criteria addresses our integration dilemma.

Solution

Using global components allows us to leverage the strengths of our distributed teammates.

Second, global components provide a crisply defined freedom line for the allowable use of site-specific institutionalized processes.

The global component approach effectively allows us to leverage the best of two worlds — mature site-specific processes for development down inside the global component, and a well-defined single system architecture supporting a managed system integration.

6.5.3 Does the Global Component Approach Contradict the Virtual Concept?

In the preface we asked the reader to step outside his box and imagine the possibilities. A vision of an integrated virtual project where a distributed workforce employs project agreed to tools, infrastructure, and management strategies was then presented.

One might ask at this point if our global component approach contradicts this vision? We think not. In fact, the recommended approach provides the optimum path to achieve this vision.

All projects, collocated or distributed, have process freedom lines. Through the global component's specified architecture constraints, along with the RFPM and the CPDM, a virtual project defines precisely where this freedom line exists. As a consequence, it also defines where seamless commonality must exist as well.

6.5.4 Terminology Clarification

Global components should not be confused with other software constructs commonly referred to within today's software industry. The terms package, category, computer software components, and components (as used in component-based architecture) all have specific meanings, and are each different from our global components. For more information on these terms and a more detailed discussion of how they relate to global components, refer to Appendix B.

6.5.5 *Three Key Characteristics of the Global Component*

There are three key identified characteristics of the global component:

- Complete life cycle product
- "Sell-off" potential
- Process freedom line support

6.5.5.1 *Complete Life Cycle Product*

A key to the global component is its complete life cycle characteristic. That is, a global component includes artifacts from each life cycle phase (requirements, design, code, test). This has the potential for applying a complete, mature site set of processes to the component's development.

6.5.5.2 *Sell-Off Potential*

A global component product can be sold off internally on the project. For example, a global component could be sold off from a software group to a systems group, or from a remote site sub-team to a team located at the main project site. This is a key characteristic in support of systems integration.

6.5.5.3 *Process Freedom Line Support*

A key characteristic of a global component is its support for a process freedom line. You can also think of the freedom line as providing two levels of process:

- Local process level
- Global process level

Local process level
"Local process level" refers to those site-specific processes below the freedom line that can be employed in the production of a global component. Local

processes may utilize site-specific infrastructures and site-specific support capabilities. However, constraints do exist in the production of global components. For example, a global component's development must comply with the RFPM, and the CPDM requirements. Beyond this constraint, site-specific development is encouraged to leverage to the maximum extent possible mature site-specific institutionalized engineering procedures and practices.

Global process level

The global process level is primarily an integration level. This is the level where attention is paid to customer deliverables. If in the document production tale we had a well-defined global level, the needed consistent quality checkpoint on our customer deliverable would have been in place. As a final note, we strongly encourage maintaining the global process level at the industry open and standard level (use of standards that are accessible to all the organizations involved) with regard to methodologies, tools, and languages. It is the global level where potential miscommunication across sites primarily exists. See Figure 6.2 for a diagram of the local and global process.

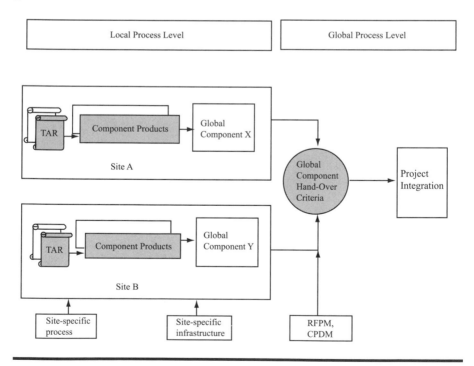

Figure 6.2 Local and Global Processes

6.6   Analysis and Recommendations

After analyzing the tales in this chapter, related recommendations are found in three areas:

- Tasking
- Quality
- Integration

6.6.1 Tasking

We have two recommendations with regard to tasking.

6.6.1.1 Recommendation 1 — Clear Task Definition

Task definition, especially those that cross site boundaries, need documented TARs with component-products identified. For more details on this recommendation, refer to the discussion in Chapter 4 on component-product definition through the use of a CPDM and TAR.

6.6.1.2 Recommendation 2 — Clear and Singular Assignment of Responsibility and Accountability

Of equal importance to clear task definition is the clear and singular definition of the responsible and accountable manager. Experience indicates that direct communication between senior engineers, like Frank in our tale, and engineering personnel is strongly encouraged. Senior engineers provide critical mentoring for less experienced personnel. However, the TAR MUST be assigned and statused through one, and only one, responsible and accountable manager.

This crucial point cannot be over-emphasized. Responsibility is given to managers to ensure personnel are appropriately tasked, but accountability is too often misplaced on virtual projects. Accountability means liable for analysis or explanation. Often on virtual projects managers have responsibility "on paper", while other personnel in the organization are held accountable. When personnel in the organization, like Frank in our tale, plead with engineers to complete a task, it is a warning sign of misplaced accountability.

When managers are not held accountable for ALL the tasks of their personnel, priorities rapidly get misplaced. When accountability is missing, we lose motivation, double tasking increases, and product quality rapidly degrades.

Based on our experiences, if a task requires close supervision, then the manager and engineer should be collocated. Collocation is always recommended over attempts to share management responsibility and accountability across physically distributed sites.

6.6.2 Quality

Earlier in this chapter we asked the question:

> *Is the customer really setting a new quality standard?*

We believe that the best way to determine the answer to this question is by asking the customer directly. But do we know who to ask? Stated differently, do we know whose opinion counts?

As we saw in Chapter 5, having the customer participate directly on your development team can be a two-edged sword. In our tale Frank was quick to reply that the customer was in agreement with the quality approach taken in the document. He even used the name of the customer representative, Will Brown. But was Will Brown the right person to speak on behalf of the customer with regard to a formal deliverable product?

Engineers — including customer engineers — have opinions, but when a customer deliverable is involved one should always be cautious with regard to agreements. We recommend working through your program office and, if necessary, contractual channels to get any such changes documented appropriately.

6.6.3 Integration

Earlier in this chapter we asked the question:

> *If there is a new quality standard being set, then how do we communicate it consistently to our full team, regardless of its physical location?*

Solution

The global component approach provides 5 key benefits.

Our global component approach addresses this issue. Through this approach a freedom line is recognized. The freedom line recognizes the existence of varying site cultures, and where commonality is required. The global component approach provides the following benefits:

- Leverages site-proven mature processes.
- Allows for the effective use of existing site assets.
- Provides clear and consistent criteria for product development at each location.
- Focuses our limited resources on key cross-site product integration.
- Provides consistent and needed quality checkpoints across project sites.

The goal on virtual projects is not to throw away years of evolutionary process maturity at each site, but rather to leverage it. Furthermore, by allowing individual sites to employ proven existing processes, we can focus our limited project resources where they can do the most good. Our experience indicates that focus needs to be at the system integration level. This can provide the consistent quality checkpoint that was missing in our tale. By documenting the global component hand-over criteria in the RFPM we communicate our approach to the full team.

6.7   Conclusion

In conclusion, the clear definition of tasks, along with single-chain responsible and accountable management is critically important to the success of virtual projects. Furthermore, we cannot afford to redevelop and re-mature our processes and procedures for each distributed project. Experience has shown that attempts to transport existing mature processes is fraught with difficulties.

A more effective approach has been found through focusing on work split and recognition of a global integration level with well-defined product hand-over criteria. By recognizing a process freedom line we can leverage existing mature processes, and, at the same time, gain the most practical and achievable common process for our limited resources.

CHAPTER 6 KEY POINTS SUMMARY
Culture historically provides "frame of reference" for product quality
On virtual projects "culture-based" quality "frame of reference" rapidly breaks down
Procedures only small part of process deployment
Mature organizations find phase-based work splits difficult
Component-product = Task "piece-part" product
Global-component = Site level product
Use global components to reduce system integration risk
Use global components to leverage teammate strengths
Global components provide five (5) key benefits

References

1. Royce, Walker, *Software Project Management*, Addison-Wesley, Reading, MA, 1998, p. 86.
2. Haywood, Martha, *Managing Virtual Teams*, 1998, Artech House, Boston, p. 64.
3. Karolak, Dale Walter, *Global Software Development*, IEEE Computer Society, Los Alamitos, CA, 1998, pp. 35–46.

7 Eight Practical and Affordable Steps to Set Up and Maintain a Successful Virtual Project

f there exists a single recurring theme throughout this book, it probably could best be described as

"Who does what, when do they do it, and what products do they produce?"

On the surface this may sound simple, but as we have seen differing backgrounds and experiences give rise to unexpected pitfalls.

7.1 Eleven Virtual Project Pitfalls

The real reason behind many collaborative failures — as stated in the introduction — rests in failure to take timely and effective action to resolve real underlying root causes of problems. In many of these cases, the actions required are not as complex or costly as one might think.

In this chapter the eleven common pitfalls we have observed on multiple virtual projects are summarized. Eight are expressed in terms of a failure to take one or more specific actions, or delaying actions too long. The other three relate to initiating the wrong action, or initiating an action at the wrong time. Related recommendations were summarized earlier in the overview. These recommendations are discussed further in the 8-step plan that follows, along with more detailed information regarding potential pitfalls, sub-steps, and more detailed related recommendations. See Table 7.1 for an enumeration of the pitfalls and a cross-reference to where further discussion can be found in the 8-step plan.

Table 7.1   Pitfalls and Discussion Cross-Reference

Pitfall Decription	Step	Chapter
Failure to address the loss of traditional collocated informal activities	1, 2, 7, 8	7.3, 7.4, 7.9, 7.10
Forcing the definition of work split prior to architecture definition	2	7.4
Delaying the definition of work split too long	2	7.4
Failure to define clearly and unambiguously remote site tasking responsibilities	1, 2, 5, 6	7.3, 7.4, 7.7, 7.8
Let's use the most mature process	4, 5, 6	7.6, 7.7, 7.8
Failure to define and deploy critical virtual team rules and virtual communication rules	4	7.6
Failure to establish clear lines of product responsibility deep into the virtual organization	1, 5, 6	7.3, 7.7, 7.8
Utilizing a "pure-IPT" organizational structure on a virtual project	5, 6	7.7, 7.8
Failure to establish clear work split prior to detailed planning	2	7.4
Failure to test the concept of operation of a newly established virtual organization	7	7.9
Failure to deploy an effective project-tailored virtual culture	8	7.10

7.2   Introduction to the Eight (8)-Step Plan

Return for a moment to Figure 1.1 in Chapter 1. It isn't very difficult to draw up a static high-level organizational chart. As can be seen in the figure, many similarities across organizations exist at this level. But, as we have seen, when one digs a little deeper, a different picture emerges. The potential for differing views on how an organization actually operates on the inside is limitless. Because of this situation, a key to virtual collaborative success is the effective communication of a view of the organization we have not yet discussed — a dynamic view.

It is anticipated that the reader will use this plan as guidance in setting up a new — or verifying an existing—virtual organization. As we move through each step envision how you expect your organization to actually operate in practice. This dynamic view is important because it provides insight into how the groups within your organization will interact. It is also the view from which much miscommunication can quickly be uncovered by project leaders before costly errors are made. In step 7 we will utilize this view to simulate an organization that ensures our project leaders share a common dynamic vision. The 8 steps, along with sub-steps when applicable, are summarized in Table 7.2.

Table 7.2 Eight-Step Plan Summary

Section	Step	Step Description	Sub-Steps
Sect. 1	Step 1	Establish high level project organization	Assign team leaders Develop charters and define responsibilities Initiate RFPM
Sect. 1	Step 2	Establish work split	Establish approach (subsystem, phase, other) Establish initial system architecture Establish CPDM and global component criteria Define work split
Sect. 1	Step 3	System planning	System build planning Requirements allocation Integration plan
Sect. 1	Step 4	Special tasks	Infrastructure Project rules
Sect. 1	Step 5	Establish third level of organization	N/A
Sect. 1	Step 6	Detailed planning	N/A
Sect. 2	Step 7	Testing the organizational concept of operation — dynamic view	N/A
Sect. 3	Step 8	Execution phase warning signs	N/A

7.2.1 How to Use the Material in this Chapter

This chapter is solution oriented. It may contain more details than some project leaders need to know, which is why the overview was included in the front of the book. To aid the reader in utilizing this material most effectively the chapter is partitioned into three major sections.

7.2.1.1 About Section I – Project Creation

Section I, Project Creation, includes the first six steps of our eight-step plan. It encompasses all the steps necessary initially to create a new virtual project. In this section you will learn not just what needs to be done, but the recommended sequence of activities along with pitfalls associated with executing critical steps out of order. Knowing the pitfalls is important to project leaders who must make decisions and set priorities related to early project activities.

7.2.1.2 About Section II – Project Dynamic Testing

Section II, Project Dynamic Testing focuses on establishing a common vision for the execution of the project. This may be the most important section for project leaders because it focuses on the effective communication of project activities, including tasking and customer communication. Section II is equivalent to step seven of our eight-step plan.

7.2.1.3 About Section III – Execution-Phase Warning Signs

In Section III we identify warning signs that all virtual project leaders should be aware of and be prepared to take action to resolve when observed. These warning signs are based on some common pitfalls seen on past virtual projects.

It is worth noting that the 8 steps are not all executed sequentially. For example, steps 2, 3, and 4 occur in parallel, and step 8 never ends. Also, while we describe our recommendations using steps, success on virtual projects cannot be achieved through a "cookbook" approach. See Figure 7.1 for a diagram of the 8-step plan showing step dependencies and sequencing.

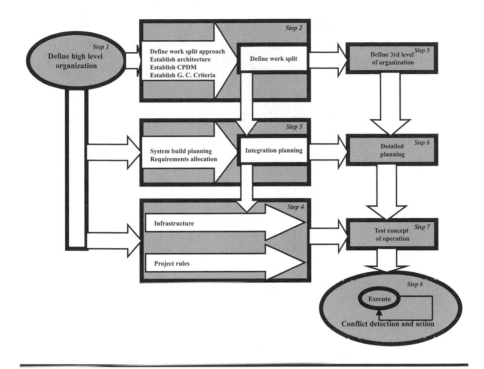

Figure 7.1 Eight-Step Plan

Section I
Project Creation

7.3 Step 1 — Establish High Level Project Organization

The high level project organization includes the top two project levels. This organization must address all activities at all planned locations for the project. The top level of the organizational structure consists of the project management team. Members of this team, supported by senior system engineers, establish the second level of the organizational structure.

The second level of the organization should consist of a system engineering team and a set of product teams, each focused on a well-defined customer deliverable product(s). The system engineering team should be given the responsibility for all the system engineering management activities common across all deliverable products. This includes infrastructure, process, and integration responsibilities. Each product team should be accountable for the construction of their product(s) in accordance with the guidance provided by the system engineering team. See Figure 7.2 for the recommended high level organizational structure.

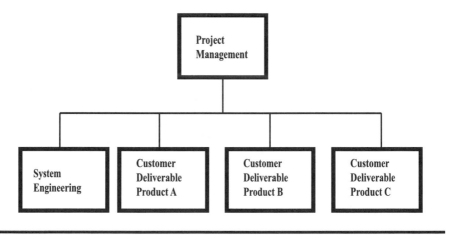

Figure 7.2   Recommended High Level Organizational Structure

7.3.1   *Assign Team Leaders*

In this sub-step we identify and assign team leaders for the second level of the project organization. On collaborative projects this step is often more difficult than on traditional projects. This is due to the added complexity of multi-site and multi-organization involvement. Collaborative project team leaders should be chosen based on the following focused criteria:

- Strong communication skills
- Open mind — willingness to consider alternatives
- Strong conflict management and resolution skills
- Technical management experience, knowledge, and desire

7.3.1.1 Select the Best and Train the Rest

Solution

Use ONE AND ONLY ONE LEAD for each second level team.

Select the best available candidates based on the focused criteria. Where weaknesses exist, utilize formal training and on-the-job mentoring as needed. Of primary importance is the selection of ONE AND ONLY ONE LEAD for each second level team.

While this point may seem obvious, some collaborative projects — especially those with two or more strongly cultured organizations — have attempted to share team leadership across organization or site boundaries. When one thinks about it, it isn't hard to understand why such an approach might be attempted.

First, we all desire the best qualities in our team leaders and often ideal candidates are difficult to find. Due to the characteristics of virtual projects, a few of the ideal qualities may be found in a candidate from one site, while the best remaining qualities are found in someone who happens to reside at a different location. In these cases we understand why one might want to "create" the best virtual leader by combining qualities from different people at different sites. Nevertheless, we highly discourage the sharing of team leadership duties, but this does not mean discouraging the sharing of project leadership itself.

7.3.1.2 Hierarchical and Roving Leaders

Solution

Ensure responsibilities of roving and hierarchical leaders are clear to all team members.

While sharing team leadership responsibilities may solve certain immediate problems on a virtual project, our experience indicates that over the long haul it tends to foster many of the negative characteristics of a schizophrenic project discussed in Chapter 2. It is important to realize that a good team leader need not be the strongest technical individual, nor must that team leader exhibit superhuman capabilities. Project leadership responsibilities — as distinguished from team leader responsibilities — can be, and are encouraged to be, accessed through many sources.

Max DePree in his book *Leadership is an Art* refers to two types of leaders: hierarchical and roving.[1] Max tells us that "roving leaders take charge, in varying degrees, in a lot of companies every day." This is often the case on virtual projects as well. Rarely, on a virtual project, does one person hold all the expertise needed to solve a given problem.

But Max also tells us that leaders also understand "who should be listened to and when."[1] This is an important point on virtual projects. A clear distinction should be made between leaders who lead through influence (mentors) — roving leaders, and those who have ultimate accountability and say for a project's deliverable products — team leaders (hierarchical leaders).

The leadership of the project should discuss this issue together early. Ask the following question with all the key project leaders present (hierarchical and roving):

> *How should an engineer handle a forceful comment from a roving leader if the engineer doesn't agree with the comment?*

It may seem obvious to us that the engineer should discuss this with his manager, but on a virtual project these situations can occur with much greater frequency than in other situations, and often in the heat of battle, the engineer finds himself short of time.

It is for this reason that we advise the project leaders to draft a written statement on this subject and place it in the RFPM under project critical issues. On traditional collocated single-organization projects such formality would not be required, nor even advised. This is because the existing organizational subculture normally takes care of communicating this type of information effectively. Unfortunately, solutions to this issue can vary so widely across different organizations that when they are allowed to collide on a virtual project, serious team conflict can result in a short period of time. This subject is discussed further in step 7.

It doesn't need to take much time for leaders to discuss this issue and then draft a brief statement capturing the team strategy. More importantly, this action can help avoid destructive and costly team conflict later when the project can ill afford it. This is one example of a traditionally informal piece of information that needs to be documented more formally in a virtual environment.

7.3.2 Develop Charters With Clearly Defined Responsibilities

Solution

Develop written charters with clear responsibilities.

Having charters be clear with respect to responsibilities is much easier to say than do. When it comes to actually writing a team charter it is not easy to achieve both crispness and clarity at the same time.

While charters should be high level, they should not mislead. If you are a level-two team lead, don't be lulled into believing that once you have completed your charter and YOU understand what YOU wrote that others will see the boundaries of your responsibilities as clearly as you do. Consider the following guidance to help minimize potential miscommunication.

Solution

Minimize the use of organizational, or site-specific, terms or acronyms.

Be conscious of and try to avoid the use of terms or acronyms in your charter that those from outside your organization may not understand or may misunderstand. Any term that needs clarification (i.e., architecture as discussed in Chapter 3) and directly affects the scope of your produced products should be added to the definitions section of the RFPM (discussed in Chapter 4). But don't add terms that are only needed for you or your internal team. Remember that the focus of the RFPM is on areas likely to cause miscommunication across organizational or site boundaries.

Solution

Take the definition of responsibility a step further by referencing a CPDM.

Virtual project charters should avoid vague responsibility statements such as "responsible for the development and maintenance of the architecture." Charters should reference actual customer deliverable products or reference a CPDM where clearly defined component-products and responsibilities are provided. The CPDM may not yet exist at the time the charter is developed, but if a CPDM is planned (and we recommend it), then it still can be referenced from the charter.

On traditional single-organization collocated projects this added formality with respect to product and component-product responsibility is not as crucial. In these environments component-product expectations are communicated through informal means (as discussed in Chapter 1). On today's collaborative projects, where multiple corporate memories are more likely to exist, these traditional informal communication mechanisms can no longer be relied upon as heavily.

7.3.3 Initiate RFPM

Solution

Develop an RFPM incrementally.

As discussed in Chapter 4, the RFPM should be developed incrementally. However, many of the pieces of the RFPM, including the CPDM, project rules, and site-specific infrastructure information need to be developed early. It is for this reason the initiation of the RFPM is included as a part of step 1. As stated in Chapter 4, the RFPM does not duplicate information readily available through other sources, but rather provides key information traditionally passed on through informal means.

7.4   Step 2 — Establish Work Split

We have observed two common pitfalls with regard to work split:

- Delaying the definition of work split for the wrong reasons.
- Forcing the definition of work split prior to prerequisite task completion.

Delaying the work split definition for the wrong reasons can have devastating effects on a virtual project, because work split definition drives almost everything including process, tools, infrastructure, and support services as well as end-product responsibilities.

Projects that fail to understand critical work-definition dependencies can quickly get into trouble trying hard to move forward without knowing where they are going. But before discussing the wrong reasons for delaying work split definition, let's first discuss key prerequisite tasks that must be accomplished before an effective project work split can be defined.

7.4.1   Establish Approach (Subsystem, Phase, Other)

Solution

Understand the work split issues.

First, before defining an effective work split, a work split approach must be established. As was discussed in the previous chapter, there are advantages and disadvantages to each approach. The right approach for your project depends on project-specific factors. Among these factors are skills availability at specific sites where work is planned. Use the information in Chapter 6 as a guideline to establish your own approach.

While recommending a subsystem work split approach, particularly when strongly cultured organizations are involved, it must also be recognized that choosing a subsystem approach increases the criticality of the next step — establishing an initial system architecture.

7.4.2 Establish Initial System Architecture

Solution

Architecture first.

A common work split pitfall is choosing a subsystem approach, and then jumping straight to defining the subsystems. Unless you have a great deal of experience building similar systems in the past, defining subsystems this way often leads to trouble.

Sound subsystem definitions depend on well-thought-through architectures with clearly identified constraints. When time is not allocated early to produce a sound architecture, subsystem owners often revert to defining their own subarchitectures inside their individual subsystems. This not only increases complexity and cost, but also dramatically increases the integration risk.

7.4.2.1 Political Pressure on the Architecture Contractor

Often, due to the criticality of architecture — especially when multiple contractors are involved — enormous pressure on the architecture-responsible contractor can result. This pressure may be more political than technical. In this environment be prepared for the emergence of the tiger team as discussed in Chapter 5.

While getting the architecture defined early is important, it is even more critical to the ultimate success of the project that it be done right and accepted by the full team. Not taking the necessary time to assimilate the ideas of all team members will only serve to fuel destructive project conflict and architecture rejection. Be sure to consider collocation during the critical creative stage for key architecture team members. Refer to Chapter 2 for more information on architecture and potential pitfalls in defining the architecture. As seen in the architecture tale in that chapter, there exists more than one way to define the term architecture. Ensure responsibilities are clearly established in charters, in particular, the responsibility for defining the components (or subsystems) as this activity drives the definition of the third level of the organization (step 5).

7.4.2.2 Skill and Experience Required during Front-End Stage

Solution

Use small group of senior personnel during critical front-end stage.

Too often in the early project stage we find the wrong skill and experience level of personnel assigned to challenging new collaborative ventures. Up front you need a small group of senior experienced architects, not junior programmers. Personnel brought onto a project at the wrong time not only contribute to low productivity, but also feed a negative project attitude at one of the most sensitive and crucial project stages.

7.4.2.3 Capturing and Crisply Communicating the Architecture

One of the keys to a successful architecture is capturing its definition in a format that can most effectively be communicated to others. An industry standard representation is advisable.

It is also worth noting that far too often we see significant gaps between architecture definitions and subsystem designs. These gaps — in our opinion — exist because task definitions failed to clearly indicate where the architecture ends and subsystem design picks up. The CPDM can bridge this gap.

7.4.3 Establish CPDM — A Bridge From Architecture to Subsystems

Solution

Use CPDM to drive out architecture gaps.

In Chapter 4, the CPDM as a bridge from corporate procedures to project-specific information was discussed. It can also be thought of as a bridge from the architecture to the subsystems. This is because inside the CPDM we identify precisely what the architecture-related component-products are, and also what the system design component-products are. The CPDM acts as a forcing function driving out early in the project architecture-subsystem design gaps — the ones that typically cause integration problems.

7.4.3.1 Establish Global Component Criteria

If a subsystem-based work split approach is employed, the global component approach (refer to Chapter 6 for more details) provides consistent product hand-over criteria from the development-responsible team to the established integration-responsible team.

This approach allows individual sites/organizations to develop, test, and document a chunk of the system separately. The global component approach is particularly appealing to those looking for ways to leverage existing proven local processes inside teaming organizations. This strategy is advantageous when multiple sites with proven life-cycle development processes exist.

On the other hand, if a phase-based work split approach is chosen, then work products will need to be defined at the lower component-product level, rather than at the tested software chunk level.

7.4.3.2 What Skills Do Personnel Assigned to Develop the CPDM and Global Component Criteria Need?

The CPDM and the global component criteria should be developed by an individual who is familiar with the project methodology and the customer deliverable requirements. The CPDM must be approved by the project leadership. Refer to Chapter 4 for more details about the CPDM.

7.4.3.3 Relationships among CPDM, Work Split, and Tasking Risk

If a subsystem-based work split approach is chosen, then the CPDM can be maintained at a higher level. This also allows for more local process freedom. On the other hand, if a phase-based approach is chosen it becomes more critical to define lower level component-products as tasking miscommunication can become a greater risk.

7.4.4   Define Work Split

Once the work split approach is established, the initial architecture defined, and the CPDM and global component criteria established, then work split can be defined. If a subsystem approach has been chosen, defining the work split is analogous to defining the global components. We have completed our discussion of the prerequisite tasks to defining work split. It is now time to turn our attention back to the first pitfall identified earlier in this section with regard to work split.

7.4.5   Delaying the Definition of Work Split for the Wrong Reasons

Often we hear the words:

> "We can't define the work split yet, because we haven't completed the architecture."

When you hear this message heed it as a warning sign. There are sound reasons to hold off work split definition. Those have been discussed. However, holding off work split definition any longer than absolutely necessary will fuel mistrust at a project critical stage when we need to be focusing on building those necessary interpersonal bonds.

While it is true that a subsystem-based approach to work split places the architecture definition directly on the critical path, it must also be recognized that the architecture is an evolutionary product and will continue to be refined throughout the project life cycle, based on lessons learned and integration feedback.

The initial architecture definition, as best we know it in the early project stages, must be documented and placed under control. This should include the initial definition of the actual subsystems. From this point forward changes must go through project leadership approval since impact to existing designs may result.

7.5   Step 3 — System Planning

The third step in our eight-step plan, System planning, consists of three sub-steps: System build planning, Requirements allocation, and Integration planning.

7.5.1   System Build Planning

The system build plan is a high level planning activity which is usually assigned to a senior engineer within the systems engineering group. This plan sets the top level build strategy for the project. The plan should include

- A high level schedule showing the number of planned builds with start and completion dates.
- A high level description of the proposed functionality of each build.
- Key strategies for each build.

You can think of the system build plan as the top level engineering road map on the project showing where key activities from a build perspective occur. Key strategies identified should include early project process-oriented builds that focus on proving out development environment tools, document production steps, and the fundamental initial target architecture.

Early process builds take on a particularly important role on virtual projects because of the lack of proven past patterns of successful operation interacting with all the teams involved. Functionality in the early builds is usually limited to existing products planned to be reused largely in an "as-is" state, or with minor modifications. Subsequent builds lay in additional functional capabilities.

System build planning occurs in parallel with the work split definition, but must take into consideration planned teaming arrangements and multiple development sites.

7.5.2   Requirements Allocation

In parallel with the development of the system build plan, the high level system requirements from the customer are reviewed, refined, allocated to the product teams identified in step 1, and allocated to builds based on the build plan. Refined requirements are placed under control in a requirements management database in accordance with project processes. This is an important step early in the project to help each organizational entity understand at a high level what its group is responsible for.

7.5.3   Integration Planning

The integration plan takes the build plan as an input, along with the work split allocation (global components) and creates the plan for integration of the global components. You can think of the integration plan as one that describes the sequence of steps involved in integrating each of the identified global components into customer end-product deliverables. The integration plan addresses not only the what (global components), and when (schedule of planned turn-over), but also the where (at which site(s) will integration take place).

The integration plan feeds the detailed planning activity of each product team. While the product teams plan out the details of designing, building, testing, and documenting their global components to meet the planned integration with other global components, they also provide feedback to the integration planning activity based on lower level planning constraints.

The criteria for global component hand-over for integration should be either included in this plan or referenced from it in a higher level system engineering management plan. It is important to realize that global component definitions can be affected by work split decisions. Our goal — to the maximum extent possible — is to keep global component responsibility at a single site and single organizational level. While integration planning can proceed, to an extent, in parallel with work split definition, its completion is dependent on the work split. Refer to Appendix K for additional virtual project system planning assistance.

7.6 Step 4 — Special Tasks: Infrastructure and Project Rules

We divide step 4 into two parts: infrastructure and project rules. In the first part of this section we examine closely just what infrastructure is and how to determine what the infrastructure project needs are. In the second part we establish the project rules that were discussed at length in Chapter 5.

7.6.1 What is Infrastructure and How Do I Determine My Project Needs?

The project infrastructure, as used in this book, can be partitioned into three components:

- Hardware
- Software
- Support

Hardware

The hardware component includes the development environment hardware and the integration hardware. For each, the following should be addressed:

- Number of processors
- Type of processors
- Memory
- Mass storage
- Communication and configuration

Software

The software component includes the development environment and integration tools such as:

- Requirements management tools
- Design tools
- Compilers
- Test tools
- Configuration management tools
- Debuggers
- Load management tools

Identify modes of operation including

- Development environment
- Test environment
- Integration environment

Support

The support component includes

- Configuration Management (CM)
- Quality Assurance (QA)
- Technical Publications
- System Administration (backups, network management, load management)

Often, on virtual projects, two competing infrastructure views exist. On one side is the project's seamless viewpoint. This is the side that believes an engineer ought to be able to sit down at a work station at any location of the project and do his job. This view attempts to make all infrastructure components as common as possible across all sites. On the other side is the view that desires to leverage existing mature processes and supporting infrastructures at each site as much as possible. This view attempts to drive each site to maximum site-specific infrastructure independence.

On the surface, each view has merit. Unfortunately infrastructure issues too often end up draining precious project resources that could be better utilized on end-product activities. In practicality, tight budgets usually drive virtual projects to find creative ways to leverage existing site infrastructures. This can be done with an eye to finding a balanced solution that doesn't cause unacceptable integration risks. This leads to a freedom line approach to infrastructure, similar to what was seen in Chapter 6 when dealing with process. But this also leads us to a question:

How do we go about determining where to establish the infrastructure freedom line?

The steps to finding the answer to this question is what the first part of step 4 is about.

7.6.1.1   Four Key Products for Analysis

Solution

Use the four key products to aid in determining infrastructure needs.

We have identified four key products each of which helps in determining the overall infrastructure answer. In this section we describe how you can employ these four products to reach the right infrastructure answer for your project.

- Work split approach
- CPDM
- Global component criteria
- Integration plan

Work split approach

The work split approach is the first element to examine to aid in establishing the infrastructure project approach. If a subsystem approach has been chosen, then it is likely that a significant part of the existing local infrastructure can be leveraged at each site where subsystems will be developed. This includes existing development environment hardware, software, and support services (QA, CM and technical publications). If, on the other hand, a phase-based approach is chosen, then the use of existing site-specific infrastructure becomes less likely. Additional constraints on the infrastructure are provided through the CPDM and the global component criteria.

CPDM

Does the project require specific tools to be employed for requirements management, design, coding, testing, configuration management, or other engineering activities? The CPDM is employed to answer these questions. In this capacity, the CPDM not only helps the engineer do his job, but also aids site-specific infrastructure planning.

Global component criteria

Does the project require that the software be tested on a specific hardware platform before turnover for integration? Hardware platform constraints should be identified up front in the project as part of the global component criteria. By examining the global component criteria site infrastructure planners can determine quickly if project-specific target platforms (SUN, DEC, HP, Silicon Graphics...) will be required.

If a remote site is not using the project's chosen target platform, then added integration risk results. Each project should examine this risk and document its position as part of the global component hand-over criteria. Be aware of the trade-off. Requiring target hardware reduces integration risk, but may drive up remote site infrastructure costs.

Defining the global component criteria and CPDM up front not only improves plan accuracy, but it also helps avoid conflict late in the project. When not addressed early and documented, choices of platforms, compilers, and tools can all cause serious project conflict and ultimately reduced productivity.

Integration plan

After establishing the development environment infrastructure needs, we turn our attention to integration. Different integration approaches carry cost-risk trade-offs. Use the project integration plan to identify planned integration sites.

While a single integration site may reduce overall project integration hardware cost, it may increase overall project cost when one considers travel, and increased integration time due to latent defects. Be aware that integration facilities — especially those at a different site from where the software was developed — usually do not provide an optimum environment for engineers to isolate and fix defects.

As an alternative an integration build up through a sequence of mini-integrations planned at key development sites is preferable. Again, there is the cost-risk trade-off to consider. While this approach allows for earlier and potentially more effective defect identification and resolution, it can drive up the cost of integration hardware, and may lengthen the planned schedule.

Integration is a challenge for most virtual projects. Be cautious of planning a big-bang single integration. While it may appear optimum on a schedule, oftentimes it is the most costly approach in the long run.

7.6.1.2   Sample Problem Scenario

Now let's take a moment to look at a short scenario. Suppose you are working on a virtual project that includes two mature organizations (SEI level 3). Each organization has its own established processes, and its own favorite tools and platforms, along with established and proven internal CM, QA, and technical publications support operations.

Let's also suppose that a subsystem approach to work split has been chosen, and one of the contractors, the ACE company, has been selected to be the integrator of an existing application that is planned to be reused. Along with the integration role, ACE is also responsible for changes that will require modifications to approximately 10% of the 1 million lines of C++ code in the existing application. Although the customer wants reuse, they are also concerned about effective support for the system for the next 20 years. So what do you do?

7.6.1.3   Sample Problem Solution

Recall that earlier (Chapter 5, Section 5.1.8.1) we defined productivity as "the effectiveness with which resources are utilized." Productivity involves more than a line of code per hour count. It involves support issues as well, which include the effectiveness with which we utilize our processes and infrastructures and our people.

Undoubtedly, in this sample scenario, both organizations involved have strong cultures. In this case, because we were able to split work at a subsystem level and because the organizations involved have mature processes, a strategy that looks to maximize site-specific freedom and use of existing available and proven infrastructure components is recommended. It is important to realize that the maturity and track record of the organizations involved are critical factors upon which we base our recommendation.

Of course, specific questions will need to be answered and documented in the CPDM and global component criteria to reduce the integration risk associated with this approach.

Example questions that will need to be answered include

> *Will the project require ACE to test and verify the application with a specific compiler?*
>
> *Will the project require ACE to test and verify the application on a specific platform?*
>
> *Have all architecture constraints been identified?*
>
> *Is a formal interface specification required between the reuse system and other subsystems?*
>
> *Will the design and documentation be acceptable in the existing form or must ACE convert this information to a new project standard tool?*

Long-term project support issues will be addressed through the answers to these questions. Once again, the development of the CPDM and the global component criteria will act as a forcing function to ask the right questions early, and get the needed agreements documented. Additional infrastructure checklist questions are provided in Appendix H.

7.6.1.4 What Should You Do When Your Infrastructure Won't Support Your Plan?

In this section we have demonstrated a systematic way to determine project infrastructure needs. Following the process described should paint a clear "infrastructure needs picture" for a specific project or site. When you are done you may decide this is a picture you would rather not see.

Nevertheless, we strongly urge you to complete this effort and document the results. Then take the facts to upper management if warranted. If it is clear that the real infrastructure needs of your project plan cannot be achieved, then don't try to fool yourself about it. Our experience indicates that infrastructures don't just appear and holding onto unrealizable project expectations usually leads to trouble. Instead, take action to change your plan — and do it now! And here is specifically what to do.

Go back to the end of Chapter 2 and re-read what Ed Yourdon said about triage. Now with triage in mind, the most important thing to do with limited infrastructure dollars is to address the real issues facing your engineers — particularly at remote sites.

And when it comes right down to it many of the real issues involved are not all that complex or expensive. If you don't believe it go back and read the tale about Don Martin in Chapter 5 (Section 5.2.2). In many cases it's the little things that have the greatest effect on an engineer's productivity and attitude toward his job. And remember that setting the bar high is good, just don't put it out of reach where all it can do is add team frustration and low morale to an already difficult project.

7.6.2   Project Rules — Communicating the Lessons

Whenever a new technique or tool-set arrives on the software scene (i.e., object-oriented design) those who apply it first go through what has been called the "early adopter" syndrome. In a nutshell this refers to the pain one endures in learning through trial and error what works best, and what to avoid. Out of these early adopter experiences lessons learned briefings are often produced in an attempt to transfer valued lessons to others. Lessons learned knowledge transfer is usually more informal than formal. Our experience with what we have learned on virtual projects indicates that greater payback could be achieved through a controlled degree of increased formality.

Too often projects build up with new personnel who start right in making many of the same mistakes made by their predecessors. While this condition has been witnessed in the past on collocated projects, new communication barriers on virtual projects caused by distance and differing backgrounds serve only to worsen the situation. Documented project rules through an RFPM is one example of the type of increased formality to which we are referring.

The need for more formal definition and documentation of project rules (including rules on the use of virtual communication mechanisms) was discussed at length in Chapter 5. But documenting rules is only a first step. If they are to take hold, project rules must not only be established, they must be communicated to all team members early and they must be enforced.

Solution

Use mentoring for on-the-job guidance.

People will follow rules if they see the value. This implies a need to also communicate insight into why each rule exists. One of the best ways to convey this is through mentors and project leaders who vigilantly monitor project activities providing on-the-job guidance that effectively demonstrates in real situations how, where, and why the rules are best applied.

Use the guidance provided in Chapter 5 as a framework, but don't limit your rules to the examples provided. Discuss, and agree on what rules make sense for your team. Consider the experiences of others as described in this book, but recognize the value of your own experiences by turning them into rules that will help you avoid making your own mistakes again.

Solution

Use rules, but not too many.

One caution — don't get carried away with creating rules. Don't make the list too long. It is critical that all team leaders buy into the rules. Once the list is approved, post it where it is accessible to all, and only update it after testing out a new one that all agree will help the project.

7.7   Step 5 — Establishing the Third Level of the Organization

The third level of the organization is where the bulk of the engineering activities take place. This level is comprised of smaller working teams inside the second-level deliverable product teams. Each third level working team has responsibility for one or more global component products. The global component products (see Chapter 6) are defined consistently with the architecture and identified in the integration plan. The third level of the organization is sometimes referred to as the global component team level.

Solution

Collocate global component teams to the maximum extent possible.

To the maximum extent possible, all members of a given global component team should be collocated. Global component team members must interact frequently and informally on a daily basis during the development cycle. Global component responsibilities should not cross-organizational boundaries, if possible. This can aid in reducing unhealthy internal team conflict. Methods to help detect unhealthy team conflict are discussed in step 8.

The primary focus of the global component team is to produce a quality product that meets the established global component hand-over criteria. If the global component teams are to function effectively, a key chain of events must be followed prior to team creation.

As previously discussed, the architecture first drives the work split. Once the work split is clearly established, then — and only then — should the third level teams be initiated. Once the third level teams are identified and their leaders assigned, detailed planning of the teams' activities can commence.

This sequence may seem out of order to some. Nevertheless, on virtual projects, when a different order is followed a variety of project difficulties can quickly surface. This is discussed further in step 6, detailed planning.

7.8 Step 6 — Detailed Planning

If you try to do detailed planning before the work split definition is clear, then be prepared to do it again. Building a detailed plan that is executable requires consideration of critical resources. This includes both infrastructure and personnel, both of which are site-specific.

Third-level team leads should work with second level managers in completing detailed plans. This collaboration is important for third level team buy-in. Because the global component team should be collocated, the third-level team leader cannot be assigned until the site-level work split has been completed. Another reason why the third-level team lead should collaborate in the detailed planning is because different organizations have different cultures when it comes to detailed planning. Leaders need to be particularly sensitive to this issue.

7.8.1 *Cultural Differences in Approaches to Detailed Planning*

Solution

Be aware of varying leadership styles to detailed planning.

Some organizations delegate the bulk of the detailed planning activity to the third-level team lead. In these organizations the second level manager creates an intermediate level schedule with key review dates and major milestones at the global component level, but delegates the detailed planning down to the global component team level.

In other organizations, second-level team leads take on the full detailed planning task allowing their third level teams to concentrate totally on the technical work. There is also a third variant where a single engineering manager plans all engineering activities down to the detailed level.

Virtual project leaders should be keenly aware of these variant leadership styles. It might even be worth an open discussion with the first and second level team leaders present to ensure everyone understands ahead of time what approach will be taken.

If your second level leads come from a delegating-culture and your top engineering manager is a do-it-all-alone detailed planner, and you haven't discussed this openly ahead of time, be alert for team leadership mistrust at a most critical point in your project.

7.8.1.1 *Architecture Relationship to Leadership's Common Vision and Trust*

Solution

Be aware of the relationship between architecture and planning.

The trust issue among team leaders referred to above, if not dealt with in a timely fashion, can rapidly affect a team's performance if the project architecture is not in place prior to detailed planning. One might not think it so important that architecture precede detailed planning, but when the architecture definition is unclear, detailed planners are often forced to make architectural assumptions.

Without a better architectural definition to go on, one can expect those assumptions to be based on the prior experiences of the detail planner. When leaders have different architectural experiences and develop plans independently based on those experiences, leadership tension will rise rapidly even before the project is out of the planning stage. We want our leaders to share a common vision that can be communicated to the full organization. A leadership agreed-to-architecture must come first, if this common vision is to be realized.

7.8.2   A Closer Look at Three Prerequisite Tasks

There are three primary inputs to the detailed planning step:

- CPDM
- Global component criteria
- Integration plan

In the following paragraphs the role each of these inputs play in the detailed planning activity is examine more closely.

CPDM

Many team leads do not view planning as a fun part of their job. As a consequence, it can be very frustrating when a team lead discovers his plans must be reworked because his assumptions were wrong. While re-planning is unavoidable in certain cases, much of the re-planning efforts our clients conduct could have been avoided. If you understood the concept of a CPDM and placed a priority on producing this simple but valuable product up front, then it can save the detail planners significant re-work. The CPDM indicates the answers to many questions about which detail planners find themselves making assumptions.

As an example, if your engineering staff is unfamiliar with the project's chosen software methodology, or the programming language, or design tool, then it is likely your staff will require some level of training. Training takes time and can impact detailed plans. Furthermore, if the required design tools or compiler are not yet available through the site infrastructure, then the time it takes to purchase, ship, install, and test could also impact your planned activities. Stated differently, the CPDM defines in a concise fashion key pieces of information that need to be considered when putting together a detailed plan that actually has a chance of being executed successfully.

In Chapter 4 (Section 4.4.2) we discussed the importance of the CPDM as a forcing function to surface these types of infrastructure-related needs, as well as potential training needs. Often CPDMs are not produced early because the project has not made key decisions in terms of tools and/or methodology. However, if you are starting down the detail planning road and this is the case, then take this as a warning — your plan may well be at risk. Besides forcing the definition of key issues early, the CPDM also provides a vehicle to aid in effective task communication for both current project personnel and those who will come later.

Global component criteria

The CPDM provides key and concise information to aid in planning and producing component-products. Similarly, the global component criteria provide key and concise information for planning and producing a global component (focus of third level team's activities). The global component criteria provide key constraints that need to be taken into consideration during the detailed planning step. An example could be the requirement to test on a specific target hardware platform.

> *Will the specific target hardware platform be available at the chosen site in time to meet the detailed schedule?*

This is the type of question the global component criteria force us to ask during the detail planning stage. When critical path constraints are not recognized and actively worked early, the risk of effectively executing one's plan can rise rapidly.

Integration plan

Successful detailed development plans must be built around the constraints of integration plans. The integration plan conveys the overall project plan for integrating the global components. This includes specific functionality required in each global component in each planned incremental build. Trying to build a successful detailed plan without an integration plan is like trying to hit the target with a blindfold on. If the integration plan is late, plan on reworking your detail plan.

Integration plans should also identify planned sites where integration will occur. This will affect travel plans and budgets for personnel to support the project integration phase. If the integration is planned at your facility, then you had better be planning the acquisition of the integration infrastructure as well.

7.8.3 First Things First

Pushing a team to do detailed planning before all prerequisite tasks are complete can actually do more harm to the project than good. Driving detailed planning activities out of sequence not only runs the high risk of rework, but can also foster unhealthy project conflict at a time when leadership unity is critical.

Section II
Project Dynamic Testing

7.9 Step 7 — Testing the Concept of Operation of the Project Organization

New virtual projects will not instantly operate as efficiently as single-site organizations that have taken years to mature internal processes. Strong teams with strong interpersonal bonds where responsibilities and expectations are understood and owned do not just happen. Through key activities virtual team growth can accelerate rapidly. One of those key activities is conducting a walkthrough of the concept of operation of the project's organization.

Consider setting aside a 2- to 4-hour block of time for project leaders to walkthrough key organizational scenarios. You can think of an organizational scenario as a thread through the organization. The leadership team should be collocated for this activity. When project leaders discuss openly and face-to-face potential problem areas, not only is the organization helped, but crucial interpersonal bonds among leaders can also be quickly strengthened.

Try to focus this activity on organizational interactions that are unproven. These are typically found in areas where culture differences are likely. For example, leaders from different organizations — especially those who may have differing management styles — should discuss openly their visions of the organization with respect to tasking, product reviews, approvals, and product hand-overs. These are all areas where cultural differences can hinder productivity.

Don't put off sensitive discussions. If you know of areas where potential problems might exist, especially those that may be caused by differing cultural views, get the right leaders together as soon as possible, and keep the interaction going on a regular basis until agreements are reached.

Often at the start of a virtual project leaders do not know where to begin leadership discussions. This is especially true when their own past experiences have been limited to a single culture. To facilitate these meetings the following five potential hot-spots which have been known to cause difficulties on past virtual projects should be closely examined:

- Task direction
- Task management
- Cross-site or cross-organizational interactions
- Integrated engineering responsibilities
- Customer communication

7.9.1 Task Direction — When Roving Leaders and Hierarchical Leaders Collide

Earlier in this chapter we discussed hierarchical and roving leaders. Different leadership styles can have a dramatic effect on how real work actually gets accomplished on a given project.

In some organizations tasks are initiated strictly through the hierarchical leadership chain. In these environments roving leaders provide guidance to engineering personnel. Roving leaders in strict hierarchical organizations know the difference between guidance and direction. They are aware of the difference between their roles and that of the hierarchical leader. In particular, roving leaders in strict tasking organizations are cautious to ensure their guidance is not construed as conflicting with task direction from the hierarchical side. Engineers in strict hierarchical organizations look to the hierarchical side when task scope is in doubt, and look to roving leaders for guidance on their choice of solutions.

In other organizations the hierarchical leadership chain may take on a looser tasking role. In these organizations the hierarchical leader may actually look to a roving leader to provide the specific day-to-day task direction. In these environments an engineer may actually perceive a roving leader as the individual who provides the real task direction.

It is important to realize that each of these models can work. They work because in each case expectations are clear. Engineers know who to turn to when clarity of direction or guidance is needed. But when the two models collide on the same project, trouble usually ensues. Let's take a closer look at what we mean.

Recall from Chapter 1 how new people learn about an organization's expectations of them. Engineers watch and talk to other engineers as they do their jobs. Through this informal communication they learn a significant part of what will be expected of them in the organizational environment. Understanding where to go for task direction and guidance is learned in a similar way.

Figure 7.3 shows a strict hierarchical tasking model. In this model managers task and status engineers directly and regularly. Roving leaders understand this model and they know their roles within it. The engineers understand it and know what is expected of them, as well as what to expect from both their hierarchical and roving leaders. When new people come into this organization they see the model and begin to follow it. The organization functions predictably and continues to do so as personnel changes occur.

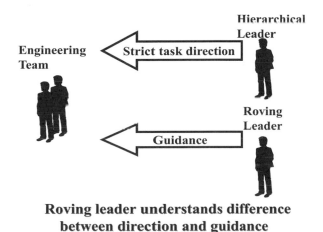

Figure 7.3   Strict Hierarchical Tasking Model

Figure 7.4 shows a loose hierarchical tasking model. In this model the engineering team looks to the roving leader for day-to-day direction. The hierarchical leader has tasked the engineering team, but in this organization the task direction is usually at a higher level. In this case detailed direction, as well as guidance, come from the roving leader. In this organization when new people come in they see the model and execute to it. The organization functions predictably and continues to do so when personnel changes occur because the pattern of expectations is clear. It is a different pattern from the strict hierarchical organization, but because it is followed consistently, the organization functions predictably.

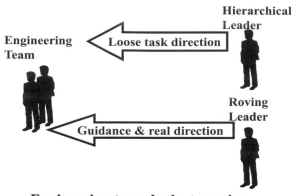

**Engineering team looks to roving
leader for real direction**

Figure 7.4   Loose Hierarchical Tasking Model

In Figures 7.5 and 7.6 we see two situations that can occur when organizations employ a strict and a loose hierarchical tasking model together. In Figure 7.5 there is a manager from the strict hierarchical tasking organization, and a roving leader from the loose hierarchical tasking organization. In this case, both the hierarchical leader and the roving leader expect to drive the team technically day-to-day. This results in a collision of styles and a condition called "double-tasking." When this combination of models comes together engineers are driven to work long days striving to complete tasks from two sources. It is not uncommon to find that goals from each source conflict, requiring tasks to be reworked.

Solution

Recognize the signs of double-tasking and take action to resolve it.

In Figure 7.6 there is a manager from a loose hierarchical organization, and she has a roving leader to help her who has come from a strict hierarchical organization. In this case no clear direction is provided to the engineering team on a consistent basis. When new people come into this project they see no consistent pattern. Different engineers may see different expectations and therefore the organization does not operate in a predictable fashion.

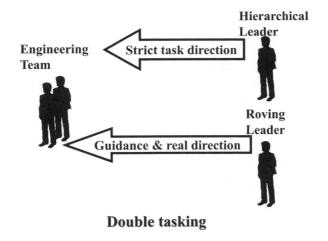

Double tasking

Figure 7.5 Hybrid Strict Hierarchical Tasking Model

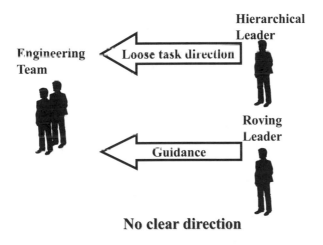

No clear direction

Figure 7.6 Hybrid Loose Hierarchical Tasking Model

Solution

Recognize the signs of "no tasking" and take action to resolve it.

The situation described above is not unusual in level one capability maturity model (CMM) rated organizations, but it can also occur when two highly mature organizations with different tasking models team up.

Team leaders should discuss openly their organizational tasking model experiences. Recognize the characteristics of the organization and get it out on the table early. If differing approaches exist talk it through until a consistent strategy is reached. Then, document and place the results in the RFPM so others know what is expected.

7.9.2 Task Management — A Strict vs. Integrated Approach

Different organizations often have differing cultures with respect to task management. Task management, as used here, refers specifically to the management of task scope. There are two task management models: the strict model and the integrated model. The difference between the two models can be demonstrated by examining the risk management process and its relationship to engineering activities inside an organization.

When risks are initially identified on a project, they are usually sent to a risk management board where they are reviewed and prioritized. If it is agreed by the risk management board that the risk requires closer attention, then someone — often a senior system engineer — is assigned to develop an associated risk abatement plan.

The senior engineer next analyzes the risk, conducts appropriate cost-benefit trade-offs, and develops a recommended action plan. After the plan is accepted by the board, the risk is entered into the active risk management system. Once the risk abatement plan has been accepted by the board, the next step is for the organization to implement the recommended actions. It is the actual process by which these actions turn into real engineering tasks that we want to focus this discussion.

In some organizations product teams are immediately triggered into action by the acceptance of the risk by the risk board. These organizations tend to have a culture that views the risk management process as an integrated part of the normal engineering process. (See Figure 7.7.)

Other organizations, however, view task scope from a more narrow perspective. These organizations often require a written authorization from the program office to proceed with what could be viewed as additional tasks caused by the new risk abatement plan. (See Figure 7.8.) While task scope

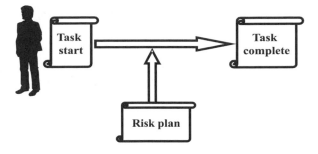

**Risk abatement plan flows in
as an integrated activity**

Figure 7.7   Integrated Task Management

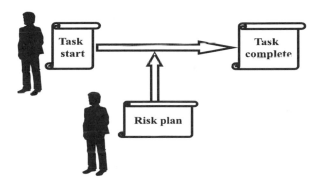

**Risk abatement plan implementation
requires strict program office approval**

Figure 7.8   Strict Task Management Approach

can, in cases, be a judgement call, organizational cultures can play a significant part in influencing the way teams view their responsibilities.

What is important for virtual project leaders to understand is the existence of these differing views and how they can affect the actual work for which a team believes it is responsible. Many leaders often come to virtual projects with very definite task management models on these issues already fixed in their heads. These expectations are often based on their own past experiences, but often this information isn't written down or well communicated. These expectations can be a crucial part of what lies at the root of leadership struggles and mistrust on virtual projects.

It is crucial that you get these issues out on the table. Talk about them with all leaders present. Do you want your project to have a strict or an integrated approach to task management? Once your leadership team decides which approach is right for your project write it down and put it in the RFPM so other new people who come on the project later will know, too. Through these techniques you may not be able to replace what a single-site organization has taken years to accomplish, but you can begin to build your own "virtual" project culture and you can do it rapidly!

7.9.3 Cross-Site or Cross-Organizational Interactions — Using a Checklist

When two sites that have not previously worked together team up the leaders from each side should meet to discuss and share their expectations. One of the most common reasons why two sites need to work together is to integrate global component products developed at each site. Use the following checklist in these cases to ensure the key issues are addressed.

Checklist in preparation for global component product integration:

- Is the global component product criteria established and agreed to?
- Are the requirements for both products clear, documented, and controlled?
- Has agreement been reached on the design methodology and documentation?
- Has agreement been reached on the language and compiler?
- Has agreement been reached on testing approach?
- Are the architectural constraints well defined and agreed to?
- Has agreement been reached on the platform for testing prior to integration?
- Has agreement been reached on the integration platform?
- Has the integration site been agreed to?
- Does the integration site have the required infrastructure needs?
  - Hardware
  - Software
  - Support
- Have members of the other site/organization been invited to appropriate reviews?

- Has agreement been reached on the integration schedule?
- Has agreement been reached on the specific requirements to be tested at integration?
- Has the approval process been agreed to?

Add to this list your own specific areas of concern. The earlier the leaders begin discussions the better. Be aware that when leaders meet to discuss these issues they are setting a communication model that often carries over into the rest of their teams. Engineers learn more than technical expectations from their leaders. When leaders demonstrate respect for leaders from remote sites, this behavior often carries over to their teams. The reverse is also true.

7.9.4 Integrated Engineering Responsibilities — Using a Checklist

In the past, separate and distinct organizational entities often existed to provide support and specialty engineering services. With integrated product teams, responsibilities for many of these functions are moving back inside the product teams themselves. Because of this change in responsibility, team charters should be reviewed carefully to ensure all responsibilities are well understood. Explicit statements ought to be included in team charters to address these responsibilities. Use the following checklist to ensure critical responsibilities that sometimes get missed when new virtual project organizations are established are each covered.

- Have the following responsibilities each been addressed?
  - Security
  - Safety
  - Reliability
  - Maintainability
  - Supportability
- Have all the infrastructure needs been addressed?
  - Hardware
    Oftentimes on virtual projects integration hardware needs are not adequately planned because responsibility is unclear in the early project stages.
    - Development environment hardware
    - Integration hardware

- Software
  The software component includes the development environment and integration tools such as:
  - Requirements management tools
  - Design tools
  - Compilers
  - Test tools
  - Configuration management tools
  - Debuggers
  - Load management tools
- Support
  Ensure responsibility for each of the following support areas is addressed:
  - Configuration Management (CM)
  - Quality Assurance (QA)
  - Technical Publications
  - System Administration (backups, network management, load management)
- Does your group own any processes?
  - Life Cycle System and software processes
    Ensure that ownership exists within the project organization for each of the following life-cycle phase activities and related products.
    - Requirements
    - Architecture
    - Design
    - Test
    - Integration
    Use the CPDM as a cross-check on the organizational responsibilities.

7.9.5   Customer Communication — Establishing a Well-Defined Policy

Customer communication is critical to the success of any project. In today's world with a focus on integrated product teams there often exists a close working relationship between contractor engineering personnel and customer personnel. However, virtual project leaders should be aware that differing views exist on the best way to handle engineering-customer communication.

First, all projects should recognize that there exists two fundamental communication categories:

- Formal
- Informal

Within the formal category there can exist a variety of types. The following is intended only as a sample:

- Customer deliverable products
- Action item responses
- White papers
- Status reports
- Review minutes

This process may actually be more complicated on a virtual project due to the need for a local or organization-specific approval process prior to full project approval of formal items being released to the customer. Also recognize that different organizations often have differing cultures with respect to customer interactions. It is therefore important that team leaders discuss and agree upon a formal customer communication process which considers the appropriate types of information for your project.

Be aware if you are not the prime you really have two customers on the project. You will need to meet the prime contractor's expectations as well as the end-customer's expectations. Make sure the approval process is well defined early and documented where the entire team can access it in the RFPM. (See Figure 7.9.)

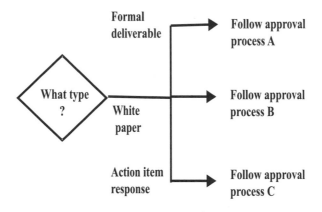

Figure 7.9   Customer Communication Approval Process

Section III
Execution-Phase Warning Signs

7.10 Step 8 — Execution with a Focus on Conflict Management

Discussing face to face with your leadership team the implications of a loose hierarchical tasking model or a strict task management approach isn't always an easy thing to do. But these topics are easier to talk about before they become serious hindrances to the team's productivity. By following the first seven steps, you should be well prepared to execute a successful virtual project. To review, we have:

- Established an organization with clear responsibilities
- Defined work split
- Established a project build and integration plan
- Established well-defined piece-part products at the site/organizational level in support of our plans
- Established criteria for completion of piece-part products in support of plans
- Established detailed plans and task definitions to build piece parts addressing common task miscommunication areas
- Addressed infrastructure needs in support of those tasks at each site
- Established key project rules in support of effective communication
- Held leadership face-to-face discussions testing our common project vision

We are now prepared to execute the project. Throughout the first seven steps we have been sensitive to pitfalls experienced by others. Nevertheless, conflict must still be anticipated. To help project leaders in handling this conflict, a number of virtual project-specific conflict warning signs were identified.

7.10.1 The Non-Technical Side of Project Execution

So far in step 8 we have focused on the technical process side of execution. Throughout this book we have emphasized many non-technical or cultural factors that can hinder project success. Because on virtual projects we anticipate increased conflict and because this conflict often can be intense, conflict resolution skills become increasingly key to project success.

Plenty of published material is available on conflict management[2,3] on the market today. It is not the intent here to duplicate this valuable information, but rather to share with potential virtual project leaders some of the specific signs of conflict that are common across a number of complex virtual projects. Related recommendations are also provided.

7.10.2 Two Forms of Conflict

When dealing with conflict it must first be recognized that conflict in itself is not something to be discouraged. Often it is by working through conflict that the best solutions are found. We actually want to encourage healthy conflict among our teammates. This type of interaction is necessary if we are to achieve our goals of a "best of the best" solution. Nevertheless, in practice, this notion of encouraging and supporting healthy conflict often presents a dilemma for project leaders. This dilemma can be stated as follows:

Problem

How does a project leader distinguish the healthy form of conflict — which when left alone will strengthen a team — from the destructive form which when left alone can tear a team apart? (Restated from Chapter 2.)

7.10.3 A Sign of Healthy Conflict

A number of projects use the following pattern with respect to conflict:

- A valid issue is raised.
- The issue is worked through by the team — often with intense and lengthy discussions.
- One or more solutions are proposed, discussed further, and eventually a consensus is reached.
- The team accepts the solution and moves on to its next challenge.

This pattern is a sign of healthy conflict.

Some have asked:

How does the intensity or frequency of a conflict relate to the health of that conflict?

It has been our experience that the difference between healthy conflict and destructive conflict isn't a function of intensity or frequency. Conflict can exist daily in a healthy project environment, and — at times — it can be intense. What is key is the pattern of reaching solutions acceptable to the team that allow the team to move on. When healthy conflict is at work a track record of team-accepted solutions grows.

7.10.4 Key Warning Signs of Destructive Conflict

Too often, on virtual projects, the pattern doesn't fit the healthy model. In the following paragraphs are four warning signs of unhealthy conflict. If you detect these signs, do not wait. We repeat this recommendation and say it louder. DO NOT WAIT. When you detect ANY of the warning signs described below, immediate action should be taken by the appropriate project leader. When unhealthy conflict is allowed to persist — for even a short period of time — it can cause irreparable harm to the team.

It is worth noting, however, that the detection of unhealthy conflict on a virtual project is not in itself cause for alarm, as long as timely and appropriate action is taken. Due to the differing experiences of personnel and lack of strong interpersonal bonds on most virtual projects, some unhealthy conflict can be expected. This is particularly true in the early stages of the project when work split, reuse strategies, and architecture choices are still unclear. The mistake that is too often made is not taking timely positive action to eliminate these problems at their root.

7.10.4.1 Warning Sign 1 — Repeating Issue

The first, and probably the most common, sign that destructive conflict exists on your project is the repeating issue sign. This is the case where:

- A valid issue is raised.
- The issue is worked through by the team.
- It is believed that a consensus has been reached and the issue put to bed.

- One week or one month later the same issue returns.

Does this sound familiar? Have you ever sat in a meeting and thought you were sitting through a re-run of an old movie? When you sense the repeating issue warning sign, here is what you do:

Solution

Work by consensus.

First, check that the issue was indeed previously resolved by the team. It may have only been discussed without consensus being reached. But don't forget that consensus doesn't mean that everyone gets to vote, or that everyone necessarily likes the outcome. It does, however, require that team member voices get heard. Consensus is based on the idea that team members can live with solutions they may not like as long as their ideas are honestly listened to.

Second, verify that the result was documented, and that the agreed to solution received leadership approval and was placed in the RFPM under the critical project issues. This may sound overly formal. Let's discuss the formality issue a bit further.

The need for increased formality

Of course, not all team decisions require formal documentation. In fact, we couldn't afford to document every decision the team makes. Leaders must use their judgement on these issues. But if the repeating sign is clearly hindering the team's progress, it is a good bet that a more formal treatment of this issue may be appropriate.

In the case when the repeating sign involves a hotly contested issue, and the results have not been documented, assign a person to complete this task. If team consensus has not been reached, then raise the issue up the organizational chain, if necessary.

The issue may even require a small team to go off and work it. But if this tiger team approach is used, don't forget the discussion on this subject back in Chapter 5.

There may be a situation where good work was done by a small group, but the results were never shared and assimilated by the larger group. This is a common reason why issues keep coming back.

Solution

Don't force formal documentation too soon.

Be careful not to force formal documentation of an approach if assimilation and team acceptance haven't occurred. This not only won't solve the issue, it may actually make it worse. When small groups make decisions without listening to the thoughts of teammates, particularly when the small group is all from the same site or same organization, small conflicts rapidly grow.

Solution

Keep the full team in the loop.

If it is decided that the small team approach is the right approach, then that team should have representation from all critical project viewpoints. Once a potential resolution is found, the small team should present its proposed solution to the full team prior to any final decision being made. One technique used very effectively is for the small team not to completely solve the problem, but rather identify two or three alternative solutions and then allow the larger group to make the final decision. This approach demonstrates a true willingness to work through the power of the team and can go a long way to strengthen a team that may be struggling to establish its value and identity.

Solution

What to do if the issue continues to repeat.

Once the issue has been resolved by the team and documented in the RFPM, if the repeating issue sign continues, then the appropriate manager should confront the individual in a direct manner and as close in time to the incident as possible.

In this case the manager should tell the individual that the issue has been addressed and a solution has been agreed to by the team. Refer the individual to the RFPM to read the resolution. Then look the person straight in the eye and say that he (or she) is hindering team progress by continuing to discuss this matter.

If the individual objects, make it clear that he is not being asked to agree with the decision, only to live with it. If he states that he cannot live with it, then the appropriate manager should take action IMMEDIATELY. Possible actions could include mentoring the individual in team rules and collaborative skills. It is also possible that the individual may need to be taken off the project. This is a sensitive judgement call for the manager. The manager must in this case balance the nature of the conflict, and the track record of the individual.

It is important to give a team time to assimilate new approaches, but don't wait too long or you may find that the harm done can't be fixed. Healthy conflict is always acceptable, but you should never allow personnel to break agreed-to team rules.

7.10.4.2 Warning Sign 2 — Non-Compliance With Team Information Sharing Policy

The second most common sign that destructive conflict exists is non-compliance with the team's information sharing policy. This situation was discussed at length in Chapter 5.

Solution

Write down your policy and deploy it.

The team information sharing policy should be discussed early in the project. Reach agreement on what the team is willing to share externally, and under what conditions that information can leave the team. But in all cases, in process information — that is, information relevant to issues on which the team has not yet reached a consensus — should be kept inside the team. Then write down the policy and place it in the RFPM.

If a manager becomes aware of a situation where an employee is not complying with this rule, then the manager should privately bring this matter to the employee's attention. Refer the individual to the RFPM. Make sure he(or she) is aware of the rule and why it is important.

In this case the manager should explain to the individual that personnel on this project don't have long-established interpersonal bonds and to build team trust requires that everyone demonstrate team loyalty on all possible occasions. In particular, this means not talking about sensitive team issues, or talking about other team members' views on an issue especially when a team member is not present.

Steven Covey, in his book *The Seven Habits of Highly Effective People*, states that "one of the most important ways to manifest integrity is to be loyal to those who are not present. In doing so, we build the trust of those who are present."[4] Because of the distance factor on virtual projects, there are often many opportunities to demonstrate this loyalty to our team.

After explaining why this rule is important, the manager should ask the individual directly if he will comply with the rule in the future. If the individual does not believe he can do this, then the manager should IMMEDI-ATELY take action. Once again, the team should NEVER accept personnel who refuse to follow the team rules. As a leader you will do more to earn the respect of your team by taking a tough stand on the right side of the issue.

7.10.4.3 Warning Sign 3 — "They're Out to Steal Our Business" Message

This is really a special case of warning sign 2, and should be handled similarly.

Solution

Take the direct approach.

Don't put off having a direct discussion with an individual who is talking loosely about the business motives of one of your teaming organizations. I cannot tell you how many times I've heard the "they're out to steal our business" paranoia popping up in conversations inside organizations.

In this case the manager should explain to the individual that it is part of today's business model to team with organizations, and compete with them at the same time. The existence of competition should not affect our loyalty to a teammate.

If the individual is convinced that someone from another company is using information from your project inappropriately, then ask him if he has objective evidence. Usually there is no real evidence, there is just a feeling about it.

If the feelings persist and are echoed by other personnel, then it may be worth discussing openly with a manager from the other organization. Often when someone feels this way from one company the same feelings exist with personnel in the other company. Don't be surprised if you open up communication with a manager from the other company and find out he is dealing with the exact same issue. In any event, the straightforward open discussion approach is likely to strengthen the relationship with the other manager which will help your project in the long run.

7.10.4.4 Warning Sign 4 – The Quiet Sign

To be perfectly honest, if you've noticed this warning sign, it may be too late to help your team. When a usually vocal team becomes quiet, it can be a sign of agreement, but it can also mean that the culture fatigue has just become too much and they are on the verge of giving up.

Solution

Look for the unofficial tiger team.

If you observe this sign, immediately look for an unofficial tiger team operating on the edge of your organization. Experience indicates that there is a good chance you will find at least one.

Often a prime cause of personnel frustration is the rejection of hard work without good reason. If an unofficial tiger team is operating on your project, do your homework before you act — but do it fast. Find out under whose authority the team is operating and what purpose they serve. The organizational teams must be driving the project. They have the authority, responsibility, and accountability. Do not allow your project to be driven by those who work around the organization, rather than through it.

If there is a valid reason for the tiger team, then get it out in the open. Let the full official team know why it exists, and how the results of that activity will flow back through the defined organizational processes. Often these situations occur because of critical schedule crunches, but there is never a valid reason to leave the team in the dark feeling their efforts are unimportant to the project.

7.10.5 Preventative Maintenance

In cases where destructive conflict is detected, actions, as discussed above, should be taken immediately. Waiting will only make the situation worse. But solving the immediate problem is not the only step to be taken. We also need to look for root causes and correct them where possible to keep the problem from recurring.

7.10.5.1 Warning Signs Of Non-Compliance with Preventative Maintenance Techniques

Using causal analysis techniques, the existence of destructive conflict often can be traced to a failure to effectively apply fundamental preventative maintenance techniques. Many of these techniques have been discussed earlier in this book, but we summarize them here for completeness.

Solution

Deploy the techniques discussed in this book.

While failing to employ these techniques may not cause immediate harm to your project, timely corrective action can reduce the number of incidents of destructive conflict that have to be dealt with in the future — and it could just save your project altogether.

Warning sign 1 — Team members not following agreed-to rules.

Developing, documenting, and gaining leadership approval of project rules is only the first step in the deployment of project rules. Leaders must ensure team members are trained in the use of these rules as well. Furthermore, it is up to leaders to monitor teams for compliance with agreed-to team rules. This must be continual throughout the execution stage of the project. Training, and monitoring personnel to ensure the application of rules are integrated into daily work patterns, is a critical part of process deployment and ultimately to project success.

Warning sign 2 — Team members not using RFPM.

The RFPM is of no value, if it is not employed. Process engineers can define processes, but there is little they can do to deploy them. Team members listen to their leaders. If the leaders do not communicate the importance of using these vehicles (like the RFPM) in everyday operation, then they simply will not be used. When the RFPM is not being used, first look to the leaders to ensure they are setting the right example and sending the appropriate signals to the team.

Warning sign 3 — TARs not being used effectively

Project leaders must document and monitor tasks to ensure the communication pitfalls discussed earlier are not occurring. This implies the use of TARs in a disciplined fashion demonstrating task acceptance, and regular task statusing. The TAR should demonstrate a history of communication between the manager and the engineer ensuring task expectations are understood.

We discussed task assignment pitfalls in Chapter 3. In Chapter 4 we described recommended enhancements to the TAR to aid in avoiding miscommunication. Many virtual project difficulties can be traced to inconsistent task direction. Leaders must communicate with co leaders ensuring consistency of project vision. Leaders must also set appropriate examples by working through the organization, not around it.

7.11 Conclusion

Max Depree[1] tells us in his book that "intimacy is at the heart of competence." To demonstrate what he means he tells the story of a man who went to his regular restaurant for lunch only to find it unusually busy. While he managed to get a menu, before he could order he realized he would be late getting back to work. As a result he decided to skip lunch. On his way out he casually mentioned this to the cashier. That night the owner of the restaurant showed up at his house unannounced with enough dinner for two nights and told him he was providing it free of charge.

The techniques discussed in this chapter may not be the most exciting. They are about as exciting as a restaurant owner taking dinner to one of his customers.

We've talked about team rules, about documenting team decisions, and about clearly documenting task assignments. And we've talking about listening hard to your team, and doing whatever it takes to let team members know their views are important in every possible situation.

As mentioned earlier in this book, the techniques that help virtual teams most are not all that complicated. As stated at the start of this chapter, we are talking about who does what, when do they do it, and what products do they produce. In the final analysis, it is the team members who must execute, but it is the team leaders who must create the lighted path and provide the needed encouragement that allows them to succeed.

CHAPTER 7 KEY POINTS SUMMARY
Use ONE AND ONLY ONE LEAD for each second level team
Ensure responsibilities of "roving" and "hierarchical" leaders clear
Develop written charters with clear responsibilities
Minimize the use of organizational, or site-specific, terms or acronyms
Take definition of responsibility a step further through CPDM
Develop an RFPM incrementally
Understand work split issues
Define Architecture first
Use small group of senior personnel during critical front end stage
Use CPDM to drive out "architecture gaps"
Use four key products (see section 7.5) to aid in determining infrastructure needs
Use Mentoring for on the job guidance
Use rules, but not too many
Collocate global component teams to the maximum extent possible
Understand potential impact of varying leadership styles
Understand relationship between architecture and planning
Recognize the signs of "double-tasking" and take action to resolve
Recognize the signs of "no tasking" and take action to resolve
Work by consensus
Don't force formal documentation too soon
Keep the full team in the loop
Know what to do when an issue keeps repeating
Write your policy down and deploy it
Take the direct approach
Always be on the look out for unofficial "tiger teams"
Deploy the techniques discussed in this book

References

1. DePree, Max, *Leadership is an Art*, Dell, NY, 1989, pp. 48–49.
2. Mastenbroek, W.F.G., *Conflict Management and Organization Development*, Chichester, J. Wiley, 1993.
3. International Conference on Industrial Relations and Conflict Management, *Conflict Management and Industrial Relations*, Kluwer-Nijhoft, Boston, 1982.
4. Covey, Stephen R., *The Seven Habits of Highly Effective People*, Simon and Schuster, NY, 1989, p. 196.

8 | Conclusion

In the preface to this book we asked you to step outside your box — for just a moment — and imagine the possibilities. We then painted a scenario of a project moving forward as a single integrated team right from day one. That vision included subcontractors working as an extension of a prime contractor's own workforce, using project agreed-to tools, infrastructure, procedures, and strategies.

To understand the critical importance of succeeding in a multi-site/multi-corporation environment one only needs to examine the changes taking place inside today's workforce. According to a recent study conducted by the U. S. Bureau of Labor Statistics, approximately 25% of all workers age 16 or over have been with their current employer 12 months or less. The same study also indicates that the average worker is now expected to change jobs every 5 years.[1]

These statistics paint a picture of an increasingly mobile work force. The 20-year employee holding a wealth of corporate knowledge inside his head may well be a corporate asset of the past. At the same time, corporations are experiencing an increasing demand for software-intensive solutions produced from a combination of existing products and new development. This, in turn, is driving a greater demand for personnel with increasingly specialized software skills; that is, skills geared toward specific software products. Compounding this demand is the seemingly neverending shortening of cycle times to enter and succeed in new markets.

Within this demanding environment, even the largest of our mega-corporations are finding they can no longer maintain inside their own corporate walls all the critical skills necessary to compete in many new markets. As a result, today's companies are being driven to reach out in a cooperating manner to organizations previously viewed only as competitors.

8.1   The Virtual Company

Inside this dynamic environment the Virtual Company provides great potential for new business opportunities through rapid access to a deeper pool of personnel with broader skills. Through virtual collaboration two major obstacles of the past — distance and company boundaries — are removed. Nevertheless, while the required technologies exist, many corporations continue to face significant implementation-related challenges in moving their organizations toward productive virtual operations.

8.2   Summarizing Our Approach to the Collaborative Challenge

In the introduction to this book we presented four common collaborative problems identified by Booz-Allen research:

- Cultural incompatibility
- Leadership struggles
- Lack of trust
- Inbred notions of competition

While most agree with these findings, few practical answers have been forthcoming to date to resolve these dilemmas. Through our analysis of past collaborative projects as captured in the pages of this book, we have gained valuable insight into real underlying root causes. Our efforts, which admittedly have relied more on heuristics than science, have demonstrated that beneath surface level symptoms lies a tightly interconnected web of technical and non-technical factors. More importantly, by exposing these factors and their relationships to one another, we have been able to identify practical and affordable actions that project leaders can take today to help guide their virtual projects on a path to success.

8.3   A Final Note on the Informal Side

In this book we have examined closely how work actually gets done in traditional collocated engineering environments. In the process we have found ourselves analyzing to some depth the role played by the informal side of the engineering process. Some have expressed concern that this focus may encourage an increase in uncontrolled, unmanageable, unmeasurable project activities. In actuality, our intent has been the opposite; that is, to bring to light how reliance on informal activities fails us in the virtual world. Equally important has been our intent to provide manageable alternatives that can aid you, the reader, in avoiding these pitfalls in the future.

8.4 Virtual Project Strategies of the Future

In his book, *Systems Architecting of Organizations*, Eberhardt Rechtin tells us that excellence depends on context and he gives us an example based on the Hewlett Packard organization. Rechtin tells us that HP "proved unable in the 1970s to build profitable, large-scale, complex systems." He then explains that the difficulty was traced to "divisional autonomy; a strength in individual product lines, but a weakness in system integration."[2] This same lesson on the critical importance of "context" to success is equally applicable to virtual projects of the future.

We have witnessed through our tales the enormous productivity drain that often occurs when traditional collocated techniques are inappropriately applied in a virtual world. We have watched as attempts to coerce proud, mature, successful organizations into following out-of-context foreign prac tices have resulted in leadership struggles, mistrust, and destructive compet- itive team conflict.

Clearly, our virtual project strategies of the future must seek out creative ways to more effectively tap the strengths of our teammates in a manner that considers the full context of each of our teammate's resources.

Organizations that have attained advanced process maturity levels have done so for reasons that extend beyond documented procedures alone. Pro- cess maturity implies an enabling organization with a supporting infrastruc- ture and people who work within that structure — rather than around it — to solve real problems.

Nevertheless, to tap this strength requires recognition of, as well as an effective method to manage, the associated integration risk. This is the risk of products coming together across divergent organizations and fitting into a single integrated system that meets the customer's needs.

8.5 Making the Strategy Work

Throughout this book we have identified specific pitfalls, but have also sug- gested practical solutions. Many of the pitfalls have been traceable to the lack of a single integrated corporate memory. This was discussed earlier in the book.

To implement a strategy that works requires that we focus our attention on the critical points where people and products come together across divergent organizations and/or sites. This is the intent of our proposed Rapid Filtered Project Memory (RFPM) which focuses on the project-specific critical information that is most vulnerable to task miscommunication across organizational boundaries. The RFPM can be viewed as a first step toward a Virtual Culture.

8.6   Summarizing the Virtual Culture Concept

A virtual culture is a simple, yet powerful concept. Unlike site-specific cultures that have grown informally, and at their own pace, virtual cultures require more proactive management attention. Virtual cultures are more tangible, more product oriented, and more formal than traditional site-specific cultures. They must provide crisp, clear product and process definitions at those critical points where products and people come together across diverse organizations. If they are to take hold it is critical that our virtual cultures receive full team leadership support.

8.7   Sample Products from a Virtual Culture

In the appendices to this book there are 24 products, along with examples of their uses. Each one is provided specifically to address one or more of the common pitfalls identified in Chapter 7 and discussed in earlier chapters. A cross-reference is also provided as a guide for the reader to sections where related pitfalls are discussed. These products are a starting point for your project's virtual culture. Below is a summary of the products included in the appendices:

- Templates
  - Virtual Project Organization
  - Rapid Filtered Project Memory (RFPM)
- Forms
  - Global Component Criteria
  - Global Component Identification and Responsibility
  - Component Product Development Matrix (CPDM)
  - Task Assignment Record (TAR)

- ■ Infrastructure Common Requirements
- ■ Criteria
  - ■ Virtual Team Leader Selection Criteria
  - ■ Entry Criteria for each of 8 steps in setting up a virtual project
- ■ Warning signs
  - ■ Destructive conflict
  - ■ Non-compliance with preventative maintenance techniques
- ■ Checklists
  - ■ Cost guidance
  - ■ Build plan
  - ■ Integration plan
  - ■ Global component integration
  - ■ Infrastructure
  - ■ Component Product Development Matrix
  - ■ Virtual Project Organization
  - ■ Operational Models for leader discussions
  - ■ Virtual Team Charter
- ■ Rules
  - ■ Virtual team
  - ■ E-mail
  - ■ Teleconferencing
  - ■ Leadership/manager

8.8   The Philosophy of a Virtual Culture

The philosophy of a virtual culture is based on clear definitions of work products at the points where tight coupling across organizations must exist. A well-defined virtual culture should support not only the integration of products across organizations, but also a freedom-line concept allowing individual teaming organizations maximum and effective usage of their internal resources.

The freedom line concept is a natural byproduct of a well-defined product-oriented virtual culture. First-generation virtual projects have demonstrated that we cannot rely on word of mouth or chance hallway meetings for communication of critical project information.

Our intent through the virtual culture is not to replace site-specific organizational cultures that have grown and matured over years and are today a crucial part of what makes a mature organization mature. In fact, we do not believe one can replace, nor should one even try, strong and proven site-specific organizational cultures. Virtual cultures serve a different purpose. They provide a key missing link.

8.9 Virtual Cultures of the Future

Effective virtual cultures of the future must be complementary to, rather than competitive with, long-standing site-specific cultures. While this may sound simple, experience has shown that its implementation requires painstaking attention to detail in establishing clear and crisp agreed-to terminology, product definitions, product attributes, required tools, and agreed-to project critical issues that only constrain teammates where absolutely necessary to meet the needs of the end-product customer deliverables. The criticality of leadership support in achieving an effective product-oriented virtual culture should never be underestimated.

8.10 What Should You Do Now?

What we recommend that you do now depends on the current state of your virtual project. In Figure 8.1 is a flowchart to help you determine the next step to take.

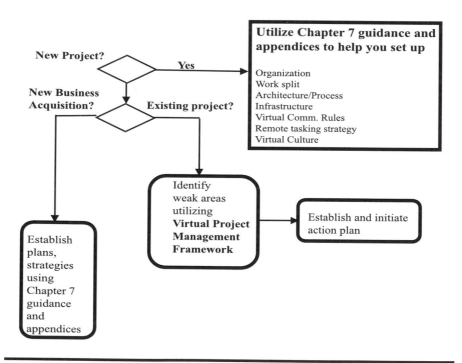

Figure 8.1   Determining Your Next Step

8.10.1 New Projects

If the project is new, utilize the guidance provided in the 8-step plan in Chapter 7. To help set up the project and to establish an initial virtual culture, refer to Appendices A through J.

The products provided in the Appendices, along with the guidance in earlier chapters, can help get the project started on the right path. However, do not use these products directly "out of the box."

Your project leadership team should work together to tailor this material to the specific project's needs. Recognize that this is not something that can be done quickly, although using the guidance provided can give a significant jump-start in leveraging the lessons from many predecessor virtual projects. Nevertheless, anticipate work assignments, actions, follow-up and ongoing maintenance and awareness training to effectively implement the recommendations provided.

To help guide your efforts, in the introduction to Appendices C through I there is a cross-reference to the appropriate sections of the book that describe related pitfalls and other rationale for use of the associated products.

Be aware that this process is only a first step. You are putting in place a key framework to aid in executing a successful virtual project, but effective deployment will require continual leadership guidance and follow-up.

8.10.2 Existing Projects

If the project is already underway and you don't have the luxury to start over and fix things you now know you would do differently, you can still use the material provided in this book and in the appendices. However, in this case, we suggest you employ our Virtual Project Management Framework to help assess the current project state.

8.11 The Virtual Project Management Framework

You can think of the virtual project management framework as a four-level maturity framework specifically developed for virtual projects. (See Figure 8.2.) Each level is described further below.

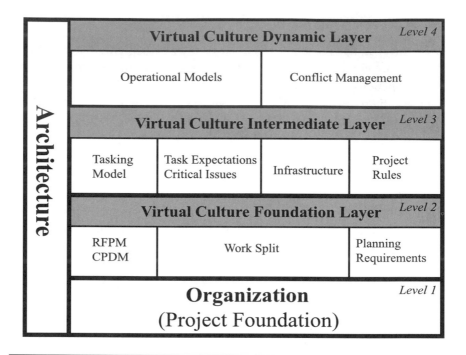

Figure 8.2 The Virtual Project Management Framework

8.11.1 Level 1 — The Organization

The organization, or project foundation, provides the first level of the framework. This corresponds to step one of our eight-step process.

8.11.2 Level 2 — The Virtual Culture Foundation Layer

The second level, the virtual culture foundation layer, provides the virtual foundational elements: work split, setting up the RFPM, defining CPDMs, and planning. This level relates to steps 2 and 3 of our process.

8.11.3 Level 3 — The Virtual Culture Intermediate Layer

The third level, the virtual culture intermediate layer, is where we find our tasking model, infrastructure, and project rules.

8.11.4 Level 4 — The Virtual Culture Dynamic Layer

Level 4, our dynamic layer, is where we encounter operational models and conflict management issues.

8.12 How to Use the Framework

The virtual project management framework can help evaluate an existing project by providing guidance to determine the key questions to ask to help isolate critical areas. Related questions include, but are not limited to:

- Is the technical architecture well-defined and controlled?
- Are the foundational elements in place and working effectively on the project?
  - Work split well-defined?
  - Build and integration plans in place?
- Do we have a sound intermediate layer?
  - Are tasking and task expectation clear and working effectively in remote situations?
  - Are the common elements of infrastructure well-defined and in place?
  - Are we utilizing our virtual communication technologies effectively?
    - Have rules been defined and are they being followed?
- Is our dynamic layer operating effectively?
  - Are we taking appropriate action when the warning signs of destructive conflict appear?

Some have argued that the dynamic layer is really a foundational element, and therefore should be on the bottom of the framework rather than the top. We have chosen to place the dynamic layer at the top level because the real reason unhealthy conflict (leadership struggles) exists is failure to take the key actions most often found in the bottom three layers of our framework.

It is also worth noting that we have portrayed architecture as integral to each level of our framework. This reflects the criticality of architecture as both a fundamental building block, and a common point of reference for all project decisions. By addressing the real underlying issues, and by addressing them in the right order and in an integrated fashion, we provide our best chance for project success.

References

1. Gannett News Service, "Job hopping by young workers increasingly common," August 29, 1999.
2. Rechtin, Eberhardt, *Systems Architecting of Organizations*, CRC Press, Boca Raton, FL, 1999, preface p. v.

APPENDICES

Introduction

In the appendices that follow you will find:

- CPDM Guidance
- Terminology
- Templates
- Forms
- Sample Forms
- Criteria
- Warning Signs
- Checklists
- Rules

Our intention in providing this material is to aid the reader in the process of setting up a new virtual project. This material can also be used as a guide in assessing an ongoing project.

We recommend that you tailor the templates, forms, criteria, warning signs, and rules based on your own experiences and the specific needs of your project. In particular, the rules, and warning signs provided are intended to provide the reader with a starting point based on observations from past virtual projects.

To help in guiding the decision-making process Table C.1 is a cross-reference between the products provided in the appendices and the chapters and sections of the book where associated pitfalls or rationale are discussed.

Appendix A: Component-Product Development Matrix(CPDM) Implementation Guidance

A.1 Example of Potential Task Miscommunication — Requirements Specification

Historically, English language specifications have been employed to develop formal testable requirements specifications. Today "Use Cases" are becoming more popular and are being employed in many organizations as an alternative to the more traditional and formal English language specifications.

This movement to decreased formality of requirements specifications, however, is by no means universal. We see certain organizations continuing to hold firmly to the more traditional and formal specification approach, while still others have chosen a hybrid (combination of both) approach. Due to variances in approaches, as seen in the requirements, architecture, and database areas (and these are only examples — more exist), on virtual projects we need more effective methods to communicate chosen approaches. In particular, on virtual projects, the informal mechanisms relied upon in the past tend to break down. This is a primary motivation for the use of a component-product development matrix. See Table A.1 for an example of two requirements component-products: System Requirements and Use Cases. They are discussed further in the requirements Section A2.1. Table A.2 provides an example of a data requirements sheet component product.

Table A.1 Example of a Component-Product Development Matrix (CPDM)

Component-Product	Description/Reference	Tool/Form	Phase	Location	Responsibility
System Requirements	Ref. Rqts Procedure	DOORS	Requirements	DOORS Database	SE
Use Cases	Ref. UML Methodology	Rational ROSE	Requirements	SEN	SE
Database Requirements	Ref DB Reqts Procedure	Data Reqts Sheet	Requirements	SEN	SE
High Level Packages	Ref. UML Methodology	Rational ROSE	Preliminary Design	SDF	Arch
Top level Design rationale, risks	Ref. CPDM	Microsoft WORD	Preliminary Design	SDF	Arch
Process Arch. Diagram (PAD)	Ref. "Use Cases Combined with Booch OMT UML"	Rational ROSE	Preliminary Design	SDF	Arch
Process to Class Alloc Diagram (PCAD)	Ref. "Use Cases…" text	Rational ROSE	Preliminary Design	SDF	Arch
Process Interaction Diagram (PID)	Ref. "Use Cases…" text	Rational ROSE	Preliminary Design	SDF	Arch
Major Classes, Methods, and Attributes	Ref. UML Methodology	Rational ROSE	Preliminary Design	SDF	Arch
Major Classes, Methods, Attr	Ref. UML Methodology	Rational ROSE	Detailed Design	SDF	SW
Database Design	Ref. DB Design Proc.	E-R Modeling Tool	Detailed Design	SDF	SW
Critical algorithms	Ref. Design Procedure	WORD, ROSE	Detailed Design	SDF	SE
Interaction Diagrams	Ref. UML Methodology	Rational ROSE	Detailed Design	SDF	SW
Detailed Classes, Methods, and Attributes	Ref. UML Methodology, detailed design procedure	Rational ROSE	Detailed Design	SDF	SW
Detailed design rationale	Ref. CPDM	Microsoft WORD	Detailed Design	SDF	SW
Detailed algorithms	Ref. Design Procedure	WORD, ROSE	Detailed Design	SDF	SW
Component assumptions, risks	Ref. Design Procedure	Microsoft WORD	Detailed Design	SDF	SW

Table A.1   Example of a Component-Product Development Matrix (CPDM) (Continued)

Component-Product	Description/Reference	Tool/Form	Phase	Location	Responsibility
Program Design Language	Ref. PDL Procedure	Source Code Editor	Detailed Design	SDF	SW
Code	Ref. Coding Standard	Language Compiler	Code and Unit Test	SDF	SW

Table A.2   Data Requirements Sheet: Component-Product Example

Data Item Name	Data Item Description	Constraints/Ranges
Name	Personnel name with middle initial	25 Characters
Social Security Number	Standard SSN format	With dashes
Courses Completed	Linked list of all courses completed	4 A/N digit identifier
Courses in Progress	Linked list of all courses in progress	4 A/N digit identifier
Grades	Linked list of grades and related course.	Range 0 to 100%. Needs to be available for all courses, or just those completed

A.2   CPDM Implementation Guidance

A.2.1 Requirements

As mentioned in Section A.1 of this appendix, we have found requirements definition and documentation to be a likely area of miscommunication due to today's varying approaches within different organizations. In Table A.1 two requirements-related artifacts are identified. The artifact referred to as System Requirements is produced following a traditional requirements definition process. For this artifact, English language requirements are entered into a requirements management database through a tool called DOORS, as identified in the table.

There also exists a "Use Case" artifact produced in accordance with the UML methodology, which is rapidly becoming a universal standard modeling language for object-oriented systems. The use of standards in the CPDM, such as UML, is highly encouraged.

By constructing requirements artifacts and placing them in a CPDM with the appropriate attributes, one can communicate concisely:

- What requirement component-products a project has agreed to produce
- What tool(s) is(are) used in support of requirements management
- What phase the requirements artifact is produced in
- Where the artifact is maintained
- What specific organizational entity is responsible to ensure the artifact is produced when required

A.2.2 Detailed Design

In examining closely many corporate level standard detailed design procedures, design guidance, the type many software engineers in the trenches need on a daily basis, is missing. This type of guidance includes answers to the following questions:

- Where **specifically** does preliminary design/architecture end, and detailed design begin?
- Where does detailed design end, and the coding begin?
- Are header files done as part of detailed design, or the coding phase?
- Is PDL required? If so, is it placed in the header file? Is there a PDL standard?
- When is the PDL required?
- How much detail do we provide in the Object Model?
- Are there low level methods that are only documented in the code?
- Are we using the code auto-generation feature of the object-modeling design tool?
- How are the Object Model and the PDL maintained consistently?
- Do we have a naming convention?
- Are there any limitations on the use of the object modeling tool?
- What is the complete set of detailed design artifacts required to enter the coding phase?

These are the types of questions many software engineers ask when it comes to actually doing their assigned work. Many of the answers to these questions cannot be found in corporate procedures because the answers are **project specific**.

The development of a completely tailored project-specific detailed design procedure is often costly to build and maintain. On the other hand, a CPDM can answer many of these questions in concise and cost-effective manner.

A.2.3 Code

When it comes to the coding phase there is greater likelihood of a corporate coding standard that can be applied directly to the project. Nevertheless, there are still project-specific questions that need to be answered and communicated consistently across the team. Coding issues that may require project-specific information include

- File header formats
- Naming conventions
- Compiler-specific dependencies
- Hardware dependencies

The strict use of a standard coding guide (i.e., ANSI) is highly recommended, along with a compiler that meets this standard. Compilers that support multiple hardware platforms are also recommended. Although today you may be focusing on a single hardware platform it is always a good idea to develop portable software and utilize a compiler vendor that allows you to keep future options open.

A.3 Sample CPDM for a Reusable Piece of Software

The primary reason for allowing multiple CPDMs to be approved on the same project is in support of the reuse of existing software products. When it has been deemed cost effective to reuse an existing software component, it is likely the component may have been developed in a different language or requires support tools different than those chosen for the newly developed software on the project. In these cases a CPDM should be created and approved indicating what software development/maintenance requirements have been placed on the reusable component by the project. Table A.3 provides a sample CPDM for a reusable software component.

Table A.3   Sample Reusable Software Component CPDM

Component-Product	Description/ Reference	Tool/Form	Phase	Location	Responsibility
System Requirements	Ref. Rqts Procedure	DOORS	Requirements	DOORS Database	SE
Database Requirements	Ref DB Reqts Procedure	Data Reqts Sheet	Requirements	SEN	SE
High Level Packages	Ref. UML Methodology	Rational ROSE	Preliminary Design	SDF	Arch
Process Arch. Diagram (PAD)	Ref. "Use Cases Combined with Booch OMT UML"	Rational ROSE	Preliminary Design	SDF	Arch
Process to Class Alloc Diagram (PCAD)	Ref. "Use Cases…" text	Rational ROSE	Preliminary Design	SDF	Arch
Code	Ref. Coding Standard	Language Compiler	Code and Unit Test	SDF	SW

Note that in Table A.3 the System Requirements component-product is still called out, along with a database requirements component product, three architecture component products, and the code. What is noticeably missing is the requirement for Use Cases, detailed design, PDL, and algorithms. This example is not intended to reflect a recommendation for component-products for reusable software. Its only intention is to demonstrate the flexibility of the CPDM in crisply specifying your agreed-to project requirements.

Refer to Appendix E for more CPDM examples.

Appendix B: Definitions

Artifact-Evolutionary Approach: A popular approach to software development based on an incremental build approach where a pre-defined artifact set is partially completed during each build.

Associative Memory: The process used by engineers to abstract by recognizing familiar features in current problems that may be similar to features in problems they have solved in their past.

Component: The term Component is often heard today with regard to component-based architectures. A component has a clear specification. It is executable, like the global component, but a component, as used, doesn't necessarily include other related life-cycle artifacts, such as requirements, source code, design artifacts, and test cases. All of these related artifacts are an essential part of a global component.

Component-Product: Any piece-part artifact produced by one group in the organization upon which another group depends.

CPDM: Component-Product Development Matrix. A table that lists specific artifacts (component-products) to be developed, along with the following artifact-related attributes:

- Brief description of artifact or reference to description
- Tool(s) used to develop artifact
- In what project phase the artifact is developed
- Location where artifact is maintained
- Project-specific organizational entity responsible for artifact

Computer Software Component (CSC): The term Computer Software Component (CSC) has been used in the past as a management aid to define and document a chunk of software. CSCs may or may not be executable, unlike global components, which are executable and testable.

Corporate Memory: Whatever system your team has in place to retain the knowledge to repeatably manufacture your product.

Culture: Emphasizes the fundamental framework which people take for granted in their social and occupational activities.

Global Component: A logically related set of component-products that meet the following criteria:

- Contains a well-defined set of requirements
- Includes design component-product artifacts
- Includes source code component-product artifacts
- Includes standalone test component-product artifacts (test cases, and results)
- Is executable and testable
- Meets a set of specified architecture constraints

Global Process Level: The integration process level.

Hierarchical Leaders: Project team leaders with ultimate responsibility and accountability.

Immature Organization: An organization that exhibits the following characteristics:

- Even if the software process has been specified, it is not rigorously followed, or enforced
- Activities are reactionary — focus on solving immediate crisis (fire-fighting)
- Schedules, budgets are routinely exceeded
- Product functionality and quality often compromised
- No objective basis for judging product quality exists

Incremental Build: A popular approach to system development whereby each phase of the life cycle is repeated a number of times, with each complete cycle addressing a coherent subset of the total system requirements.

Local Process Level: Site-specific processes below the freedom line that are allowed to be employed in the production of a global component.

Mature Organization: An organization that has the following characteristics:

- Processes fit the work actually done by engineers
- Managers have visibility into actual product development and quality

- Engineers understand the value in following the processes
- Support infrastructure exists

Package: The term package, as used within the UML modeling language, is defined to be a logical collection of classes. It is an analysis and design construct. A global component includes analysis and design artifacts (such as a package), but it also must include implementation artifacts (code), and other related documentation artifacts as well.

PAD: Process Architecture Diagram. A standard architecture diagram described in the text *Use Cases Combined with Booch, OMT, UML*.

PCAD: Process to Class Allocation Diagram (PCAD). A standard architecture diagram described in the text *Use Cases Combined with Booch, OMT, UML*.

PID: Process Interaction Diagram. A standard architecture diagram described in the text *Use Cases Combined with Booch, OMT, UML*.

Productivity: The effectiveness with which resources are utilized.

RFPM: Rapid Filtered Project Memory. Used to address the lack of a single integrated corporate memory.

Roving Leaders: Those who lead through influence (mentors), rather than through the direct hierarchical chain.

Schizophrenic Project Memory: The condition that occurs when multiple competing vibrant and growing subcultures supported by multiple and conflicting experiences exist within the same project.

Self-Directed Team: An integrated product team approach coupled with a reduction of external management support.

Software Architecture: The structure of the components of a program/system, their interrelationships, and principles and guidelines governing their design and evolution over time.

Task Assignment Record: Mechanism used in some organizations to formally define an engineer's task.

Tiger Team: A temporary working group formed with a specific objective and a stringent schedule. Tiger teams exhibit the following five characteristics:

- Small
- Temporary
- Collocated
- Tight schedule
- Clear and limited objectives

Triage: To sort.

Trigger Points or "Light-Bulbs": Unplanned knowledge discovering points.

UML: Unified Modeling Language. Universally accepted object-oriented standard modeling language.

Appendix C: Templates

This appendix has two templates. See Figure C.1 for a Virtual Project Organization Template. See Figure C.2 for a Rapid Filtered Project Memory Template.

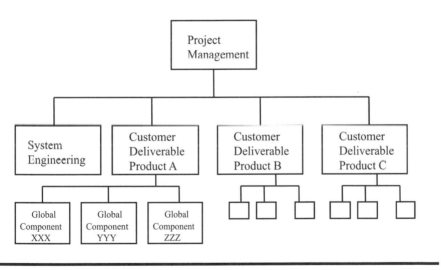

Figure C.1   Virtual Project Organization Template

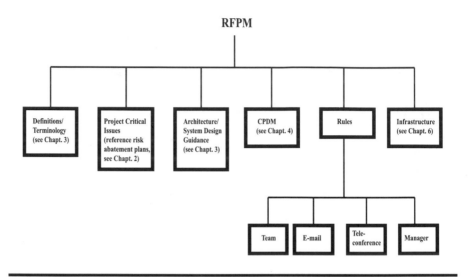

Figure C.2   Rapid Filtered Project Memory (RFPM) Template

Table C.1 Product to Chapter Cross-Reference

Appendix	Product Identifier	Chapter
C	Virtual Project Organization	1; 3, 3.3; 7, 7.3
	Rapid Filtered Project Memory (RFPM)	2, 2.6; 4; 5, 5.3
D	Global Component Criteria	6, 6.5
	Global Component Identification and Responsibility	6, 6.5
	Component Product Development Matrix (CPDM)	4, 4.3, 4.4, 4.5, 4.6; 7, 7.4
	Task Assignment Record (TAR)	1, 1.6; 4, 4.4
	Infrastructure common requirements	7, 7.6
F	Virtual Team Leader Selection Criteria	5; 7, 7.3
	Entry Criteria for each of 8 steps in setting up a virtual organization	7
G	Destructive conflict	2; 3; 5; 7, 7.9, 7.10
	Non-compliance with preventative maintenance techniques	7, 7.10
H	Costing guidance	Frequently Asked Questions
	Build plan	7, 7.5
	Integration plan	7, 7.5
	Global component integration	6, 6.5; 7, 7.7, 7.8
	Infrastructure	7, 7.6
	Component Product Development Matrix (CPDM)	4, 4.3, 4.4, 4.5, 4.6; 7, 7.4
	Virtual Project Organization	7, 7.3
	Operational models for leader discussions	7, 7.3, 7.9
	Virtual team charter development checklist	7, 7.3
I	Virtual Team	5, 5.1, 5.3; 7, 7.6
	E-mail	5, 5.2, 5.3; 7, 7.6
	Teleconferencing	5, 5.2, 5.3; 7, 7.6
	Leadership/manager	5, 5.1, 5.3; 7, 7.6

Appendix D: Forms

This appendix contains forms that can be employed in support of planning and task management on a distributed project. Use the forms provided as a starting point, tailoring them to your project's specific needs. Forms provided include

- Global component criteria form
- Global component identification and responsibility form
- Component product development matrix form
- Task assignment record form
- Infrastructure common requirements form

Global component criteria form	
Contains a well-defined set of requirements	
Includes design component-product artifacts	
Includes source code component-product artifacts	
Includes standalone test component-product artifacts (test cases, results)	
Is executable and testable	
Meets a complete set of specified architecture constraints	
Architecture constraint 1:	
Architecture constraint 2:	
…	
Architecture constraint N:	

Global component identification & responsibility form	
Global component identifier	**Responsible site/team**

Component-product development matrix form					
Artifact	Description/ Reference	Tool/Form	Phase	Location	Responsibility

Task Assignment Record form

Project Identifier	
Department Identifier	
Task Identifier	
Task Authorization	
Responsible Manager	
Assigned Engineer	
Budget	
Planned Start Date	
Planned Complete Date	
Actual Complete Date	
Task Description	
Component-Products Produced	
Dependent Component-Products	
Status/Comments —	
Status/Comments –	

Infrastructure common requirements form	
HARDWARE:	
SOFTWARE:	
SUPPORT:	

Appendix E: Sample Forms

Global component criteria example	
Contains a well-defined set of requirements	
Includes design component-product artifacts	
Includes source code component-product artifacts	
Includes standalone test component-product artifacts (test cases, results)	
Is executable and testable	
Meets a complete set of specified architecture constraints	
Architecture constraint 1: Must execute on a SUN target platform	
Architecture constraint 2: Must employ the XYZ Application Programmer Interface (API) for all system service needs	
Architecture constraint 3: Must employ the services identified in the VVV specification for all external component interfacing	
Architecture constraint 4: Must employ the services and guidance provided in the RRR Database Designers Guide in the design and access of all system databases	

Component-product development matrix example					
Component-product	Description/ Reference	Tool/ Form	Phase	Location	Responsibility
System Requirements	Ref. Rqts. Procedure	DOORS	Requirements	DOORS Database	SE
Use Cases	Ref. UML Methodology	Rational ROSE	Requirements	SEN	SE
Database Requirements	Ref DB Reqts. Procedure	Data Reqts Sheet	Requirements	SEN	SE
Major Classes, Methods, Attributes	Ref. UML Methodology	Rational ROSE	Detailed Design	SDF	SW
Database Design	Ref. DB Design Proc.	E-R Modeling Tool	Detailed Design	SDF	SW
Critical Algorithms	Ref. Design Procedure	WORD, ROSE	Detailed Design	SDF	SE
Interaction Diagrams	Ref. UML Methodology	Rational ROSE	Detailed Design	SDF	SW
Detailed Classes, Methods, and Attributes	Ref. UML Methodology, Detailed Design Procedure	Rational ROSE	Detailed Design	SDF	SW
Detailed Algorithms	Ref. Design Procedure	WORD, ROSE	Detailed Design	SDF	SW
Component Assumptions, Risks	Ref. Design Procedure	Microsoft WORD	Detailed Design	SDF	SW
Program Design Language	Ref. PDL Procedure	Source Code Editor	Detailed Design	SDF	SW
Code	Ref. Coding Standard	Language Compiler	Code and Unit Test	SDF	SW

CPDM architecture example

Component-product	Description/ Reference	Tool/ Form	Phase	Location	Responsibility
High Level Packages	Ref. UML Methodology	Rational ROSE	Preliminary Design	SDF	Arch
Top Level Design Rationale/Risks	Textual Description	Microsoft WORD	Preliminary Design	SDF	Arch
Process Architecture Diagram (PAD)	Ref. "Use Cases Combined with Booch OMT UML"	Rational ROSE	Preliminary Design	SDF	Arch
Process to Class Allocation Diagram (PCAD)	Ref. "Use Cases…" text	Rational ROSE	Preliminary Design	SDF	Arch
Process Interaction Diagram (PID)	Ref. "Use Cases…" text	Rational ROSE	Preliminary Design	SDF	Arch
Major Classes, Methods, and Attributes	Ref. UML Methodology	Rational ROSE	Preliminary Design	SDF	Arch

Sample Task Assignment Record

Project Identifier	Z234
Department Identifier	Database Engineering
Task Identifier	TYYY
Task Authorization	Contract Charge Number
Responsible Manager	Charlie
Assigned Engineer	Fred
Budget	160 hours
Planned Start Date	June 26, 2002
Planned Complete Date	July 31, 2002
Actual Complete Date	
Task Description	Produce Data Model for Z234 project
Component-Products Produced	E-R Data Model and DDL—refer to CPDM for details
Dependent Component-Products	Data Requirements Sheet (SE)
Status/Comments —	Week ending June 19—Assigned engineer Anticipate two day slip due to late delivery of dependent component product.
Status/Comments --	Week ending June 19—Responsible manager Slip will not impact project critical path

Appendix F: Criteria

This appendix provides criteria to aid in the selection of virtual team leaders, and to assist leaders in evaluating a project's readiness to enter each of the eight steps identified in Chapter 7.

Virtual team leader selection focused criteria	
Strong communication skills	
Open mind—willingness to consider alternatives	
Strong conflict management and resolution skills	
Technical-management experience, knowledge and desire	

Entry criteria to step 1—define high level org.	
Identification of project leadership team	

Entry criteria to step 2—define work split	
High level organization established	
Program manager, system engineering lead, and product team leads assigned in accordance with team lead criteria	
Charters written with clearly defined responsibilities in accordance with virtual team charter development checklist	
Rapid Filtered Project Memory (RFPM) initiated	

Entry criteria to step 3—define system planning	
Same as step 2	

Entry criteria to step 4—define special tasks	
Same as step 2	

Entry criteria to step 5— define 3rd level of org.	
First evolution of architecture established and placed under baseline control	
CPDM approved	
Global component criteria approved	
Work split established	

Entry criteria to step 6— detailed planning

First generation of architecture defined and placed under baseline control?	
Work split approach and decision complete?	
CPDM complete and approved?	
Global component criteria complete and approved?	
Build plan complete?	
Integration plan complete or in process?	

Step 7—Define entry criteria to test the organization

Project rules approved and deployed	
Infrastructure plan approved (includes all sites)	
Remote task assignments defined through Task Assignment Records (TARs)	
Integration plan baselined	

Step 8—Define entry criteria for project execution

Requirements baselined	
Integration plan baselined	
Third level of organization established with team leaders assigned	
Detailed planning complete	

Appendix G: Warning Signs

Destructive conflict warning signs	
Repeating issue sign	
Non-compliance with team information sharing policy	
"They're out to steal our business" message	
The "quiet sign"	

Warning signs-non-compliance with preventative maintenance techniques	
Team members not following agreed to rules	
Team members not using RFPM	
TARs not being used effectively	

Appendix H: Checklists

Costing guidance checklist	
Partition costing task into two pieces:	
a.) Global Component Development cost	
b.) Integration cost	
a.) Global Component Development cost	
Estimate cost of development of assigned global components for your site based on historical data utilizing following guidance:	
Use the CPDM and Global Component Criteria in considering the following development cost factors:	
Is the project leveraging local site established processes?	
Is the project leveraging a local existing and proven infrastructure?	
Does the architecture constraints require the development team to utilize a test platform that they do not have prior experience with?	
Consider the team's prior experience with respect to additional specified architecture constraints	
Does the development team have prior experience with the required programming language and compiler?	
Does the development team have prior experience with the required development methodology and tool set?	
b.) Integration cost	
Is integration planned for a remote site?	
Consider tool availability at the remote site	
Test tools	
Configuration management tools	
Consider change process at remote site	
Has a proven change process been established at the remote site?	
Consider the potential costs associated with processing changes through two change management systems	
Consider travel costs to remote site	

Build plan checklist	
Number of builds identified?	
Strategy for each build identified?	
Start and stop dates (high level schedule) for each build identified?	

Integration plan checklist	
Have all global components and site responsibilities been identified?	
Have all planned integration sites been identified?	
Has the required infrastructure to support all planned integration sites been identified?	
Will the required infrastructure be available to support the integration plan?	
Has the change management process during integration been established?	
Have entry criteria to integration been established and agreed to?	
Have trade-offs of "mini" integrations been considered?	
Has the impact of "overlapping" builds been considered in the plan?	

Checklist for global component integration

Global component product criteria established and agreed to?	
Are the requirements for all products clear, documented, and controlled?	
Has agreement been reached on design methodology and documentation?	
Has agreement been reached on the programming language and compiler?	
Has agreement been reached on the testing approach?	
Are the architectural constraints well-defined and agreed to?	
Has agreement been reached on the platform for testing prior to integration?	
Has agreement been reached on the integration platform?	
Has the integration site been agreed to?	
Does the integration site have the required infrastructure needs?	
_ Hardware?	
_ Software?	
_ Support?	
Have members from all key sites been invited to appropriate reviews?	
Has agreement been reached on the integration schedule?	
Has agreement been reached on the specific requirements to be tested at integration?	
Has the approval process been agreed to?	

Infrastructure checklist	
HARDWARE:	
Development environment	
Test environment	
Integration environment	
Target environment	
Host environment	
Configurations (centralized, federated, distributed)	
SOFTWARE:	
Requirements management tools	
Design tools	
Compilers	
Test tools	
Integration tools	
Debuggers	
Configuration management tools	
Load management tools	
SUPPORT:	
Configuration management (CM)	
Quality Assurance (QA)	
Technical Publications	
Systems Administration (backups, network management, load management)	

CPDM checklist	
Does a CPDM exist for all products under development?	
Is the description of each component product clear?	
Has the responsibility for each component product been allocated to an existing team in the organization?	
Is this allocation consistent with the team charters and has the team accepted the responsibility?	
Has the tool and/or format required of each component product been agreed to?	
Is the tool available as part of the site infrastructure where the component product will be developed?	
Has the phase when each component product will be completed been identified?	
Does the assigned team accept the responsibility to produce the component product in the identified phase?	

Checklist for setting up a virtual project organization	
Is the responsibility for each end-product deliverable clearly assigned to a single integrated product team in the organization?	
Are the products of the system engineering organization well-defined?	
Is the relationship between the system engineering organization and the end-product teams well-defined and captured in charters?	
Do the organizational team leaders meet the virtual team leader focused criteria?	
Are the third level organizational teams defined and have clearly defined (global component) responsibility?	
Do team charters identify specific product level responsibilities (or refer to a CPDM with this information)?	
Has the use of site-specific terms been minimized in team charters?	
Are the third level teams collocated?	
Are all component products that are the responsibility of each third level team defined?	
Does an approved CPDM exist for all work being done for each third level team?	
Does an approved global component criteria exist providing the criteria for a successful product hand-over?	

Operational models for leader discussion checklist	
Tasking model (strict vs. loose—hierarchical, roving)	
Tasking model (strict vs. loose—new tasks (risk management) entering process	
Customer communication (formal deliverables, minutes of meeting, action items, white papers) process	

Virtual team charter development checklist	
Minimize the use of organizational, or site-specific, terms or acronyms	
Avoid ambiguous responsibility statements	
Reference a CPDM for clearly defined component-product responsibilities	

Appendix I: Rules

Virtual team rules	
Abide by team information sharing policy	
Use collocation for critical front-end design activities	
Minimize the use of tiger teams	
When tiger teams are employed, use full team as a "checkpoint"	
Respect team members at all times	
Listen to team members first	
Recognize that "having a say is different than having a vote"	

E-mail rules	
Establish and employ project distribution lists	
Establish format and response rules	
Try not to use e-mail for task assignments, but when necessary follow-up with phone call	

Teleconferencing rules	
Ensure speaker is near receiver and all participants can hear	
Minimize use of mute button	
Provide handouts and presentation material early	
Be aware of presentation style issues that are not conducive to teleconferencing (i.e., pointing to slide)	

Leadership/manager rules	
Be aware of messages to personnel that "limit" dedication to a task or give "double" message	
Give team authority as well as responsibility for team decisions	
Use tiger teams with caution, always involving full team participation in at least a review role	
Utilize "conflict" warning signs to help in determining appropriate intervention point	

Appendix J: Frequently Asked Questions

The questions provided in this appendix have been posed to the author by virtual project leaders and reviewers of this book. Some of the answers extend beyond the book's current material representing the latest thinking on virtual project management strategies.

J.1 Management Questions

1.1 Question: *The book is titled "Virtual Project Management," but it contains technical information that goes beyond what is traditionally thought of as management issues. Why is this information included?*

Answer: In virtual environments the difficulties often faced can be traced to the point where an issue is categorized as technical or managerial. For example, many consider work split, organizational issues, risks, and tasking of personnel as management issues. On the other hand, architecture and infrastructure are viewed as belonging to the technical domain. Nevertheless, work split decisions have a profound impact on site-specific infrastructure needs, and these decisions can fracture a sound architecture.

While many think of architecture as technical, it is also tightly coupled to the organization and to cost and schedule. Architecture is also an effective task management tool which helps coordinate and communicate task expectations.

While many tend to look at a problem from the management or the technical perspective, it is the integrated perspective that often is most critical to virtual project success. Throughout this book we have attempted to take the integrated perspective, and in doing so it has, at times, required talking about technical and management issues as if they are one. In reality, the management and technical side are two tightly interconnected sides of the same problem.

1.2 Question: *Some of the recommendations in this book appear contradictory. It recommends a strategy of leveraging the strengths of teammates, but at the same time alludes to a single integrated team employing common tools, infrastructure, and technical and management strategies. How can we have both at the same time?*

Answer: To understand the answer to this question requires a discussion of the freedom line concept. First, it must be understood that all processes in all organizations have freedom lines. Even within highly structured single-site organizations a point at which freedom is exercised exists. Key to the recommended strategy for virtual projects is the adoption of a project freedom line concept implemented at the points where products and people must come together across different organizations or sites.

Many of the recommendations in this book have been directed at resolving miscommunication associated with two key points where products and people must come together on virtual projects. These points include

- Front-end architecture
- Global component hand-over point for integration

When recommending common tools, infrastructure, and technical and management strategies it is with respect to these critical points. This allows the granting of freedom inside the development of each global component at each site. By clearly defining points of commonality, we also establish where freedom can exist. This leads to an optimum balance of leveraged teammate strengths and a single common approach to manage integration risk.

1.3 Question: *Do you think managers can be trained to allow desirable conflict, or is it just an innate characteristic of certain managers?*

Answer: By training managers to recognize key warning signs of both healthy and destructive conflict managers can learn when it is best to intervene, and when the team should be allowed to work through an issue without external intervention.

1.4 Question: *The purpose of step seven of the eight-step process is unclear. Is the purpose to change certain managers' style of management?*

Answer: The purpose of step seven isn't to change any individual manager's management style. The purpose is to raise the awareness of the full leadership team to the existence of differing management styles and how these styles can affect day-to-day engineering operations. Leaders should discuss openly their expectations with respect to the following activities:

- "Direction" vs. "Guidance" for tasking an engineer
- The role of hierarchical leaders vs. roving leaders within the organization
- How new work gets "triggered" into action within the organization (i.e., risk review board decisions)
- The approval process for all types of communication (including artifact delivery) with the customer

These issues affect real day-to-day engineering operations and can often cause leadership struggles on virtual projects. Our goal is for project leaders to discuss and agree on a concept of operation for the organization.

Within long-established collocated organizations these subjects are normally communicated informally to new project personnel. They are part of the organizational culture, and are usually taken for granted. Since many leaders on virtual projects are brought together from differing backgrounds, often they do not share common engineering organizational expectations and therefore tension can rise rapidly.

Project leaders should draft a brief statement documenting the results of their discussions. Leaders often come and go on projects. It is important that the vision of the organizational operation be captured. What we are talking about is the basis for a project's virtual culture. By discussing these issues and reaching agreement, leaders will better understand co-leaders expectations and will more readily adapt their own styles to fit the leadership team's agreed-to concept of operation of the organization.

1.5 Question: *I understand the concept of a freedom line, but can you give any additional guidance on establishing this line?*

Answer: There isn't a one-size-fits all answer to this question. You have to examine the characteristics of your project and, in particular, evaluate the characteristics of each of the sites within the project. Use the following guidance in assessing your project to help find the right freedom line point that provides the optimum chance for success.

General guidance

As more freedom is given to each site you increase the chances of leveraging site strengths and reducing mistrust and leadership struggles, but also may be adding cost and/or project risk. The more freedom each site operates with the greater the likelihood of increased cost in three areas:

- Infrastructure
- Architecture
- Integration

Each of these three areas is discussed further below.

Infrastructure guidance

Decisions regarding the freedom line could decrease the project's infrastructure costs, but it could also have the opposite effect on the project's total cost. For example, allowing a site the freedom to use existing capital assets for development can decrease the overall project development environment hardware and software licensing costs. But this must be weighed against the added risk to integration.

Assess the following infrastructure areas where cost may be affected due to the degree of freedom given to each site:

- Development environment hardware
- Test and integration hardware
- Software licenses
- Support functions
  - Configuration Management
  - Quality Assurance
  - Technical Publications

Architecture guidance

By giving increased freedom to individual sites during design and development, we move closer to a *system of systems* approach. This can be beneficial to leveraging strengths, but it can also be costly if allowed to go too far. For example, a systems of systems approach can leads to architectures inside of architectures. Depending on the specific situation, this can be very costly to maintain over the life cycle of a given project. On the other hand, if a given site has a proven mature product and architecture and a proven track record integrating with other contractors, then the system of systems approach may be the optimum choice.

Integration guidance

A key point often overlooked in the early stages of virtual projects is the impact of freedom line decisions on the cost of integration. In general, the more freedom granted early, the greater the likelihood of integration difficulties. In a system of systems where subsystems are designed to operate inside a local architecture, experience has shown there is greater likelihood of integration difficulties.

If the integration plan calls for a big-bang single integration, do not underestimate the potential added integration costs due to:

- Engineering lack of familiarity with integration infrastructure (software, hardware, and support)
- Added cost of configuration management
- Added cost due to travel

These issues are discussed further in the questions on incremental development and configuration management.

1.6 Question: *Can you characterize the single most common cause of leadership struggles and what we can do to address it?*

Answer: Leadership struggles most often center around project control issues. Leaders have expectations based on their own experiences. These expectations can range from big picture architecture-related issues to small task-related issues. These struggles are usually rooted in one of the areas addressed within the virtual culture concept.

When leaders see activities that don't fit their expectations they often view them as lost project control. This is where much of the project tension often begins. The best way to address this situation is for leaders to talk through their project expectations with other leaders. When leaders communicate on a regular basis and reach common expectations, the full organization functions more effectively. Refer to the question on the purpose of step seven of the eight-step process for additional information on this subject. Also refer to the RFPM, which is an example of how to implement part of a virtual culture, for tangible recommended solutions.

1.7 Question: *It has been my experience that integrated product teams (IPTs) do not work well. For example, some managers use the IPT concept as an excuse to give one person a job that really requires two people. Making the team responsible for everything results in less real responsibility being owned. How do your recommendations for virtual projects address this situation?*

Answer: Over-tasking of personnel is a complaint often heard in IPT environments. The intent of an IPT is not to give individuals more work, but rather to achieve integrated solutions. Nevertheless, we recognize the overwhelming super-human demands a pure integrated team concept places on workers.

It is unrealistic to expect each engineer to be capable of analyzing each problem from all the perspectives needed. In practice, it is more effective to recognize "heads up" and "heads down" positions within the organization.

"Heads up" people are the systems engineers who look across the entire system at common issues. "Heads down" people are those focused on solving specific problems. "Heads-down" people are usually assigned to a specific global-component team. Our recommendation for a freedom line and the establishment of focused level 3 organizational teams helps partition tasks into more effective manageable pieces which, in turn, ease the overwhelming demand on individuals within a pure IPT environment.

J.2   Customer Questions

2.1 Question: *The primary focus of this book seems to be on what the contractor needs to do. Are there things that the customer can do to help virtual projects succeed?*

Answer: In theory, the customer (or customer representative) is part of the integrated team and therefore the solutions we are recommending are equally relevant to the customer as well. In reality, we recognize that the same rules do not always apply to our customers as apply to ourselves. Nevertheless, on virtual projects the issues we face with a customer are often similar to those faced with teammates who have differing backgrounds and experiences.

Team members need to work through the team to communicate with other team members — and this includes the customer. It is up to each of us to communicate our ideas effectively to all of our teammates, including the customer, to gain support. From the customer perspective this implies working through the defined organization as well.

J.3   Rules Questions

3.1 Question: *Are the rules listed in Chapter 5 and in Appendix I intended to be a complete set of rules for the project?*

Answer: The rules identified in this book are a ***starting point*** for the full set of rules a project will need. These rules have been based on experiences from first-generation virtual projects. They focus on resolving common pitfalls associated with virtual-project-specific issues. As such, these rules are not intended to represent all the rules the project will need.

Take the lists provided in the Appendices and tailor them to the specific needs of your project. The final set of rules you arrive at must be a set that the complete team — especially the team leaders — can live with and fully support.

J.4 Work Share Questions

4.1 Question: *Is work share the ultimate point of friction that causes a virtual team to fail?*

Answer: Oftentimes this appears to be the case. Too often subtle work share issues inappropriately underlie engineering decision-making. This is why it is critically important to execute engineering activities in their proper sequence. A sound architecture and an organization with clearly defined responsibilities provide the fundamental framework for effective coordination and communication of work share responsibilities.

Do not put off work share decisions any longer than necessary, but don't make work share decisions purely from the political perspective either. Consideration of both the technical architecture and the organizational architecture is critical for work share decisions to be effective and for ultimate project success.

J.5 Team Questions

5.1 Question: *Do you recommend the use of integrated product teams (IPTs) on virtual projects?*

Answer: Integrated product teams should be employed at the customer deliverable level, but to achieve the most effective operation we don't recommend IPTs in their purest form. The customer-deliverable product teams should operate as IPTs in the sense that they are responsible for ensuring the end-product meets all of the customer requirements. However, certain common services should be provided by non-IPT service teams; for example, a separate System Engineering Team (not an IPT in the pure sense) looks across the product teams and provides common system engineering services. In practice, this is more effective than having each product team be directly responsible for its own system engineering services.

We also recommend the use of third level global-component teams below the customer-deliverable product level. The global-component teams focus on testable components that are integrated into the final products. Each global-component team should be collocated. Refer to the organizational recommendations in step one of Chapter 7 for more information.

5.2 Question: *I don't see the value in traditional integrated product team training. I am a private person. I don't invite people from work to my home except on rare occasions. Spending time getting-to-know my teammates doesn't do much for me. What kind of training do you recommend for virtual teams and is it any different from traditional IPT training?*

Answer: To solve the culture issues raised in this book we do not recommend focusing valuable training time on "getting-to-know" your teammates from remote locations. One cannot force interpersonal relationships through training. What we do recommend is a more tangible product-oriented leadership team effort where agreement is reached on the virtual culture. A virtual culture includes

- Templates
- Forms
- Criteria
- Warning signs
- Checklists
- Rules

Through this leadership training tailored tangible products are produced and agreed to be used on the project by the team leaders. Each product has been included to specifically address one or more of the identified common pitfalls observed on first-generation virtual projects. See Chapters 7 and 8 and the Appendices for more information.

J.6   Culture Questions

6.1 Question: *People learn using different styles. Are there different problem-solving styles as well? Are problem-solving styles the same as culture? If so, how does one take advantage of alternative problem-solving styles?*

Answer: Different problem-solving styles do represent a part of what is thought of as culture. The key to taking advantage of alternative problem-solving styles is coordination and integration. This requires that key people be collocated during critical project times for assimilation of new ideas. This is discussed at length in Chapter 2.

6.2 Question: *Could you clarify what you mean by a virtual culture?*

Answer: Majken Schultz tells us that culture concepts emphasize fundamentals that we take for granted and that culture is characterized by strongly held beliefs based on experience.

When referring to a virtual culture we do not mean to imply a culture for virtual projects that replaces the local site-specific cultures to which Schultz refers. It is not in the best interests of virtual projects to attempt to replace local cultures. This will only add to project struggles and mistrust.

As stated previously, it is our goal to leverage the strengths of our team-mates and those strengths include their critically important identities and related cultures. But leveraging strengths is not enough to ensure a virtual project will succeed.

There exist critical points at which products and people from divergent sites must come together, and, at these points, we need well-defined and agreed-to rules. This is the purpose of the virtual culture — it establishes those critical agreements at the points where product and people must come together to produce a single integrated product.

6.3 Question: *You stated that you use the Virtual Project Management Framework to help find potential problems on existing projects? Could you describe in more detail how this is done?*

Answer: On existing projects the first step is to understand what is working well and what isn't working so well and why. This is accomplished through discussions with those in the organization (both managers and engineers). In the process of these discussions we listen for **key patterns** based on the four levels of the framework. This technique allows us to quickly assess where the most critical weaknesses on the project exist. We recommend starting this process with architecture.

The following questions are associated with the common patterns we look for based on our framework:

- Framework Level 1
  - Is the architecture fundamentally sound?
  - Is the architecture responsibility clear within the organization?
  - Do the architecture and organization complement one another?
  - Is the architecture being used effectively to coordinate and communicate responsibilities?
  - Are the architectural component-products well-defined, understood, and mapped to the third level of the organization?
  - Are there gaps between the architecture and design?
  - Is there an architecture terminology problem across different organizations on the project?
- Framework Level 2
  - Is work split well-defined?

- Is the work split consistent with the architecture?
- Do each of the sites clearly know their responsibilities?
- Are requirements being managed and have they been allocated to sites?
- Are build plans and integration plans in place?
- Are all the architectural constraints clearly defined and written down where new personnel can access them when they come on the project at remote sites?
- Framework Level 3
  - Are we leveraging our teammates' strengths in each of the following areas?
    - Domain knowledge
    - Process
    - Infrastructure
    - Organization
  - Is the project effectively utilizing virtual communication technologies?
    - Rules in place?
  - How well does remote tasking work on the project?
    - Use TARS?
    - Clear component-product responsibility?
- Framework Level 4
  - Do our project leaders have a common vision for the operation of the organization?
    - Leader-engineer tasking/guidance interaction
    - New work trigger-mechanism into execution
    - Customer interactions
  - Are leaders recognizing the warning signs of healthy and unhealthy conflict and taking appropriate and timely actions?

The questions listed above give an indication of how we systematically analyze an existing project. What is most important in this process is what to do when weak areas are identified. This is the point at which the product-oriented solutions provided in the appendices aid in putting effective remedies in place. Some of the key products employed include

- Level 1 Products
  - Architecture CPDM
  - Terminology in RFPM
  - Critical project issues in RFPM

- Level 2 Products
  - Global component criteria
  - Global component identification and responsibility form
  - Build plan Checklist
  - Integration plan Checklist
- Level 3 Products
  - CPDM
  - Rules
  - TARs
  - Infrastructure common requirements form
- Level 4 Products
  - Leader's statement in RFPM on organizational interactions
  - Warning signs checklist

6.4 Question: *Over the past ten years industry has been moving away from extensive costly and difficult to maintain documentation. With your recommendations for what you call a virtual culture are you suggesting that we need to return to the days of extensive formal documentation?*

Answer: Our recommendations are not inconsistent with initiatives to streamline traditional costly documentation approaches. However, on virtual projects there exist ***critical specific*** areas where more formal documentation is required. The emphasis here is on the ***critical specific*** part.

We are only suggesting increased formal documentation at those critical coordination points where people and products must come together. These are the points at which we cannot rely on traditional site-specific informal cultures to resolve issues as they have in the past. These are also the points where analysis has shown first-generation virtual projects have experienced the greatest communication failures.

6.5 Question: *Are you saying that the reason we fail when we attempt to move a mature process to a different physical location is because we fail to move the informal side as well as the formal?*

Answer: Actually it is the reverse. When we fail to proactively define a virtual culture we end up with multiple informal cultures colliding. The reason many efforts to move mature processes fail is due to this collision of informal taken-for-granted cultural information. This is what underlies much of the mistrust and leadership struggles we have observed.

The intent of our RFPM is to provide more formal documentation of critical information — but only that critical information associated with key cross-organizational/site coordination points.

J.7 Design Questions

7.1 Question: *It seems that many of the virtual difficulties we face relate to opinions about a design being right. Is there an analytical way to assess design correctness?*

Answer: As discussed in Chapter 2, the design process relies more on heuristical methods utilizing past experience than on analytical techniques. Our experience indicates that the correctness of a design, in practicality, rest mostly in the eyes of the designer and the reviewer. This itself presents a potential conflict when the reviewer's experiences don't match those of the designer. This is a large part of the dilemma we face.

This is also why it becomes increasingly critical for our virtual project team leaders to exhibit the characteristics of open-mindedness and willingness to consider new alternatives when working with teammates from organizations with differing experience bases.

On the other hand, while the correctness of a design may always contain a degree of subjectivity, by documenting the project's critical issues in the RFPM, and tightening up task definitions through the techniques recommended in this book, we can substantially reduce the miscommunication that so often leads to divergent views related to design correctness.

J.8 Costing Questions

8.1 Question: *Can you analytically prove that projects will realize a cost savings by using the techniques advocated in this book?*

Answer: It is difficult, if not impossible, to analytically prove a cost savings due to any particular factor, or set of factors. This is because of the inability to hold external factors constant during the measuring process.

However, the vast majority of experienced engineers and managers to whom I have spoken recognize the immense productivity gain that results from avoiding the pitfalls of first-generation new technology projects. The recommendations in this book are all focused on the reduction of inefficient resource usage — both products and people — which is certain to result in substantial cost savings on later generation virtual projects.

J.9 Process Questions

9.1 Question: *It appears you are co-mingling two very different and powerful ideas. One is a proposed TECHNICAL PROCESS to handle virtual projects,* *while the other relates to PEOPLE MANAGEMENT issues? Is there another book we should be reading to understand more of each of these sides?*

Answer: Actually there may be more than two different and powerful ideas being co-mingled in this book. Part of the purpose in this book was to demonstrate the tightly interrelated nature of architecture, process, and management in achieving an effective integrated solution.

This question is similar to one asked about technical and management issues. Refer to that answer for more information.

9.2 Question: *Could you provide more information about how a CPDM might be employed on a commercial off-the-shelf (COTS) integration project?*

Answer: In the past, software development plans have been oriented toward the development of new software. These plans have usually required methodology and tool-set specific component-products. When reusing existing assets, constraining component-products to a specific methodology and tool-set is often inappropriate. The CPDM provides a flexible and easy-to-implement technique to identify methodology and tool-set requirements that works equally well for both newly developed and reusable assets.

In the case of COTS, a CPDM could identify requirements, and test component-products to be produced in accordance with the standard project methodology. At the same time, design and code component-products could be identified, but not constrained by tool-set or design approaches.

This would allow a commercial vendor to package design and implementation information in accordance with their own established internal policies. By focusing the CPDM on the requirements and test component-products we provide the flexibility necessary to effectively manage, control, and employ off-the-shelf or reusable products.

9.3 Question: *Why do we need a maturity framework specific to virtual projects? Isn't the Software Engineering Institute Capability Maturity Model (SEI CMM) sufficient for all software efforts?*

Answer: The focus of the SEI CMM is on the maturity of software processes at a single site and within a single organization. With multi-site multi-organization virtual projects new issues arise that are not adequately addressed by the SEI CMM.

For example, two highly mature SEI CMM rated organizations may together operate at an immature virtual level because of intense leadership struggles for control and significant mistrust due to competition. The SEI CMM doesn't address these issues.

Virtual projects require additional guidance in creating effective integrated teams from multiple organizations with differing process backgrounds and experiences. These issues are the focus of the Virtual Project Management Framework.

9.4 Question: *I don't appreciate the problems associated with moving a mature process. If I am starting a new virtual project with a level 4 organization and a level 1 organization, why wouldn't it make sense to leverage the process strengths of my level 4 organization across the entire project?*

Answer: Leveraging the strengths of your level 4 organization undoubtedly does make sense. However, the first question to ask is

> *What are the strengths that I want to leverage from my level 1 organization and what do those strengths depend upon?*

Too often this question is missed. The strengths of your level 1 organization must first be understood. Don't get caught in the trap of believing that all level 1 organizations are ineffective at doing their jobs. Often you need to look deeper inside an organization to fully understand that organization's strengths, and what those strengths depend upon.

When we say one site brings the process strength, another site brings the architecture strength, and yet another brings system integration strength, do we really understand the dependencies each of these have on the others?

The strengths of most mature organizations are dependent upon more than a set of defined procedures. Organizational maturity requires an underlying enabling organization, supporting infrastructure, and people who have been trained to use and work through the defined system. When we fail to understand the interconnected nature of the organization, architecture, process, and infrastructure, serious damage to precisely the strength we desire to leverage often results.

J.10 Architecture Questions

10.1 Question: *How are architecture constraints expressed as part of the global component criteria, and how does this mechanism help a virtual project?*

Answer: Many virtual project leadership struggles result from architecture constraint miscommunication. As an example, the development and target hardware platform is often a topic of intense inter-site battles. By working through these issues early and documenting project agreed-to platform constraints, unhealthy project conflict can often be avoided.

In Appendix E a sample global component criteria form is provided. In this example four typical architecture constraints are identified:

- Must execute on a SUN target platform
- Must employ the XYZ Application Programmer Interface (API) for all system service needs
- Must employ the services in the VVV specification for all external component interfacing
- Must employ the services and guidance in the RRR Database Designers Guide

Documenting specific architecture constraints clarifies process freedom lines and supports effective communication across remote project sites.

10.2 Question: *Could you explain how the CPDM helps avoid Architecture miscommunication?*

Answer: In Appendix E a CPDM architecture example is provided. The power of the CPDM is found in both its simplicity (approximately 1/2 page in length) and its precision in defining in tangible product-oriented terms the project's agreed-to meaning of often ambiguous architecture terms.

In the example provided six component-products are identified and assigned to the responsibility of the architecture group in the organization. From the example we also learn what phase the architecture component-products will be available and what tool will be used to develop them. Using a CPDM to define what architecture means to a given project reduces potential project conflict resulting from unclear architecture definition and responsibility assignments. See Chapter 3 for more about architecture.

10.3 Question: *In Chapter 8 within your discussion on how to use the Virtual Project Management Framework you state that architecture is integral to each level, and that it is a common point of reference for all project decisions. Can you give examples of what this means?*

Answer: Many view architecture from the technical domain. Few would disagree that it is closely coupled to design. But it is also closely coupled with process and management. This may not be as evident to some.

For example, on virtual projects one of the first management decisions is often related to splitting up the effort. But work split decisions cannot be de-coupled from the technical side. The identification of components that can be developed separately is as much a technical architecture decision as it is a management decision. It is technical because the technical architecture must support how those pieces will interconnect and integrate into a final functioning system. It is also a management issue from a project risk perspective. From the management perspective, remote developers must build to a specification. From the technical architecture perspective, all component pieces must meet architecture constraints.

The purpose of an architecture extends beyond the technical domain. An effective architecture partitions the solution in a way that aids coordination and communication of responsibilities. In this way the architecture works together with the organization to aid the definition and flow of work effort. This is normally thought of as primarily a management issue.

Referring to our virtual project management framework in Chapter 8, you will notice that architecture crosses all identified levels. It was portrayed in this fashion to emphasize its role in all project decisions — technical and managerial.

J.11 Configuration Management

11.1 Question: *I have heard that configuration management becomes more complex on a virtual project. Could you explain why?*

Answer: Configuration management does become more complex on a virtual project. This is because there are new issues to be faced that didn't exist in the single site/single organization environment. We have identified three complicating factors which are discussed further below.

Complicating factor 1

With the involvement of multiple sites, each potentially with their own internal CM processes and tools, we face the complexities of interfacing multiple CM systems with one another.

Each location may need to configuration manage their own products during development. When global-components are ready, they will need to be handed-over for integration from one site's CM system to another site's CM system. This is the first level of added complexity normally not faced on traditional collocated projects.

Complicating factor 2

During integration changes will need to be made to fix identified problems. Are changes made directly at the integration site using the integration site's CM tools and processes? If so, there is the added complexity of engineers needing to learn a different and unfamiliar system at the integration site. Furthermore, if we allow changes directly at the integration site, how do we flow those changes back into the baseline at the remote development site?

Complicating factor 3

A further configuration management complicating factor is introduced by incremental builds. Often, in an effort to reduce schedule time, increments are planned in an overlapping fashion. While this may save schedule time, it can significantly complicate configuration management by requiring the management of various components.

This occurs because of the need to make changes for "bug fixes" during integration of Build N at the same time changes are being made to add functionality in Build N + 1. When this situation arises a further complicating factor results from the need to eventually re-engineer those bug-fixes from Build N into the N + 1st build variant. Refer to the question and answer on incremental development for more information on this subject.

Varying levels of security classification can be a further complicating factor for configuration management. See the question and answer section on Security for more information on this subject.

J.12   Incremental Development

12.1 Question: *What are the major issues faced when employing an incremental development approach on a virtual project?*

Answer: This is a difficult question because incremental development is a broad topic. But, if I had to pick one major area to focus on, it would be build management. This is because build management is a multidimensional problem on virtual projects.

To start, the term *build* must be clearly defined because different organizations tend to use the term differently. Today the term is most often used to describe a slice or increment of the complete system. A build includes the execution of each of the phases (requirements, design, code, test and integration) identified in the project life cycle. Each build has a planned start and completion date and a prescribed set of functionality to be met. Five issues within build management are discussed further below.

Issue 1 — System Build Plan

The first issue one faces with respect to build management is the development of the system build plan. This plan, as described in Chapter 7, identifies:

- Planned start and finish dates for each build
- The number of planned builds to get to the complete system

- High level functionality in each build
- Key strategies for each build

The primary issue faced with system build planning is the degree of overlap between builds. Overlapping builds has the advantage of decreasing overall schedule time, but it complicates the management issue in a number of areas. This was previously discussed in the section on Configuration Management.

Consider the following issues when planning degree of build overlap:

- More personnel required to support parallel builds
- Increased likelihood of need to re-engineer changes from previous build
- Increased complexity of configuration management of multiple parallel builds
- Increased infrastructure needs

Issue 2 — Integration Plan

Within each build one must consider the planned integration activities. The integration plan takes the high-level build plan as an input, along with work split allocation to sites, and creates the plan to integrate separately developed global components. Specific issues to consider in integration planning include

- Which sites are participating in which builds?
- At what site does final build integration take place?
- Should we have mini-integration builds at specific sites before major build integration?

Issue 3 — Access to Optimum Skills and Tools

If certain sites have responsibility for multiple global components that interface with one another, it probably makes sense to do as much interface checkout as possible at the original development site where the greatest expertise and optimum development and tools support exist.

You can anticipate lower productivity when your personnel must travel to a remote site for integration. This is due to the lack of familiarity with the tools and because of the complexities of configuration management. For this reason local sites should have their own local mini-build plan, possibly even pulling in critical remote components for early integration checkout.

Issue 4 — Dealing with Cost/Risk Integration Trade-Offs

While early integration checkout is often advised, there are trade-offs to consider:

- "Mini" local integration builds cost schedule time
- "Mini" local integration builds require support personnel
- "Mini" local integration builds may require added infrastructure costs

While in many cases the added cost of an early local integration activity may be difficult to justify, for high-risk global components (those with extensive and new interfaces to other global components) the added cost may be well worth this investment. You can think of "mini" builds as risk abatement builds.

When considering the trade-offs be sure to consider the added cost of detecting defects later at final integration due to:

- Increased configuration management cost
- Cost of travel for engineers
- Cost of unfamiliar environment with non-optimal debug tools
- Added cost of re-engineering change into next build

Issue 5: General Factors for Consideration

Other issues to consider when weighing the advantages and disadvantages of a big-bang vs. incremental integration include

- Infrastructure cost
- Effect of architecture stability
- Effect of coupling of global components
- Degree of commonality of practices
- Track record of sites working together
- Track record of organizations integrating similar systems

J.13 Security

13.1 Question: *Do you have specific recommendations for the management of products with multiple security classifications on a virtual project?*

Answer: Security should be considered from day one of a virtual project. Security issues can affect the organization, the architecture, and the work split. While the development and integration of products at differing security classifications can complicate the management process, there are a number of advantages to maintaining component-products at the lowest possible security level.

In particular, the life cycle cost to maintain unclassified products can be significantly less than the life cycle cost of highly classified products. As an example, when defects are identified in COTS-related systems it becomes much easier — and less costly — to reproduce the problem and resolve it in an unclassified environment than in a classified one.

There are many strategies that can be applied when it comes to security on a virtual project. A general rule of thumb to keep in mind: *cost increases as the granularity of security managed products decreases.* But there are trade-offs to consider here.

Make sure your architecture and organization support the chosen security classification strategy. Where possible, manage security classification at the global-component level. As an example, if you have unclassified COTS software or unclassified reusable components, then try to architect these pieces into unclassified global-components. There are a number of advantages to maintaining COTS, or other reusable software, in an unclassified global-component. In particular, this strategy allows the test and sell-off of these components in an unclassified environment where problems can more cost effectively be resolved using personnel who do not require costly security clearances.

With modern object-oriented techniques today, there is high potential for maintaining most, if not all, of the classified information in datasets that can be partitioned and managed separately from the global-components that process these datasets. This strategy allows us to maintain models and implemented code either unclassified or at a reduced classification level. Thus more of the final system is integrated in a less costly environment.

Managing integration builds and change activity with a mix of component classification levels does add complexity to the build and configuration management process. However, tools and techniques are available today to effectively manage this activity without security risk and such strategies can significantly reduce overall life-cycle system costs.

J.14 Infrastructure

14.1 Question: *My biggest concern is infrastructure. One of my teammates is a PC house. But another is a SUN house. Both tell me if I force them to a different platform, it will drive far more than just the cost of hardware. How do I assess this situation and arrive at the right answer?*

Answer: Implications of infrastructure decisions can run deep. Beyond the obvious hardware costs, one finds the additional cost of tools, training, licensing, existing product dependencies, and the cost of building vendor-specific time-tested personal relationships. Here is what we recommend.

The first step is to evaluate the strengths of each of your teammates. In this process look closely at the dependency between your teammates' strengths and their current infrastructures. This includes more than just their current hardware platform. Consider also their software investment, and the software and people that are used in a support capacity (i.e., configuration management, quality assurance, technical publications).

What we expect you will find is that there are certain dependencies that are more crucial than others. It is important to dig deep enough to understand your teammates' infrastructure dependencies if you are going to make the best decision for your project — and recognize that the answer may differ for different teammates. Once you have made your decision, document the results in the RFPM so personnel brought onto the project later understand these constraints.

J.15   Remote Tasking

15.1 Question: *I am a manager and my biggest fear in using remote personnel is not knowing for sure if they are doing the right thing. Could you tell me more about how you recommend managing remote tasking?*

Answer: The accompanying diagram, Figure J.1, shows a number of influential factors that affect task success.

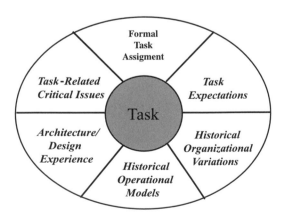

Figure J.1   Tasking Influential Factors

As the diagram indicates, the actual formal Task Assignment Record (TAR) represents only a small part of the total influential factors of a given task. Through peer-to-peer interactions an engineer learns a great deal about *task expectations* and *organizational variation*. Task-related *critical issues* and *architecture* are two others factors that are based largely on past experiences and are traditionally passed on through informal means.

Historically, task success has been closely associated with listening to the right people in the organization. This requires an understanding of the operational models of a given organization — another factor traditionally learned through informal means.

As discussed throughout this book, it is the informal side that so often breaks down in the virtual world. We have recommended a number of practical, affordable product-oriented solutions to aid in strengthening the weaknesses of remote tasking on virtual projects. These recommendations include the following, each of which has been discussed in other parts of this book:

- TAR enhancements
- Use of component-product development matrix (CPDM)
- Use of rapid filtered project memory (RFPM) to document critical issues
- Document key operational model patterns
- Use of virtual communication rules

Appendix K: The "Big Picture" Views

T his Appendix provides six (6) macro or "big picture" views of a virtual project. These views may be of interest to software and system engineers as aids in understanding project activities from a particular perspective. Also included in this section are project life-cycle views from the perspective of inside a global component. These views are included to aid project engineers in establishing a virtual project development plan. The critical functions of configuration management and security are also briefly addressed in this section.

K.1 Macro Project Perspective

When referring to the macro project perspective, we mean the big picture perspective. We have already discussed in this book all of the pieces necessary to understand this vision of a successful virtual project. To help the reader comprehend it, we provide six macro views of a project in this section. These views include:

- The engineer view
- The rules view
- The piece-part build-up view
- The component-product integration view
- The site-level integration view
- The organization-level integration view

K.1.1 The Engineer View

If you have followed the steps outlined to this point, then you know we have not required that your project employ any particular software methodology or programming language. Nor have we told you that you need to select one and only one methodology, or one and only one programming language for your project.

You don't need to use object-oriented design, document your software to any particular format, or code in any particular language to set up a virtual project following the guidance in this book. But you do need to make those decisions and document the results so engineers at each site understand expectations.

Any requirements that your project is levying on the development of software at specific sites or by specific organizations should be documented in either a component product development matrix (CPDM), or the global component criteria. Specific platform testing requirements and architecture constraints go in the global component criteria. Software methodology, tools, language, documentation, and test requirements are placed in a CPDM.

Tasks assigned to engineers should be written on a Task Assign Record (TAR). All TARs should reference a CPDM. See Figure K.1.

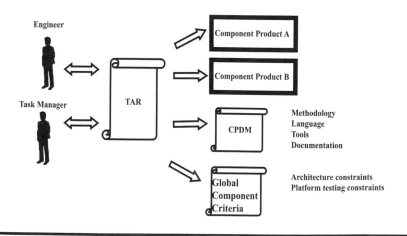

Figure K.1   Engineer View

K.1.2 The Rules View

At the macro project level we have identified just two project-level rules:

■ All global components across the project must meet the **single-project global component criteria.**

■ Each global component must be developed to the constraints of a documented and leadership-approved CPDM. The project leadership may approve multiple CPDMs for use in different project instances. How many CPDMs are approved is up to the project leadership and should be decided based on the specific requirements and needs of the project.

Rationale for single-project global component criteria

Single-project global component criteria are required across the project to ensure all global components integrate. For standalone global components, exceptions to these criteria may be granted on a case by case basis by the project leadership. The global component criteria define key required commonality in support of end-product integration.

Rationale for multiple CPDMs

While a single project CPDM is a good goal in theory, in practice on today's complex projects it is not realistic, nor cost-effective. Normally, a CPDM expresses process requirements at the language, design methodology, and tool level. Building and requiring a CPDM at this level drives process commonality. However, as discussed in Chapter 6, to leverage existing mature site-specific processes and infrastructures, there may be a better answer.

By allowing the use of multiple CPDMs, a more flexible and cost-effective project process and infrastructure solution can be supported. This includes the use of mixed languages, reuse of existing assets, and the use of commercial off-the-shelf (COTS) solutions.

Compliance with the single-project global component criteria ensures each global component (new, COTs, or reused assets) will integrate under a common architecture. See Figure K.2.

Use of commercial off-the-shelf (COTS) or government off-the-shelf (GOTS)

The approaches recommended in this book to manage and control a virtual project are in full support of reusing existing assets, including commercial off-the-shelf (COTS) and government off-the-shelf (GOTS) products.

What is critical is that the products chosen meet all the customer's requirements. In particular, be careful to ensure chosen products meet the architecture constraints, documentation requirements, and test requirements specified in the global component criteria.

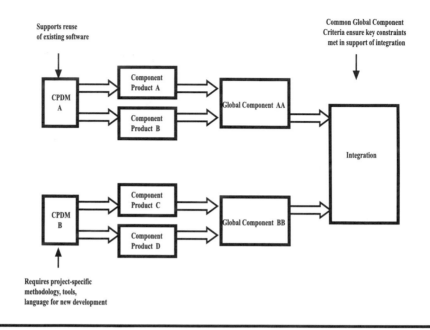

Figure K.2   Rules View

Be aware that COTS vendors can make changes in future product releases that can affect how they interface to an existing architecture. Talk to prospective COTS vendors about this issue and thoroughly test any COTS or GOTS product before selecting it.

K.1.3 The Piece-Part Build-Up View

Engineers execute assigned tasks as specified by TARs, and constrained by a CPDM and global component criteria. As a result component-product piece-parts are produced. These component-product piece-parts are then grouped together logically to produce global component-products. The global component-products are testable and meet the common global component criteria in support of deliverable product integration. See Figure K.3 for a diagram of our piece-part build-up view.

K.1.4 The Component-Product Integration View

The component-product integration view shows us the sequence in which global components are integrated into deliverable products. This is the

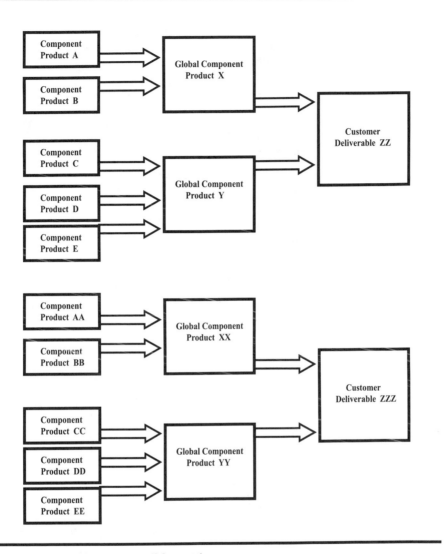

Figure K.3   Piece-Part Build Up View

traditional integration view. From this view you receive only information about the components and the sequence of planned integrations, but no information with respect to sites or organizations involved.

See Figure K.4 for a diagram of the component-product integration view. From this view one can see planned intermediate integration leading up to a deliverable product integration.

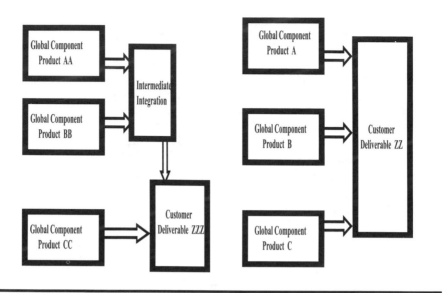

Figure K.4   Component-Product Integration View

K.1.5 The Site Level Integration View

The site-level integration view assists those involved in planning for the actual integration activities. The site integration view supports site infrastructure planning. This view also helps in planning for travel of engineers to support intermediate phase integration plans. See Figure K.5.

K.1.6 The Organization-Level Integration View

The organization-level integration view identifies where global components developed by distinct organizations are integrated together. This view helps identify where potential cultural issues may arise due to organizational differences. See Figure K.6.

K.2   Incremental Builds

Each of the six macro views described in the last section presents a single build perspective. Over the project's life each view can be thought to repeat N times, where N equals the number of builds identified in the build plan. Not all sites, global component-products, and organizations necessarily participate in every build. This depends on the build plan specific to the project.

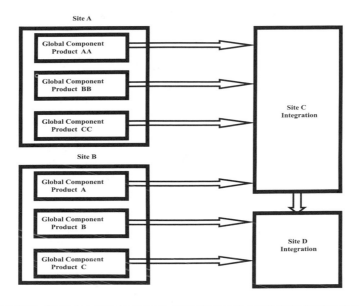

Figure K.5   Site Level Integration View

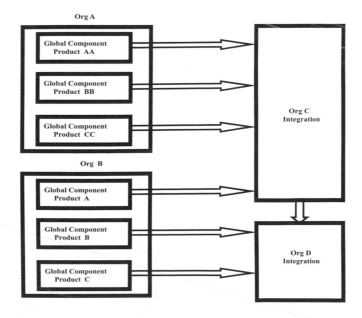

Figure K.6   Organization Level Integration View

K.2.1 The Life Cycle from Inside the Global Component Product

Deep inside each global component-product each of the activities listed below occurs:

- Requirements analysis and definition
- Top level design
- Detailed design
- Code and unit test
- Global component test

Traditionally these activities have been represented using a waterfall model. See Figure K.7.

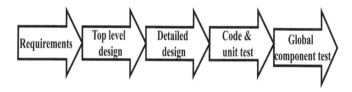

Figure K.7   Traditional Waterfall View

The waterfall view, however, has caused difficulties in the past when developing large complex software systems. In reality, the waterfall model is a simplification of the actual software development process. This was not well understood in the past.

Today, however, we understand that all requirements cannot be defined prior to the start of the top-level design activity. Likewise, we understand that we cannot complete the entire detailed design effort before writing some code to prove out certain risky design concepts. As a result, today we look at software development from a more evolutionary and incremental perspective.

K.2.2 Artifact-Set Evolutionary Software View

Today, one way we recommend viewing software development is from the artifact-set evolutionary viewpoint. This perspective has been expressed well by Walker Royce,[1] and we use it here to apply the concept to global component products, which, is an example of an artifact-set as described by Royce.

Inherent in the artifact-evolutionary view of software is the notion of incremental development. We believe this concept fits well with a multiple build approach where each build represents a slice in time of the evolving end-product.

K.2.3 Multiple Incremental Builds

Inside each build we execute each phase of the life cycle (requirements, design, code, test, integrate). Each artifact (component-product) within each artifact-set (global component-product) is only partially complete within each build, unless we are executing the final build.

Each build should have a specified focus identified in the build plan. For example, build one may be focused on requirements, architecture, and proving out the process. Build two may be focused on integrating an existing software component inside the newly defined project architecture. Build three may add specific functionality requiring some new development together with some integration with existing components.

The final build usually adds very little or no new functionality. The focus of the final build is on verification of the complete set of customer requirements, and verification of the system by the customer for its intended use.

Examining Figure K.8 we see that each artifact evolves through each build cycle. The emphasis is on requirements up front, then design — but most artifacts continue to evolve through most of the builds.

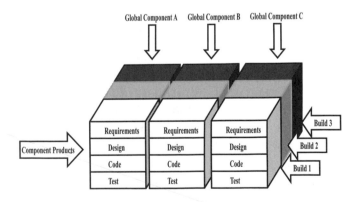

Figure K.8   Evolutionary Artifact Software View

K.2.4 *Build Overlap Trade-Offs*

For simplicity, Figure K.8 has been drawn as if the builds are sequential. In most cases, this will not be so. There are many trade-offs to be considered when planning builds and build schedules.

Overlapping builds can shorten the overall project, but does so at increased management complexity. In particular, overlapping builds may complicate load build and configuration management issues. Often multiple versions of the same software are required to be managed in these cases. This also may lead to the need to reengineer changes in one build into a later build. Overlapping builds also tends to drive personnel requirements higher.

K.3   Configuration Management

The importance of strong configuration management cannot be overemphasized with respect to distributed operations across multiple sites and multiple organizations. You can anticipate added configuration management complexity and the need for added controls at key points in the process.

As an example, consider the integration phase. Assuming more than one location is involved, you can anticipate having to process changes through two configuration management systems rather than the usual one. This, of course, depends on how tightly coupled the processes are at the two sites — which leads back to the process freedom line discussion in Chapter 6.

As part of integration planning you will need to decide where your software baseline is to be maintained. Think this through carefully. You will probably want to maintain the software baseline at the primary development environment where your best tools (i.e., debug tools) and most knowledgeable people are. But how are you going to control changes at site? The answer is probably through a local site CM system because you can't afford the time it takes to cycle each change back through a remote location.

So now you see why you probably are going to be dealing with two CM systems. Whenever your system allows changes to the same software from two locations you must be very careful, or you can quickly lose control of your baseline software.

Other issues you are likely to face include compatibility of different configuration management tools, and the management of variant versions of the same software in support of parallel overlapping builds.

K.4 Multiple Security Levels

On projects where parts of the software under development require different security classifications, another set of issues is raised by the multi-site and multi-organization factors. We recommend highly that security be taken into consideration at the time of work split decisions.

If possible, each global component should contain software that is all at the same security level. This simplifies the software management process throughout all phases. If necessary, multiple levels of security can be handled at a finer granularity, but this requires more stringently defined processes and controls throughout all phases of the development process.

References

1. Walker Royce, *Software Project Management*, Addison-Wesley, Reading, MA, 1998, pp. 83–107.

Appendix L: Synopsis of 34 Insights and 50 Solutions

I n this appendix a synopsis of the 34 Insights and 50 Solutions identified throughout this book is provided. References to sections of the book where the reader can find more information are also provided.

ORGANIZATIONAL INSIGHTS	
1. Strong subculture beliefs and perceptions tend to mold organizational views from the inside	1.3
2. The perception of key subculture groups inside of an organization is often crucial to the ultimate success of individual engineers	1.3
3. The majority of communication within organizations occurs informally. Also, some of the most critical information required to succeed is transmitted through such means	1.3
4. An engineer, if he is to be effective at his job, must understand more than how the organization is described on paper. He must understand how the organization works in practice. And he must understand the organization's expectations with respect to his specific task	1.4
5. Organizational structures are never permanent. They continually evolve through a dynamic and healthy push-pull tension often initiated from inside the organization. It is for this reason that we claim, at any point in time, how an organization really works is best communicated by those who work within it	1.5
6. The existence of organizational expectations isn't something that can be found in formal organizational procedures, yet we have found them to be highly influential in the ultimate determination of the degree of success achieved by an engineer	1.6
7. In the past the importance of the informal side of the process may not have received the attention it deserves due largely to the high visibility of an organization's process maturity goals and its focus on the formal side	1.7
8. In times of crisis personnel in mature organizations work through the organization, not around it, because they believe in it	1.8

CULTURAL & CONFLICT RELATED INSIGHTS

9. Healthy conflict, managed appropriately, invigorates a team by drawing it closer	2.
10. Majken Schultz in his book *On Studying Organizational Culture*, tells us that "organizational culture develops when members of organizations must cope with a number of more specific problems in the process of getting organizations to work." He also tells us that group identity, culture, and a sense of survival are all closely related	2.1
11. Inside collocated organizations peer pressure is often counted on as an effective vehicle to aid in rapid conflict resolution	2.1
12. The same *informal* subculture pressures that are relied upon when collocated are simply not there to solve many of the "small" problems that cross organizational and site boundaries in a virtual environment	2.1
13. Experienced engineers abstract by recognizing familiar features in current problems that may be similar to features in problems they have solved in their past	2.4
14. Individuals need incubation time for their own ideas, but also to integrate the ideas of others	2.4
15. Studies examining the frequency of interactions between teammates have concluded that when teammates must interact frequently and those interactions occur on "short cycle times" collocation offers "the greatest opportunity" for success	2.4
16. Key informal activities that "just happen" when collocated, require conscious management action when operating in a virtual collaborative environment	2.7

ARCHITECTURE, TASK MANAGEMENT, & RISK INSIGHTS

17. One's view of architecture can affect task partitioning, task expectations, and communication between manager and engineer. It also can affect organizational level responsibilities, and expectations	3.2
18. Task expectations are often closely coupled with specific organizational structures	3.3
19. Architecture often equates to "whatever the architecture team does"	3.4
20. Risk, uncertainty and critical issues depend on one's experience	3.5
21. When we see things as fundamental, we treat them differently than strongly held beliefs	3.8
22. By questioning our beliefs, we open ourselves to new possibilities that may be presented to us through the beliefs of others	3.8
23. What another culture (or organization) may see as very important, or even risky, we may have been taught to ignore as being inconsequential, or so fundamental as to not deserve attention	3.8

RFPM & CPDM INSIGHTS

24. The RFPM acts as a "forcing" function driving us to the right solution	4.
25. The act of creating a CPDM is a major part of the solution	4.7

DISTRIBUTED TEAM INSIGHTS	
26. On virtual projects supporting self-directed teams is difficult for managers who have historically exerted strong control to effect results	5.1
27. E-mail is not a synchronous form of communication	5.2
28. E-mail flooding is the result of personnel being given a new tool and insufficient training in its use	5.2
29. On virtual projects often we don't start out with either trust or mistrust	5.2
30. Many collaborative ventures fail because the process by which trust is achieved is not well-understood, or well-implemented	5.2

INTEGRATION & QUALITY INSIGHTS	
31. In mature organizations long established cultures often provide a "frame of reference" for product quality	6.1
32. Procedures are only a small part of effective process deployment	6.2
33. Mature organizations often find it difficult to work effectively with phase-based work splits	6.3
34. You can think of the component-products as the "piece-part" products of individual tasks, while the global components are the products of individual sites within a project	6.5

CULTURE & CONFLICT RELATED SOLUTIONS

1. During the critical creative design stage of a virtual project a small team of senior system designers needs to be collocated in support of rapid design integration	2.5
2. To address the need for an integrated project memory, we introduce in this book the concept of a Virtual Culture. A *Rapid Filtered Project Memory (RFPM)* is an example of one way to implement part of a Virtual Culture. The primary purpose of an RFPM is to address the lack of a single integrated "corporate memory" on a virtual project	2.6
3. Because virtual projects are composed of personnel with diverse backgrounds and experiences, it is critical that a single "project memory" be defined to aid in focusing the team in a consistent manner	2.6

ARCHITECTURE & TASK RELATED SOLUTIONS

4. We recommend consistently employing a well-defined and "agreed to" single architecture view when assigning lower level tasks	3.6
5. On virtual projects we have found that TARS, as well as the process required to complete the task assignment, may require more formally documented information. This is because on virtual projects we cannot rely on the same informal communication mechanisms that have been available in the past	3.9

VIRTUAL CULTURE RELATED SOLUTIONS

6. Write down agreements that have implications across distributed sites	4.1
7. Employ incremental-specific subdirectories	4.1
8. A well-constructed CPDM can keep remote team members on a consistent path by answering many of the most common questions that arise	4.3
9. By using a CPDM the effort required to tailor "general" corporate procedures to the unique needs of a given project can be substantially reduced	4.3
10. Providing well-defined component-product definitions with clear responsibility through a CPDM can substantially reduce remote task miscommunication	4.4
11. Using a CPDM reduces the need to change standard procedures, when project organizational responsibilities change	4.4
12. Using the dependent component-products field on a TAR, especially for dependencies that cross site boundaries, forces critical team communication early in areas where there is likelihood of task miscommunication	4.4
13. The CPDM supports integrated development teams through communication of responsibilities across physically distributed locations	4.5
14. Through the CPDM the forcing function moves away from costly formal documentation to the less costly management of component-products	4.6

VIRTUAL TEAM SOLUTIONS

15. Keep "in-process" information inside the team	5.1
16. The "quiet sign" is often a warning sign—be prepared to take action	5.1
17. Use e-mail predefined distribution lists	5.2
18. Use e-mail templates and response rules	5.2
19. Treat lack of trust as a virtual project risk	5.2
20. Set up a "rules" subdirectory within the RFPM	5.3
21. Use recommended rules based on past virtual project experiences	5.3

GLOBAL COMPONENT SOLUTIONS

22. The use of global components reduces system integration risk	6.5
23. Using global components allows us to leverage the strengths of our distributed teammates	6.5
24. The use of global components provides 5 key benefits	6.5

EIGHT-STEP PLAN RELATED SOLUTIONS

25. Use ONE AND ONLY ONE LEAD for each second level team	7.3
26. Ensure responsibilities of "roving" and "hierarchical" leaders are clear to all team members	7.3
27. Develop written charters with clear responsibilities	7.3
28. Minimize the use of organizational, or site-specific, terms or acronyms	7.3
29. Take the definition of responsibility a step further by referencing a CPDM	7.3
30. Develop an RFPM incrementally	7.3
31. Understand the work split issues	7.4
32. Define the Architecture first	7.4
33. Use a small group of senior personnel during critical front end stage	7.4
34. Use a CPDM to drive out "architecture gaps"	7.4
35. Use four key products to aid in determining infrastructure needs	7.5
36. Use Mentoring for on the job guidance	7.6
37. Use rules, but not too many	7.6
38. Collocate global component teams to the maximum extent possible	7.7
39. Be aware of potential varying leadership styles to detailed planning	7.7
40. Be aware of the relationship between architecture and planning	7.8
41. Recognize the signs of "double-tasking" and take action to resolve	7.9
42. Recognize the signs of "no tasking" and take action to resolve	7.9
43. Work by consensus	7.10
44. Don't force formal documentation too soon	7.10
45. Keep the full team in the loop	7.10
46. Know what to do when an issue keeps repeating	7.10
47. Write down your policy and deploy it	7.10
48. Take the direct approach	7.10
49. Always be on the look out for unofficial "tiger teams"	7.10
50. Deploy the techniques discussed in this book	7.10

Index